TRIBE
OF HACKERS
SECURITY LEADERS

TRIBE
OF HACKERS
SECURITY LEADERS

TRIBAL KNOWLEDGE FROM THE BEST
IN CYBERSECURITY LEADERSHIP

MARCUS J. CAREY & JENNIFER JIN

WILEY

ISBN: 978-1-119-64377-7
ISBN: 978-1-119-64379-1 (ebk.)
ISBN: 978-1-119-64376-0 (ebk.)

Manufactured in the United States of America

Library of Congress Control Number: 2020933611

10 9 8 7 6 5 4 3 2 1

Contents

Acknowledgments

Tribe of Hackers would not exist without the awesome cybersecurity community and contributors in it. I owe them tremendously for allowing me to share their perspectives on our industry.

I'd like to give a special shout-out to my wife, Mandy, for allowing me to do whatever the heck I want as far as building a business and being crazy enough to do this stuff. To Erran, Kaley, Chris, Chaya, Justin, Annie, Davian, Kai, Theo: I love you all more than the whole world!

I also want to thank Jennifer Jin for helping build the *Tribe of Hackers* book series and summit. She would like to thank her parents for supporting her and the online Tribe of Hackers community for their unwavering support of our mission.

Thanks also goes to Jennifer Aldoretta for helping me build a company that is true to our values. Shout-out to every one of the people I've worked with over the past few years.

Thanks to Dan Mandel, Jim Minatel, and the Wiley team for believing in the whole vision.

—Marcus J. Carey

Introduction

Over the last few years, there has been a frequently repeated statistic claiming that there are more than three million cybersecurity jobs left unfilled.

I don't really believe that's true—I believe we have an even bigger problem. I'll admit that we need more people who understand and can help reduce cyber risk. That number is probably significant. But who is going to lead all the people who are coming into the field? Who is going to lead the people currently in the field?

I'm an avid reader, and I like to apply what I learn in books to my life in cybersecurity. One of my favorite books on leadership is *Extreme Ownership* by Jocko Willink and Leif Babin. In the book, they use the saying, "There are no bad teams, just bad leaders."

I have a talent for over-generalizing things. So I thought to myself, "What if the real problem is a cybersecurity leadership problem?" Even if all the cybersecurity experts we needed were put into place, most cybersecurity teams would suffer from this lack of leadership.

This book is not about beating up on current security leaders. Cybersecurity leadership should start with CEOs, moving all the way down to the cybersecurity owner and their team. I use the term *cybersecurity owner* because titles vary in every organization. The cybersecurity owners are responsible for day-to-day cybersecurity operations and cyber-risk mitigation. This can be one person or multiple teams.

The cybersecurity owner and their team, processes, and technology make up the security model for each organization. Strong leadership makes the security model work to reduce cyber risk for the organization.

Every security model is different, so all security owners must make sure that they leverage the processes and technology they have in place to generate the best outcomes. This involves understanding the business, the most likely threats, how to mitigate those threats, and how to detect and respond to breaches. In this book, we will equip current and future cybersecurity leaders with strategies that help accomplish these enormous tasks.

This book is more about strategy than the tactics that are discussed in *Tribe of Hackers*, *Tribe of Hackers: Red Team*, and *Tribe of Hackers: Blue Team*. Use this book to help manage a cybersecurity program or figure out strategies that will help you improve yours. This book is for the people who have been thrown into a cybersecurity owner role and need some quick wisdom to get the job done effectively. It's also for the person who wants to eventually lead their own teams.

I hope this book gives many people the wisdom to someday be amazing leaders. It's going to be hard, because like GI Joe always ended, "Knowing is half the battle."

I want to give a huge shout-out to my friend Phil Beyer, who sat down with me earlier this year for lunch. I told him about the idea of a *Tribe of Hackers: Security Leaders* for cybersecurity management, and we immediately came up with several questions during that meeting and afterward.

Here's the list of questions we asked each contributor:

- Do you believe there is a massive shortage of career cybersecurity professionals? If so, how do we bridge the gap?
- What's the most important decision you've made or action you've taken related to a business risk? Why did you choose that path?
- How do you make hard decisions? Do you find yourself more often making people, process, or technology decisions? Why?
- What's something that you struggle with as a leader, and how do you overcome that? Is there a particular role in your career that has been the most challenging? Why?
- How do you lead your team to execute and get results? How is that different or similar to how you contribute as an individual?
- Do you have a workforce philosophy or unique approach to talent acquisition? How do you hire the right people and retain them?
- Have you created a cohesive strategy for your information security program or business unit? How do you ensure those goals are aligned with the overall corporate strategy?

- What are your communication tips for interacting with executive leadership? How is your approach different or similar to conversations with your boss, peers, direct reports, and the rest of your team members?
- How do you cultivate productive relationships with your boss, peers, direct reports, and other team members?
- Have you encountered challenges collaborating with revenue-generating teams like sales and product development? How do you approach partnerships with these teams?
- Have you encountered challenges collaborating with technology teams like information technology and software development? How do you approach partnerships with these teams?
- Do you have any favorite books to recommend for people who want to lead cybersecurity teams? How do you choose worthwhile reading material?

Thanks for reading.

—**Marcus J. Carey**
December 1, 2019

> "I'm a big motivator. I get people hyped up all the time."

Twitter: @marcusjcarey • **Website:** www.linkedin.com/in/marcuscarey/

Marcus J. Carey

Marcus J. Carey is a cybersecurity community advocate and startup founder with more than 25 years of protecting government and commercial sensitive data. He started his cybersecurity career in U.S. Navy cryptology with further service in the National Security Agency (NSA).

1

Do you believe there is a massive shortage of career cybersecurity professionals?

This is going to be a little bit of cybersecurity heresy, but I don't believe that we need career cybersecurity professionals to be able to combat the risks that we currently have and will have in the future. If I could wave a magic wand, I'd enable all information technology, computer science, electrical engineers, etc., to be more knowledgeable, responsible, and accountable for cyber risk. That same magic wand would also eliminate most cybersecurity roles except for oversight and compliance.

We bridge the gap by making cybersecurity be part of everyone's job. Each area of responsibility should have cybersecurity stakeholders, such as system administrators, software developers, network engineers, etc. They should play a more accountable role. Together as a group, they would have more skin in the game because they would be directly to blame. I've seen too many times where security teams relegated to the sidelines are somehow still blamed for breaches. To implement this, the executive team must play an extremely critical role.

What's the most important decision you've made or action you've taken related to a business risk?

The most important decision I made as founder and CEO of a software company was not to implement corporate drug testing. Every business is different for sure, and many cannot allow this. From a traditional business risk perspective, many would argue it's a huge risk, especially if you're employing bus or forklift drivers.

I'm about to make a huge generalization about the tech scene, which includes people who build technology and my hacker community. There is a lot of recreational drug use. I'm certainly not advocating or saying that people actively use on the job. I'm saying that if you want technology talent, especially in places like Austin, you may have to take this risk.

In a knowledge economy, people get paid for what they know and not what they do on the weekends. Many of the most talented builders and hackers will not apply for jobs if they have drug testing policies. These policies could be blocking talented people who can write secure code for your organization from applying to be an employee. I know there are many counterarguments to this, but it's a risk that I took and would do again in the future.

How do you make hard decisions? Do you find yourself more often making people, process, or technology decisions?

One of my favorite books is *How to Stop Worrying and Start Living* by Dale Carnegie because it taught me an important lesson that I still use today. The hardest decisions usually come with worrying about the outcome. The book instructs you to think about the worst thing that could happen and create a game plan for that scenario. It's usually going to go better than that.

To be super honest, people or personnel decisions are always the hardest. Most of the technology is about the same. Most of the processes are based on some sort of scientific method if you stop to think about it. People are hard to predict.

The most critical decisions surrounding people are probably hiring and firing. Hire for potential, not for finished products. When someone stops believing in the mission, it is time to part ways. Letting people go is tough for most of us, but I've learned time after time that it doesn't ruin good relationships.

What's something that you struggle with as a leader, and how do you overcome that?

I'm a big motivator. I get people hyped up all the time. Since I'm pumping people up and getting them super confident, it guts them when I'm critical of their performance.

I've learned to take a balanced approach where I can't hype people up so much. I also try to talk with them more often so I can microdose any criticism without them feeling like a tsunami just hit.

How do you lead your team to execute and get results?

Communication is the absolute key. I believe cybersecurity teams should really adopt the mind-set that they are a small business inside a larger organization, even if it's a small team (e.g., one person). Cybersecurity teams are in the business of risk reduction. Everything that the team implements should be with that goal. No bull, just business; your internal and external customers can smell it from a mile away.

Do you have a workforce philosophy or unique approach to talent acquisition?

I'm confident that if you hire right, anyone can learn how to perform most roles if they are given six months of on-the-job experience. When hiring, make sure that you have a minimum viable candidate in mind. So many organizations try to hire the "perfect" candidate based on exactly what they have running in their enterprise. Even organizations in the same vertical do business and cybersecurity differently.

The minimal viable candidate will be kicking butt in a few months. Hire them, train them, equip them, and they'll pay you back in spades.

Have you created a cohesive strategy for your information security program or business unit?

I highly recommend everyone check out *Traction* by Gino Wickman. He has an approach that can be applied to any business or business unit. The book is great for setting monthly, quarterly, and yearly cybersecurity goals. Align those goals with the overall corporate strategy. Have monthly and quarterly meetings to track your progress. Hold everyone—including management—to those goals. Practice extreme ownership.

What are your communication tips for interacting with executive leadership?

Be super transparent. Make sure you are telling the same consistent story to everyone. If you are caught downstream or upstream telling different stories, people will lose respect and discredit what you may say in the future.

For example, don't hype risk to get your direct reports to work harder, only to downplay the risk to management. The opposite approach is common as well. People will lose confidence in their mission as an end result. It's terrible for morale.

How do you cultivate productive relationships with your boss, peers, direct reports, and other team members?

The best relationships are built on a sense of a common goal. For a boss and peers, that mission is corporate success. A productive relationship means making sure that they have the right information to reduce risk. Notice the phrase "reduce risk," as it is impossible to eliminate risk.

Direct reports' and team members' relationships will be fostered on building each other up while reducing risk for the business. Everyone wants to experience professional growth, so by putting your personnel in positions to grow, they'll get what they need from your leadership position. Also, let them know you've got their backs at all times. They will reward you by kicking butt and taking names.

Have you encountered challenges collaborating with revenue-generating teams like sales and product development?

The elephant in the room for revenue-generating teams, such as sales and marketing, is that they will always want to jump on technology to increase sales and prospects. Development teams will see new widgets, languages, and other technology that makes their lives easier. This is a blessing to the company, which lives on revenue, and can be seen as a curse to a cybersecurity team.

The approach I recommend is that you and your team be research-driven and test these tools for yourself so you can understand how the business can use new technology as securely as possible. You have to be in the room when technology decisions are being made, and if you shoot everything down, you won't be in that room for too much longer. Either you'll move on or they'll ignore you.

Remember, your job is to allow the business to move fast without shooting itself in the foot. Cybersecurity should be a business enabler, not a hindrance.

Have you encountered challenges collaborating with technology teams like information technology and software development?

Cybersecurity professionals have gotten a bad name over the years for being the party poopers when it comes to technology. We've been downright disrespectful at times when dealing with information technology and software developers.

The best thing you can do is to make sure they understand you aren't there to say "no" to everything. Our job is to reduce risk. Sometimes that means we need to tighten up our IT chops and understanding of the software development process at the organization.

Having those people know that we are all on the same team is a game-changer. If they or anyone on your team thinks this is an adversarial ordeal, things will not go well.

Do you have any favorite books to recommend for people who want to lead cybersecurity teams?

Here are my top five at the moment. I believe we are in the people business, so mine relate to dealing with people and building teams. I choose books that inspire me to be a better person and leader.

- *Extreme Ownership* by Jocko Willink and Leif Babin
- *How to Measure Anything in Cybersecurity Risk* by Douglas W Hubbard and Richard Seiersen
- *Sapiens: A Brief History of Humankind* by Yuval Noah Harari
- *Talking to Strangers* by Malcolm Gladwell
- *Good to Great* by Jim C. Collins

"People require investment. That's our job as leaders."

Twitter: @ian_InfoSec • **Website:** medium.com/@ian_InfoSec

Ian Anderson

2

Ian Anderson is a security manager focusing on the relationships between information technology and operational technology and how those relationships work to defend industrial control systems. He is also interested in risk and governance and identity management within enterprise environments. Ian is a graduate of the University of Oklahoma and maintains GSLC, GCIH, and CISSP certifications.

Do you believe there is a massive shortage of career cybersecurity professionals?

I'm not so sure there's a shortage for cybersecurity-specific positions of 3 million+ people (a number frequently reported). The reality is that there are fewer than a million total cybersecurity jobs out there. If the deficit is genuinely that big, we would see other indicators. Getting into cybersecurity is still hard. Unlike in other disciplines, there's no clear path to joining the cybersecurity ranks. Degree programs and alternative training are still in their beginning stages. The shortage will become real when we see more prioritization around talent development over scaling existing talent.

Another reason I question the doom and gloom of the talent shortfall is the way we continue to hire for security. Companies routinely require things like the CISSP certification or multiple years of industry experience for "entry-level" cybersecurity positions. If these positions exist and companies can fill them, then there's a question as to whether the hiring organizations are feeling any effects from the talent shortfall. We should work with our HR partners to ensure the qualifications align with actual needs. Relying on the old perceptions of what makes a cybersecurity professional capable of performing a task is just repeating the mistakes of the past.

> Relying on the old perceptions of what makes a cybersecurity professional capable of performing a task is just repeating the mistakes of the past.

While I disagree with the scale of the problem, I do believe in continuously seeking and improving the overall talent available to companies for the purpose of cybersecurity. Not all security work is done by security teams. So, as the champions of security, we should be reaching out to these other teams to improve their abilities. We should also engage with schools, vo-techs, colleges, and universities to share our love for what we do and why our work is essential. Lastly, we need to give people a chance to succeed. We need to be inclusive, improve our diversity, and not allow things like degrees, certifications, or whatever else be the gatekeepers to our industry. There's plenty of room for talented people to join and participate.

What's the most important decision you've made or action you've taken related to a business risk?
One of the most important things I have ever done was to put structure around all the initiatives my teams were involved with.

It's easy for groups and leaders to get caught up in the "new hotness" or practice the age-old tradition of tool collection. In a previous role, I helped introduce the organization to a maturity framework that illuminated some intriguing insights around strengths and weaknesses.

Security teams must operate within the bounds of an organization and will, at times, follow the path of least resistance. For instance, some groups can get anything they want to be deployed to an endpoint, while some teams have an easier time changing the perimeter. It's possible to ignore the harder initiatives and focus on the things that you feel can be accomplished. We rely on our strengths potentially to the detriment of our own security capability.

Going back to the maturity framework, you may now see why this effort is so important. A balanced approach to defense will give you several benefits. One, you should have the ability to detect and respond to a wide array of threats and attacks. Second, you should have gained relationships with other teams and business units that will help you be successful in security in the long run. Reducing business risk is never done through the purchase of a blinking box or subscription service. The reduction of business risk requires partnerships, understanding, and a willingness to question our own preconceptions. A security framework helps invigorate the process of reaching a more mature environment.

How do you make hard decisions?
Decision-making starts with ensuring you have the right information at hand. That's why it's crucial to staff your teams and trust them effectively. A strong team that feels empowered and trusted will not only give you what you need to decide but also support your decision. That support could make or break you when it comes to execution.

All of us are faced with situations where we must make difficult decisions. It really doesn't matter if they're personal or business or whatever. The only thing we can do is make the best decision with the information at hand. The only caution I will give is that short-term wins aren't always the best solution. I would rather suffer in the short term for long-term success than the other way around. Nobody said this stuff was easy.

The last bit of information on decision-making I'll throw in is never forgetting you can wait. Rarely are decisions rapid and critical. A respected member of our field refers to this concept as "take two." By pausing and taking two minutes to consider the problem and different solutions, you're likely to come to a better overall conclusion. So, I guess the wisdom here is don't rush. Rushing will only get you into more significant problems.

What's something that you struggle with as a leader, and how do you overcome that?
Like most managers, I spent my time as a security analyst before being offered an opportunity to lead a team. The hardest thing for me to overcome was figuring out my role within the technical realm of my work. I used to engineer solutions, troubleshoot issues, and chase down incidents. It was a thrilling time in my career. Now, in a leadership role, these responsibilities have changed considerably. Leadership is an opportunity to give opportunities to others. I've been blessed by the quality of leadership that I've had so far in my career, and without those leaders, I would not be in the position I am in today. Maybe that's why this is so important to me. As leaders, we must raise people up to make the team and organization collectively better. While I still struggle with the desire to jump into the technical side of things, this is no longer my role. The best thing leaders can do for everyone is to stay focused on providing opportunities to others and clearing roadblocks.

> As leaders, we must raise people up to make the team and organization collectively better.

How do you lead your team to execute and get results?
I'm not sure there's any special sauce here other than listening to your team and communicating with them. My experience has been that nearly everyone wants to do good work. People like to feel empowered and have an impact on an organization. Leadership should focus on positioning people correctly and then getting out of their way. Micromanagement is the poison that ruins perfectly good teams. Poor management literally robs people of their opportunity to buy in. Facilitating my teams in a way where they feel trusted and empowered is one of my main priorities for strategic initiatives and day-to-day work.

Do you have a workforce philosophy or unique approach to talent acquisition?

In the first question about the talent gap, I talked about how it's up to leaders and their organizations to help produce the next generations of talent. This doesn't happen by only hiring people with experience. The hiring process must be people-centric; that is, we must focus on hiring good people and then training them up. People require investment. That's our job as leaders.

Hiring is also a great time to diversify your team. Diverse skillsets can move a good team into great team territory. An approach that I've seen to be successful is to bring in talent from different areas of an organization to balance out the team's skills. For instance, hiring out of an accounting or finance group can raise the team's overall skills related to the money side of the business, which has lots of advantages. Before starting down that path, be sure to get management's approval. Attackers are always thinking differently. Maybe we should do the same, especially when it comes to recruiting talented people in our field.

Have you created a cohesive strategy for your information security program or business unit?

A good strategy is one built and maintained with the partnerships of business units and organizational leadership at all levels. That's fancy manager language for "Go out and talk to people." By proper positioning of your resources (people, processes, technology), you should be aligned both strategically and operationally. I spend considerable time thinking through what our business is, what we are about, and what bad days look like. This thinking exercise prepares me to go out and validate the team's positioning with other stakeholders throughout the business. A second positive benefit of this strategy is that our business units become aligned with us and knowledgeable about what we are trying to do in terms of cybersecurity. At this point, there are no surprises that improve our chances of execution. When you're open and transparent with your partners, everything becomes more manageable.

What are your communication tips for interacting with executive leadership?

There is no silver bullet when it comes to communication. People are different, and each person is going to have their own communication styles and needs. Still, as a leader, you must be sensitive to the audience you're communicating with and tweak your approach to align with their needs. Some quick tips that I try to remember when I'm talking to stakeholders are:

- Respect people's time. Be clear about the intent of the communication. Is it for informational reasons, or does a decision need to be made?
- How is your information relevant to the recipient? Can you communicate in a way that is centered around the recipient and make it more relevant to them?
- What are some likely questions you may be asked? Do you have the necessary background information?
- Are you speaking strictly about things you know to be true? If you're speculating about something, are you clearly stating that?
- Are you avoiding using fear, uncertainty, and doubt (FUD) to drive your communications? Are you talking in terms of risk and impacts to the business/organization?

Is what you have to say better communicated via email, phone, or face to face? Face to face is such a powerful communication tool that we aren't using enough. Emails and chats are impersonal. Remember this when you have an essential decision to be made or information to communicate.

How do you cultivate productive relationships with your boss, peers, direct reports, and other team members?

There's no magic to cultivating relationships with people. The basic practices of empathy, accountability, and friendliness get you a long way. Each person is different, but bosses, peers, and direct reports will all appreciate someone who tries to understand their position, remains accountable for their actions, and is generally easy to work with.

Another skill I would recommend people work on is the skill of asking meaningful questions. There's an art for a security professional to be able to ask questions and not have it feel like an interrogation. Watching a colleague light up as they get to explain their position on an important

> People respond to leaders who they know care about them. Be one of those leaders.

issue is a rewarding experience. People respond to leaders who they know care about them. Be one of those leaders.

Have you encountered challenges collaborating with revenue-generating teams like sales and product development?

I find working with revenue-generating teams or product development teams to be one of the most rewarding challenges that security teams are offered. The groups I've encountered in my career are generally open to improving cybersecurity. Limiting the use of "no" helps develop relationships with these groups. Remember, there are many ways to mitigate risk for any given scenario. When you become a team of "no," you become a team that is circumvented. The business is going to continue to do what they need to do to be successful. Additionally, there's nothing but good things for teams that partner well with the actual components of the business that drive revenue. When you sit in this partner role, you begin to move from being strictly a cost center to becoming a force multiplier.

Have you encountered challenges collaborating with technology teams like information technology and software development?

There's always friction between security and other technology teams. Information technology has a difficult enough job without having an entirely different team pop in and point out flaws. Even if justified, any request for them is just extra work. Security must be careful that the conversations are strictly around the benefits of mitigating or remediating the risk of the current condition and not a discussion about "the ugly baby." This is where things like frameworks, metrics, and other nonbiased information sources can help paint a story about improvements and not tossing out somebody's work from the past 10 years.

Another method for managing these interactions is to have a road map and stick to it. Invite your technology and software partners to the table to help build out your road map. Then continuously communicate the status of the road map and help your partners fold your plans into theirs. Just like everything else, your partnerships will improve as you become more transparent and predictable in how you operate.

Do you have any favorite books to recommend for people who want to lead cybersecurity teams?

- *How to Measure Anything in Cybersecurity Risk* by Douglas W. Hubbard and Richard Seiersen. This is the quintessential book on moving from talking about vulnerabilities and exploits to talking about risk and impact. This book is an incredible resource for beginning to translate your security efforts into a language that executives and senior leadership can understand. This book will also help you work toward balancing your overall security deployment by ensuring resources and capabilities are appropriately distributed. This is truly one of the must-read books that all cybersecurity leaders should work through.

- *What Got You Here Won't Get You There* by Marshall Goldsmith. As we progress through our careers, we encounter new challenges. Still, instead of developing new skills, we tend to go back to the strengths that propelled us to where we are now. Maybe this is why so many engineers struggle to move into formal leadership roles. The reality is that your skills will have to adapt and change over time to meet new challenges, especially as you move into more senior positions. This isn't only true for those moving from technical to supervisory but even within technical roles themselves. The responsibilities of an architect or senior analyst are very different from the duties of junior analysts. Keeping this in mind will help ease the burden of transitions to new roles.

- *The Phoenix Project* by Gene Kim, George Spafford, and Kevin Behr. This is an excellent book about DevOps and the struggles a mythical organization faces as it tries to fix its operations. I recommend this book because it does a great job of detailing all the various elements of a business and how technology interacts with those elements. There's also the stereotypical security guy, which we should all take note of. The blunt and demanding security leader is still how we are generally viewed. We must remain conscious of the stereotypes of our field. We can ideally begin to take some corrective action and show that security professionals are great partners with a focus on helping the business succeed.

"Early in my career, I learned that sometimes the only way to manage your availability risk is to kick a hole in the wall."

Twitter: @Myrcurial • **Website:** www.linkedin.com/in/jamesarlen

James Arlen

3

James Arlen leads Salesforce Heroku's production engineering team, which is focused on delivering integrity, availability, and maturity to Heroku's fleet operations. Over the past 25 years, James has been delivering information security solutions to Fortune 500, TSE 100, and major public-sector organizations.

James is best described as an InfoSec geek, hacker, social activist, author, speaker, and parent. His areas of interest include organizational change, social engineering, blinky lights, and shiny things.

James holds the CISSP, CISA, and CRISC security certifications.

Do you believe there is a massive shortage of career cybersecurity professionals?

Well...I'm on record as being one of the first people to actually study the problem, and yes, there is a massive shortage. In 2014, I grabbed some media attention for "The Billion Dollar Problem" in cybersecurity hiring. Violet Blue published an article in ZDNet right around the time of Blackhat USA 2014 titled

"Cybersecurity hiring crisis: Rockstars, anger and the billion dollar problem" (www.zdnet.com/article/cybersecurity-hiring-crisis-rockstars-anger-and-the-billion-dollar-problem).

In 2015, my team (Lee Brotherston, Steve Manzuik, and Brendan O'Connor) at Leviathan Security Group was commissioned by Google to conduct research into some of the key questions of cloud security. You can read all of the resulting materials on Leviathan's website (www.leviathansecurity .com/cloudsecurity), but the key report to read is "Analysis of Cloud vs. Local Storage: Capabilities, Opportunities, Challenges" (www.leviathansecurity.com/s/Value-of-Cloud-Security-Scarcity.pdf).

These materials should give you lots of background, and—importantly—nothing has changed in the intervening five years. The problem is just as real and arguably has gotten worse rather than better.

Bridging the gap—making some headway against the gap anyway—will require a different approach than the one that has been taken by education and government for the last five years, which is an approach that is contrary to much of how the industry operates moment to moment. It's an approach that will not be favored by the "three religions of information security" (ISACA, (ISC)², and SANS) because it will not increase their ranks and prestige.

We need to stop trying to "create new cybersecurity professionals."

Yeah, I know. What the heck is Arlen going on about now?

My first real mentor in the field was Dr. Richard Reiner, and back in the (very) early 2000s, he often told the story of how once upon a time, companies had a "chief electrification officer" charged with figuring out how to use this new invention of commercial electrical power. You don't often hear about someone with that job anymore because it became obvious over time that the integration of new technologies into an organization was an organizational requirement and not a specialist thing.

We've spent too long with cybersecurity as a specialty rather than something that is included in a technologist and business generalist education and as a set of job responsibilities. In some of the most successful times in my career as a cybersecurity leader (and in my current position as an engineering leader, where I'm far more successful at information security/ information management than I have been in some positions in the past), I've made the difference by distributing the responsibility throughout the organization rather than holding it close in a specialist team.

This plan to distribute (or federate) responsibility for information security/information management across an organization does require that there be a central point for accountability, but it is a lot easier to staff a small tactical team of cybersecurity professionals.

Will any of this be easy? Nope. But it would work if we were to try it.

What's the most important decision you've made or action you've taken related to a business risk?
This is a really interesting question. It doesn't have a straightforward answer because "important" is a continuum related to the specifics of the time and place. Evaluating business risk is traditionally really difficult from within the confines of classic* information security/information management because by definition you're isolated from the actual business function of the organization. To answer the primary question, I'd have to rely on those times when I was able to operate as part of the business rather than as part of the IT department. Often I've been able to spend time focused on how the organization actually operates and what it does. During that time, I didn't "work in IT." I worked in power systems cybersecurity.

I think that the most important decision I've made or action I've taken related to a business risk as an information security professional was to literally kick a hole in a wall.

I should probably explain.

Unlike most of my unionized brethren, I and a few others in the security department were working late. Walking out of the building, we noticed a large volume of water rushing out of a broken faucet in a janitorial closet. Recalling the floor plan of the building, we realized that we were on the floor above the data center, and it was probably going to start raining on the racks soon. Other staff quickly ran to determine the situation downstairs and look for the water shut-off valve. I worked to redirect the water into the slop sink—but this wasn't very effective! The janitorial closet was between the restrooms, and

I knew that there was a floor drain only a few feet away that would effectively save the racks below from hundreds of gallons of water. So, I kicked a hole in the wall, giving the water a path of least resistance to the drain.

So, how in the heck is this related to the question?

Business risk relates to availability. We've had it drilled into us as information security professionals that the CIA triad is what matters, and I think we unconsciously place the elements in that specific order. The business of "keeping the lights on" is much more about the availability of the control systems! It would not have been a reputational hit but rather a regulatory one. The paperwork for having to abandon the primary control center and operate from the backup control center would be significant, but more importantly, the resulting potential for a blackout would impact many individuals.

Early in my career, I learned that sometimes the only way to manage your availability risk is to kick a hole in the wall. I don't know for sure if the work that we did that night prevented a blackout, but all of these years later the lesson of paying attention to the business is what has mattered most in my career.

* Classic information security is loosely defined as that variation of professionals who perceive themselves as IT workers who protect (exclusively) electronic systems from an engineering point of view. I've derisively referred to them in the past as the kind of workers who inhabit the "Department of No" and who perceive themselves as the thin blue line between chaos and safety or the last hope to protect all of the "losers" from themselves. In my opinion, these are the least effective and most damaging types of information security/information management professionals, reliant largely on "blinky lights and shiny things" to provide protection from information risk.

How do you make hard decisions? Do you find yourself more often making people, process, or technology decisions?

Heh. With difficulty. Always.

One of my comrades-in-arms, Trey Ford, consistently uses the phrase "Chess, not checkers" to indicate that there is a complex set of variables ahead of us and it would behoove us to play through several levels of permutations and combinations to determine whether there are obvious pathways to success.

I spend the vast majority of my decision-making time running scenarios through and looking for the less-obvious failure modes.

The decisions I make most often relate to people and process. Most technology decisions are relatively simple and don't contain nearly the same level of less-obvious failure modes.

Process decisions are entangled with people decisions most of the time. The simplest version of this is the "Make the right thing the easy thing" type of process decision. People are inherently lazy,* and I need to find the solution that takes advantage of that.

At one point in my career as a CISO, the laptop support team was getting ready to deploy a full disk encryption solution (before, this was just included as part of your operating system), and they had done a great job of implementing the software and were near the point of widescale deployment. They'd prepared a manual and training materials, and we were going over them. The manual was 18 pages long, and the training was 30 minutes long—for everyone in the company. As I went through the materials with the team, I tried really hard to distill the point that they were trying to make, and it turned out that the entire point of the materials was an attempt to prevent a sleep-related attack on the encryption system. The team wanted to get people to either power off or hibernate their laptops rather than just letting them sleep. This wasn't a technology problem. This was a people/process problem.

I asked the team what this training program was going to cost. We used an internal project rate of $150 per hour, and we had 1,000 staff members. This meant that the training cost was going to be $75,000. We were about to spend that kind of money to ensure that people didn't use the sleep mode of their laptops. I asked what the cost of deploying a Group Policy Object (GPO) to all of the laptops would be...about $5. So, I had the team drop all of the training materials and manual and reset the power management characteristics to hibernate when the lid switch or sleep button was activated and lock out the sleep mode entirely. Most people will just close the lid of their laptop when they aren't using it, and that would have the desired behavior while saving $74,995!

So, the hard decisions are the ones that require you do some deep thinking and find the way forward that optimizes the desired behavior and enforce it with a process and technology decision that makes the people decisions easier.

* Yes, you're inherently lazy. How do I know this? You have plumbing. Seriously. You don't deal with outhouses and chamber pots; you don't go down to the well in the town square and haul water back to your house. Plumbing is expensive—you're willing to work really hard to afford plumbing to avoid having the repeated daily duties!

What's something that you struggle with as a leader, and how do you overcome that?

My greatest struggle as a leader is easy to describe but difficult (for me) to work through. Put simply, I have a huge case of imposter syndrome.

I think that this is a generalized problem among a lot of my peers, and many of us hide it with a greater or lesser degree of success.

Overcoming it is nontrivial, especially when all of the external indicators suggest that you're wrong about yourself—you are promoted, people respect you, your ideas get implemented, people suggest that you should be interviewed for articles and books...you get the idea.

My internal expression of this is primarily that I'm only ever a few hours away from being fired for something I did (could be right or wrong—either way, I'm punished) and I'll never be able to find work in the field again. My next job will include the phrase "Would you like fries with that?"

The period of time during which this particular struggle was most significant really falls into two categories.

- The period when I was doing most of my industry conference talks (circa 2009–2012), and I would find myself standing in front of a crowd of thousands at Blackhat or DEF CON, and I could not internalize that I had anything useful to say.

- The other time when this has been a significant struggle is over the course of the last year or so as I've transitioned out of a pure cybersecurity role into a more generalized IT engineering role. Twenty-five years of predominantly audit, compliance, and security did teach me a few things about engineering. But was it enough? Is it enough? Am I enough?

The question "How do I overcome this struggle?" is answered simply: I haven't. I don't actually have a path toward internalizing my success. The only response I can have to my fear of disappointing those around me who depend on me is to work even harder to earn their respect and ensure that I don't make a material mistake. I suppose that's not so much overcoming as it is compensating.

I will earn my way out of being seen as an imposter by working harder and never relying on my reputation or my past deeds as a measure of my future performance.

Do you have a workforce philosophy or unique approach to talent acquisition?

Gathering and leading a team requires dedication, and it's nothing at all like being an individual contributor. Most days you should feel like you're contributing nothing other than making room for actual professionals to get things done.

Depending on the job, you probably won't have a lot of opportunity to create a new team—you'll have the team you have. Recall that they have been working together without you for some time. You will need to earn their trust and get their insight into what does and doesn't work in your new organization.

Getting them to do the work that you want done in your way is yet another negotiation, and you're going to have to suck it up and bend your normal style to suit the needs of your team. You cannot succeed without them, period. Interestingly, they can be modestly successful without you—so you'd best pay attention.

I show my team how my style works by actually living it. When things are going well, I stand behind them and make sure that they get all the credit for our collective success. If things start to go poorly, it's on me as their leader to step to the front and take the brunt of the onslaught to ensure that they have the space and clarity to actually get work done. In other terms, when things are going well, it's not your fault. When things are going poorly, it's entirely your fault.

Eventually you will have the opportunity to hire new staff—either through normal attrition or because you've successfully negotiated additional responsibility or accountability that will require additional people. Now you need to find someone who will work well with the team you have and ideally provide the talent gap you feel you're missing. I've made a habit of hiring people and tuning skillsets post-hire. I can train someone on a skill, but I can't make them more compatible with my team or my style after the fact.

For a shortcut to understanding my management style, I encourage you to read The Monkey Bagel entry called "Pumas on Hoverbikes" (monkeybagel.com/pumas.html), and either you'll get it or you won't.

Have you created a cohesive strategy for your information security program or business unit?
The corporate strategy is your goal. You don't get to operate separately from that!

What are your communication tips for interacting with executive leadership?
Communicating with executive leadership is an entire skillset of its own—although it is an extension of how I communicate with everyone.

Communicating with my boss, peers, direct reports, and the rest of the team is generally wrapped up in the idea that it is easier for me to learn their world and provide a translation from my requirements to their frameworks than vice versa. Many classic information security people believe that everyone should understand every minute detail of information security and if you can't grasp what they are saying, then the problem is clearly you. My response to this is simple—those people are just plain wrong. It is the responsibility of the messenger to ensure the message is received and clearly understood.

The importance of this clarity when communicating upward to executive leadership is magnified when you consider that information security/information management is a small fraction of the responsibilities and accountabilities of those executives. While you may find it really important to communicate that predictive execution in Intel processors is fundamentally broken (and therefore all of the "obvious" implications...), that information is not actionable or useful for those executives without some real context that places it within the framework of the operations of the business. Instead of talking about the minutia of microprocessor design, contextualize that information as the changes to business operations that will be required. Perhaps you need to increase your IaaS budget to account for reduced performance, or you need to take an extended maintenance window for patching operations. These are more easily expressed in business terms—for example, "Due to flaws in the fundamental design of the computers we use, we're going to need more of them to do the work they're currently doing." And "To ensure that we respond to the story you may have read in the paper about processor flaws, we're going to have to put the ERP system in maintenance mode for about four hours this weekend—we don't anticipate any downtime, but for a few hours we won't be able to accurately track our inventory and sales."

Context matters.

And so does the medium you use to deliver the message. "Death by PowerPoint" is pretty real—unless that's how your executive leadership expects to receive your message. I've worked in companies that love and hate slide decks. You should spend some time going through executive briefing materials created by other departments and learn what works and what doesn't!

How do you cultivate productive relationships with your boss, peers, direct reports, and other team members?

This is a really interesting question. The best way to cultivate relationships in every direction is rooted in an honest, forthright, deliberate, and precise manner. You meet your commitments when you say you will. You show compassion and understanding, remembering that you're a group of people working to accomplish the same goal. You presume that everyone is an honest broker who offers you face value. You treat everyone with respect and remember that everyone has their own story full of successes, failures, joy, and pain.

Basically, just be a good human and follow Wheaton's law— "Don't be a dick."

And buy a lot of coffee.

Have you encountered challenges collaborating with technology teams like information technology and software development?

Collaboration between groups that have differing priorities is always going to be difficult. This is probably a good point to discuss the reality that without challenges, and especially difficult ones, you aren't doing the job of balancing priorities and requirements.

If you take the time to break your priorities down into a couple of different views, you'll have an easier time communicating with other teams within the organization. Some of the handy ways I do this include the following:

- **Urgent/Important:** Draw yourself a graph with one axis as "Urgent" and the other as "Important"; then cut the resulting graph into four segments. The upper-right corner contains items that you really should work hard to negotiate into the organization's plan. The lower-left corner...don't bother doing those things. The juice isn't worth the squeeze. Everything in the remaining quadrants feels like it should matter, but it's all things that you can do when you have the luxury of time.

- **Three Risks:** Information security people like to talk about legislative risk, regulatory risk, and reputational risk. Blah, blah, blah. No one outside of the industry really understands that. Try instead: Wear an Orange Jumpsuit, Lose Your House, and Look Foolish. Amazing how easy prioritization conversations happen when you simply state: "We're not going to negotiate on any Orange Jumpsuit Risks, we can talk about Lose Your House, and of course we can negotiate on Look Foolish." Heck, I'm a Dad who spent more than 20 years driving mini-vans—I'm perfectly fine looking foolish.

Once you've been able to articulate the priorities for yourself, you can then contextualize those priorities for the business or technical teams. They've got their opinions—likely driven by "the street"/newspapers and Reddit, respectively—and those are valid opinions!

Do you have any favorite books to recommend for people who want to lead cybersecurity teams?
Choosing reading material at various points in my career as an individual contributor, manager, and leader has always been interesting indeed. There's a simplistic response in "You need to keep up with the news" (both inside the industry and sufficient general business news that you're able to be an effective collaborator with all of your co-workers outside of your specialty). A more complex response is that you need to ravenously consume information to stay on top of your game.

There are three significant categories of books that I'd offer in response to a request for recommendations:

- Science fiction is a way of reflecting our present using a framework set in the future (or a long, long time ago...) and thereby making it easier to analyze. I've gathered a lot of insight over the years from cyberpunk and post-cyberpunk novels. Picking up some Neal Stephenson, William Gibson, Charlie Stross, Cory Doctorow, or Bruce Sterling might give you some interesting ways to frame your current problem space.
- Industry manuals are another significant source of contextualization for your problem space. You need the background information necessary to understand some of the underlying theory for what you're dealing with. Here are some of the seminal texts on the topic:
  - *Security Metrics: Replacing Fear, Uncertainty, and Doubt* (Andrew Jaquith)
  - *The New School of Information Security* (Adam Shostack)
  - *Applied Cryptography* (Bruce Schneier)
  - *The Web Application Hacker's Handbook* (Dafydd Stuttard)
  - *Penetration Testing: A Hands-on Introduction to Hacking* (Georgia Weidman)
  - *Metasploit: The Penetration Tester's Guide* (David Kennedy)
- Here are books specifically about leadership (seems to be an obvious category):
  - *The Score Takes Care of Itself: My Philosophy of Leadership* (Bill Walsh)
  - *Chasing Excellence: A Story about Building the World's Fittest Athletes* (Ben Bergeron)
  - *Death by Meeting: A Leadership Fable about Solving the Most Painful Problem in Business* (Patrick Lencioni)
  - *Crazybusy: Overstretched, Overbooked, and About to Snap! Strategies for Handling Your Fast-Paced Life* (Edward Hallowell)
  - *Making It All Work: Winning at the Game of Work and the Business of Life* (David Allen)
  - *Drive: The Surprising Truth about What Motivates Us* (Daniel H. Pink)

> "My philosophy is to seek a diverse workforce, given the diversity of threats."

Twitter: @lotusebhat • **Website:** www.linkedin.com/in/markaarnold-phd/

Mark Arnold

Mark Arnold has worked in cybersecurity for over 15 years, serving 8 of those years in leadership roles. As a transformational leader, Mark has built security teams and programs, authored maturity models to optimize risk management processes, and implemented security domain practices at large enterprises and service providers.

Mark commits time to the security community as an OWASP chapter and InfoSecWorld board member, among others.

He holds industry certifications and has satisfied his intellectual curiosity with earned degrees from Stanford, Princeton Seminary, and Harvard University. He is a former competitive gymnast but, most importantly, a husband and dad, thriving on hugs.

4

Do you believe there is a massive shortage of career cybersecurity professionals?
There is a massive shortage if we believe the numbers (e.g., Cyberseek.org's listings for the United States only; I'm not

sure if similar disparities exist globally). Pipeline generation is the common response/retort to the question of resolving the shortage, especially as I reread the question. When it comes to the qualifier "career," requisition demand dwarfs the number of available career cybersecurity professions. We as leaders should not solely focus on "career" but build our desired pipelines targeting veterans, the underrepresented, those pursuing a second career, re-entrants into society, etc., in the effort to fulfill current needs. In many instances, we need to dismiss our biases to see the green fields of opportunity for the new workforce. Separately, I personally represent a growing number of leaders who have partnered with local nonprofits, and I am aware of many others (nationally, internationally) driven to create pockets of opportunities to bridge the cyber divide. We are seeing efforts to encourage cyber mindsets and philosophy in middle schools and earlier through coding, CFTs, etc., in an effort to address the demand that confronts us.

What's the most important decision you've made or action you've taken related to a business risk?
I have always attempted to contextualize security risks in the context of business risk. Very early on in my career I shed the use of fear, uncertainty, and doubt (FUD) to "scare" the business into actions or to model compliant behavior. I learned in one tenure through trial and error that executive leaders do not welcome repeated bad news without context such that when the real incident happens, the news is met with resistance and disbelief (i.e., Chicken Little syndrome). I was challenged to modify my approach to conform to the management of risk, which is the core function of the security leader. I had no choice but to choose the path of risk management to be accepted by the business speaking the language of risk management.

How do you make hard decisions? Do you find yourself more often making people, process, or technology decisions?
I try to make decisions based on risk these days. This may result in hard decisions regarding technical choices, process improvements, and resource capacity. Outside of the risk management context, I find myself making uninformed choices. Alignment with the business is key for the security leader to be successful. The "people decisions" are the hardest for me because of my passion for people. Because of this bias, in the

past I've not been aligned with the business in managing those leaders and team members to maximize success. Conversely, I have experienced reliance on the risk management profile to show the business deficiencies in security outcomes to meet overall business outcomes because of a lack of people resources to meet security outcomes, putting the business at risk.

My goal is to make decisions based on risk assessment and with an eye to managing identified risks. Often, I have made difficult decisions and technical choices, process improvements, and adjustments to resource capacity to lessen the risk to the business. Without a proper risk assessment and context, I find myself open to making uninformed choices and consequently impacting the business. Some of the hardest risk management choices have been "people decisions," given my passion for people. I have always been biased toward the success of the team and the individual resources that comprise it. However, I have experienced instances where loyalty to the "team" clouded my judgment and adversely affected business risk appetites and goals in my effort to save colleagues. I have learned the hard way to balance my "people passion" with risk management to reduce business deficiencies in the pursuit of business outcomes. In short, alignment with the business and risk management are my basis for successful decision-making.

What's something that you struggle with as a leader, and how do you overcome that?

My one leadership struggle is overzealousness to see members succeed even when they are struggling and a risk to the business. At times, I have ruled against pressure to manage someone out of a role in the hope that that team member will improve and reach a better outcome. In short, my challenge and/or kryptonite would be balancing my passion to see the good in people with managing the risk to my overall program and to the business.

How do you lead your team to execute and get results?

Marshaling resources to execute uniformly for me is accomplished through consistent team building, established meeting cadence, and trust and belief that your team can "go and do" and at the same time be recognized and rewarded for their efforts. In an individual contributor role in the past, I have tended to own the work in hopes of contributing to the whole. As a security leader, I have had to learn that I am responsible for the "whole" security outcome, and as such I have to ensure that each individual contributor is enabled to own the parts with the business outcome in mind.

Do you have a workforce philosophy or unique approach to talent acquisition?

My philosophy is to seek a diverse workforce, given the diversity of threats. This has been confirmed by a few select studies demonstrating that diversity and inclusion (D&I) environments enable improved security outcomes. Further, diversity should not be restricted to gender, ethnicity, and race but should also reflect diversity of background (tech, no-tech; degree, no-degree; certifications or no certifications). Asymmetric backgrounds should be celebrated, not spurned, in building teams of the present and future. Once you have the teams, incentivize them (through training, work-life balance, creative compensation, etc.) to earn trust and loyalty toward building relationships and synergies.

Have you created a cohesive strategy for your information security program or business unit?

I have created strategies by means of frameworks; otherwise, one is floundering around in the dark. I can admit that in my earlier stages of leadership my approach was less formalized and as a result less successful. The structure provided by the risk management approach ensures that one has laid out a measurable, auditable program that meets business outcomes.

What are your communication tips for interacting with executive leadership?

Simply this: speak the business of risk so that the business can make informed business decisions. The conversation with other parts of the business are more operations aligned, in my experience, and involve the collaborative conversations necessary to meet operational objectives and to offer security assurances and guidance as a security leader to these cross-functional stakeholders.

Simply this: speak their language, the language of business. Talk about security risk and how security both protects and enables the business so that executive stakeholders receiving the message can make informed business decisions. Further, be visible! In my experience, visible security leaders who freely and openly engage in collaborative and cross-functional conversations are more respected and highly esteemed, helping organizations both meet business goals and achieve security outcomes.

How do you cultivate productive relationships with your boss, peers, direct reports, and other team members?
I am a transparent leader, and at the outset of any tenure, I lay those "trust" stakes in the ground that I will go to battle for them as they should for me and each other. I use challenge coins as of late to establish these relationships symbolically. Further, I am careful to nurture the relationships by simply caring for their "entire" selves, which means, in part, caring about their lives beyond work (e.g., family, education, interests, etc.) so they have freedom of spirit to innovate with the knowledge that my support extends beyond the confines of work.

Have you encountered challenges collaborating with revenue-generating teams like sales and product development?
I have had these challenges, but at the same time I would qualify them as good ones. I am a seller at heart if not in practice, and I have come to understand (most recently through work at a managed service provider [MSP]) that one of my leadership roles is to enable the business, especially one that operates at high velocity. My partnerships cross-functionally required me to understand the work of the sellers on the front lines and ensure that the messaging around our security services was clear and consumable by buyers. We proactively took steps to co-own the messaging with our products group to position our sellers in the best possible way to be successful, while staying true to our security and compliance mandates.

Have you encountered challenges collaborating with technology teams like information technology and software development?
I encountered collaboration impudence in working with or attempting integration with "builders," only because in those organizations we historically lacked channels of conversation. We conceded to wait on the build teams to complete their

products and then, in draconian fashion, ground production to a halt to bolt on security at the end of build lifecycles or "scan the hell" out of everything, which deflated the morale of those teams. After many fails, I took a different tack by attempting to understand the world through their eyes. At the same time, conversations with my peers internally and externally persuaded me that there was a different path forward—build security in as a partner and collaborator, and in that way build consensus that not only met security requirements but, more importantly, met business objectives and outcomes. Aligning with the business opened up collaborative dialogue and workflow. And I would be remiss if I didn't mention Gene Kim's *The Phoenix Project* as pivotal in my collaborative evolution. Reading his book was like replaying a video of #allofmyFails and then "seeing the light" of working together.

Do you have any favorite books to recommend for people who want to lead cybersecurity teams?
When it comes to recommended cybersecurity books, I harbor bias for any books written by Bruce Schneier, Richard Clarke, and Cory Doctorow. If I were forced to choose specific tomes, those volumes would be Gene Kim's *Phoenix and Unicorn Project* volumes, and I have the *CISO Desk Reference Guide* volumes 1 and 2 nearby to consult in my daily work. If I am really stretched for a volume to read or need something relevant, I turn to CISO Rick Howard's Palo Alto Networks' Cybersecurity Canon Hall of Fame (blog.paloaltonetworks.com/2018/05/announcing-the-2018-cybersecurity-canon-hall-of-famers), which has been sourced through the community. This is how I have personally sought out relevant leadership material—through the community, fellow leaders, and mentors. I believe it is important to live outside isolation to survey other leadership styles that could have bearing on my own, hence my dependency on the broader community to "sharpen my own iron." I would be remiss if I did not mention the need to read material outside of our space, say from academia (e.g., *Harvard Business Review*, Harvard Kennedy School, and business school) and/or feast on lessons learned from leaders outside of our space like U.S. Army Retired General Stanley McChrystal (e.g., *Team of Teams: New Rules of Engagement for a Complex World*) to learn to lead in the context of chaos, or Michael Lewis's *The Fifth Risk* when managing outside of our norms.

"I've always been the type to innovate to solve business problems. By far my most important decision (and the riskiest) was to become an entrepreneur and start a company."

Twitter: @abagrin • **Website:** www.linkedin.com/in/abagrin

Andrew Bagrin

5

Andrew Bagrin is the founder and chief executive officer of OmniNet, a leading provider of firewall as a service (FWaaS) for small businesses. With more than 20 years of experience in the IT security industry, Andrew started OmniNet in 2013 to bring cloud-based, enterprise-level security technology to small businesses at an affordable price. Prior to founding OmniNet, Andrew served as the director of service provider business development at Fortinet, a network security provider. A network security expert, Andrew has been quoted in a variety of media outlets, including *The New York Times*, *Bloomberg Businessweek*, *Small Business Computing*, *Columbia Business Law Review*, and *Business Solutions* magazine.

Do you believe there is a massive shortage of career cybersecurity professionals?

It's been challenging trying to find good cybersecurity professionals. There isn't a lack of people trying to get into the field, just a lack of good ones. Part of the problem is that the

Formal education is new,
and it will take some time for
someone to become efficient
at turning out professionals
who are ready to go.

ones who grew up with
cybersecurity and have
been working hard and
learning are reluctant to
take the time to teach
the new people entering
the industry. It's often
challenging trying to explain
and teach tribal knowledge and frustrating when the student
doesn't pick it up quickly. Formal education is new, and it will
take some time for someone to become efficient at turning out
professionals who are ready to go.

**What's the most important decision you've made or
action you've taken related to a business risk?**
I'm faced with decisions every day. It's not always easy to
quickly weigh and determine the cost/risk analysis from
a business perspective. There are times when I've made
a decision to take an expensive journey in the name of
maintaining a high level of security, but have also made
a decision to reduce the security because of the barriers
it added. I've always been the type to innovate to solve
business problems. By far my most important decision (and
the riskiest) was to become an entrepreneur and start a
company. Cutting the corporate umbilical cord is tough to do
when you're making a fat paycheck and life is great.

**How do you make hard decisions? Do you find yourself
more often making people, process, or technology
decisions?**
This really depends on what the decision is to be made. There
is an optimal solution for each problem. In most cases for me,
technology or some form of automation would be my first
choice, although sometimes you need to have people involved
at first to make sure you implement the technology correctly.
In some cases, it doesn't make sense to add more technology
when a simple process can be added to an existing one. I
subscribe to the "slow to hire" concept as HR has become more
difficult to manage. Code, or technology, is usually the most
efficient decision, specifically in my area, since we work with
volumes and automation.

What's something that you struggle with as a leader, and how do you overcome that?
I have been extremely lucky in my career to mostly work with extraordinary people. This has been great, but it also inherently makes me trusting and gives employees flexibility, access, and control in many things. When I run into a situation where an employee isn't someone I've worked with for years or they're junior to the field, it's challenging for me to be patient and not get frustrated as they learn. It's taken some time for me to build up this patience and work with various skillsets.

How do you lead your team to execute and get results?
For me to properly lead a team, I need to give the team leads or people in charge of execution the control and responsibility to execute. When someone is working on executing their own plan, they are much more passionate and diligent to make sure it's executed 100 percent. The key is to work with them to make sure their plan of execution is aligned with the bigger picture. If I'm working on something as an individual contributor, I try to make sure I'm working on things that I'm passionate about. Having the drive to work on something not only makes it exciting but produces much better results. No one likes doing things they don't like.

Do you have a workforce philosophy or unique approach to talent acquisition?
I always try to hire someone I know or someone I trust knows. There are beautiful résumés, expert interviewees, etc., but at the end of the day, the person has to have a great culture fit, so getting talent that our people have successfully worked with before is a key part of getting the right employees.

Have you created a cohesive strategy for your information security program or business unit?
Our team is pretty small and very engineering-heavy. We don't have a cohesive written-down strategy or an InfoSec program in place. It's more efficient for us to communicate effectively on these types of topics to make better decisions as a team and for all of us to mature together as we discuss them. Of course, as an organization grows and there are people involved in various processes, it makes more sense to have a cohesive strategy with

a well-defined way to keep things aligned. This includes proper communication, procedures, training, etc.

What are your communication tips for interacting with executive leadership?

Depending on who you are and who you interact with, there is a difference between listening and gathering information, brainstorming ideas, and presenting well-prepared information to others. If you're in charge of solving a problem for a department, you want to listen to the actual people you are solving the problem for, ask questions, and learn if they've considered things, and why and why not. Brainstorm with peers to come up with a solution and discuss it with the team you are solving the problem for. Once you have a complete proposal, with information about why you propose it, along with an alternative, you can put together a clear presentation for executive management. They just want to know that they have the right people solving the problems in the most efficient way. The best thing you can do is make them feel that way by being thorough, but brief, and make the entire team feel like the problem was solved the best way possible. When you communicate with anyone, be yourself and respect who you're working with. I've made some poor choices that cost me by thinking and acting like I'm the smartest guy and everyone should listen to me.

How do you cultivate productive relationships with your boss, peers, direct reports, and other team members?

I'm a strong believer in interaction outside the office. If the boss, peer, direct report, etc., can get along with you on a personal level, working together becomes much easier. I'm a big fan of team events, even small ones. As long as you did your part in building a good culture and making sure there is a strong culture fit, things should fall into place pretty easily.

Have you encountered challenges collaborating with revenue-generating teams like sales and product development?

There are often communication gaps between departments such as sales, development, and product. Luckily, I've always found it easy to relate to and communicate with any department, even HR. I've worn the sales and business development hat for many years and have worked closely with product and development. Often I find myself being the liaison between these departments or I find someone to be the funnel of information, if there are challenges in communication between departments.

Have you encountered challenges collaborating with technology teams like information technology and software development?

I have personally not had many challenges. If there is a challenge, it's trying to articulate a clear picture of what the functionality of a product should be, or even why it should be that way. I believe it's important to get everyone on the same page and understand what we're truly trying to accomplish and why. Often the team members working on the project can come up with better ideas than your initial proposal, but only if they fully understand what the user experience should be and why. I try to mock up the UX/UI to paint a picture of what we want to accomplish, give some ideas of how we can accomplish it, and ask for input. By actively soliciting ideas and input, it forces developers to really think through the entire solution and understand what we're delivering and why.

> By actively soliciting ideas and input, it forces developers to really think through the entire solution and understand what we're delivering and why.

Do you have any favorite books to recommend for people who want to lead cybersecurity teams?

Tribe of Hackers! Understanding the fundamentals of the threats and defenses and why systems, processes, and procedures are in place goes a long way in leading cybersecurity teams. People are often passionate about cybersecurity, and you want to keep that flame burning. Unfortunately, I do not have any recommendations on a book to read specifically about cybersecurity teams. Still one of my favorite leadership books is *The 7 Habits of Highly Effective People*. I think it's a must for anyone in a management role.

Zate Berg

6 Zate has 25 years in tech, the last 8 in building/leading security teams/programs. He is originally from Australia and spent parts of his youth in the outback. He was in the Australian Army working in meteorology, survey, and communications. He started his journey in security at PwC and led his first team working for Bioware. He later spent some time building security programs for Bethesda/ZeniMax games. He is currently recruiting and developing great InfoSec people to "Help People Get Jobs" at Indeed.com. Zate is married with two boys and two corgis and spends his spare time in #TheShed woodworking.

Do you believe there is a massive shortage of career cybersecurity professionals?
I think there is no shortage of junior/entry-level talent who have the right skills and knowledge and who need developing so they gain the right behaviors and experience.

> "I take ethics/honesty seriously, and in our line of work we need to strive for being honest and truthful all the time."

I think there is a shortage of qualified senior talent who have the experience, knowledge, and behaviors to cover the width of securing complex environments. Finding and keeping these senior people is competitive. You need to understand what they are looking for and ensure that you, your team, and your organization can provide that. These people have often experienced a lot of organizations and know what they are seeking. Sometimes it's compensation, and often it's recognition in the InfoSec community at large or the ability to sink their teeth into solving complex, difficult problems.

These senior people are one-half of solving the shortage of career cybersecurity professionals. We need to understand how they evolved and re-create that on a global scale.

Often what we need to impart to new cybersecurity professionals is experience, and there is no course to send someone to for that.

The shift from people getting to security through experience in other technical fields to coming to security directly from degrees/courses with out-of-date curriculums is something we need to focus on addressing. Coming directly to cybersecurity is becoming the norm, but we have not yet adapted to developing these people correctly. We need to focus less on the skills they bring to the table, as we can teach that. We need to work out how we impart experience to these newcomers.

I think we do not have enough qualified passionate leaders to develop these passionate, talented people. We need more leaders who can recognize and develop the right people and pair them up with senior experienced people so they can gain that same experience quickly. This means coaching the newcomers, but it especially means finding those senior people in our field with the aptitude to teach and share their experiences with others.

The shortage exists but requires that senior cybersecurity people and cybersecurity leaders change to focus on working together to create the right environments and opportunities for developing and sharing experience. Our field cycles, we get new technologies regularly, but the fundamental vulnerabilities in systems remains mostly static.

What's the most important decision you've made or action you've taken related to a business risk?

I chose to leave a job and move on to another opportunity because the response to my making the business aware of a risk was to encourage me to misrepresent that risk to a client. I take ethics/honesty seriously, and in our line of work we need to strive for being honest and truthful all the time. That may include telling people things they don't want to hear (and having them blame the messenger) or may involve having to know when to escalate above/around a person who is intent on keeping the reality of a risk under wraps because they are accountable for it. This is a strong reason to not have your cybersecurity people reporting into your engineering/technical organization if your business is engineering technical products.

How do you make hard decisions? Do you find yourself more often making people, process, or technology decisions?

I do what I think is right for the business and my team, in that order. At the end of the day, my job is to support my team, but ultimately the goal is making sure the business is fully up to date on the reality of their cybersecurity risk.

I find myself making far more people decisions. Even process/tech decisions generally end up being people decisions. My job often means I spend a majority of my time convincing someone there is a problem, and then the actual solving of that problem is relatively straightforward in most cases.

I joke with my wife that as a self-confessed introvert and someone who doesn't really like crowds or being social, it is rather strange that most of my job is about people—hiring people, managing people, developing people, communicating with people, protecting data from people. Everything seems to lead back to people.

What's something that you struggle with as a leader, and how do you overcome that?

Definitely upward communication. I struggle with translating complex cybersecurity risks into business terminology that nontechnical execs can understand. I feel the issue here is the vocabulary. We have a wide and deep body of assumed knowledge that, if it is missing, makes communications about what we do much more difficult.

I also struggle with explaining these risks and concepts to execs I feel should already understand these concepts, given the businesses they run. If you are an executive of a company whose entire strategy and products are digital, then cybersecurity is a thing you must understand because at its core, it is a business problem.

If your role is to understand business problems and make the right choices for the success of your company, then you need two things: a basic vocabulary in cybersecurity and a strong right-hand person you can count on who will tell you the unfiltered truth about the cybersecurity risks your company faces.

The roles I found most challenging were roles where I was expected to "secure all the things" with minimal resources, many levels down inside the technical/engineering organization, and report to leaders with no ability to really understand what my group did. You are left with the accountability but none of the resources needed to do your job. It's a recipe for burnout.

How do you lead your team to execute and get results?
I follow the same four areas I ask my own managers to ask of the people reporting to them.

- *Do you know what your role is?* I give them direction on what our common goals are to achieve so they can see how their work connects to the company's top-line objectives. They can then break this down into smaller chunks for their direct reports to understand and execute on.

- *Do you have what you need to do your job?* I give them the resources, information, and cover/support they need to achieve those goals. This is where I procure the budget or head count that they need to perform their roles. This includes making sure they have things they need to make their jobs easier and reduce toil, churn, and burnout.

- *Does someone at work care about you as a person?* I make sure they know I care about them as a person and that it's important to me they are happy achieving those goals. This can include making sure someone is in the right role or understanding if they have factors outside work that might affect them.

• *Are you being developed?* I ensure they have the right development plan and support to grow so we can do more as a team. Do they need training? A mentor? Some books? Just someone to listen as they work through a problem?

Then I stand aside and let them do their job. I've discovered that sometimes my biggest contribution to achieving the goal and getting results is to *not* get involved. Every time I step in and own something I should delegate, I rob someone else of the opportunity to make decisions, take accountability, maybe learn from mistakes, and ultimately gain experience. In a time when we need to be letting more people in our industry gain more experience, I often find the best way to help my team win is to let them play the game, and I sit on the sidelines and coach.

It is important to celebrate their wins, ensure they get the recognition they deserve, and help them grow and learn from their mistakes. The more I set direction, get them what they need, and make sure they are happy and growing, the more I find we achieve great things.

Do you have a workforce philosophy or unique approach to talent acquisition?

We do an intern program each summer and get great candidates through that as well as Twitter, my team's networking, and our great recruiters. I tell the interns who come in similar things each summer.

I look for the ability to learn, the ability to communicate/teach about what you have learned, and the ability to work well with others. I'm not interested in what you've done more than three to four years ago and not that interested in degrees and certs. They are parts of who someone is, but not the only parts. I don't ignore or devalue them, but they are not a major defining piece of how I determine that someone will be a good hire.

I am interested in what you have learned lately and how you can show me you know that thing well. Much of our job is understanding something new, assessing the risks and issues with it, and then teaching/communicating that information to others. Having code in a repo or writing a blog/article or giving talks on what you have learned shows me you learned it well enough to build it, write about it, or teach it to others.

That is what our jobs are on a daily basis, so above all else, the ability to learn, communicate, and teach are the secret behaviors I look for in people I want to hire.

Technical skills are differing degrees of important, depending on the role. Experience can be a major factor for senior roles, mostly experience in what does and does not work and experience in influencing others. This is the hardest to teach; in fact, you cannot teach this.

I have had success at taking people who have those three traits, and not much security knowledge or direct skills, teaching them the knowledge/skills, and seeing them become highly effective team members.

As for retaining them, if you care about them as people, develop them, and help them achieve their goals, then retaining people becomes much simpler. You can't/won't retain everyone; sometimes it is the right thing for someone to move on. If you are providing the right kind of environment, they may return. I have several people in my organization who I have worked with two or three times and would work with again for sure if we were to separate and have that opportunity to come back together again.

Have you created a cohesive strategy for your information security program or business unit?

You must understand at its core what your business does. Generally, for most businesses, that is generating revenue/value. It could also be a social mission if, for example, you are a nonprofit, but even those generally resolve back to generating revenue. Whatever the mission of your company is, you will need to understand how it operates to achieve that goal.

Your strategy should be aligned with discovering, communicating, and mitigating the cybersecurity risks associated with achieving that goal.

For a company that collects data, builds software, or provides services online, cybersecurity is going to form a major part of those risks. Companies have finance, HR, legal, IT, or engineering departments to solve for specific kinds of business risks. If your business is digital, you need a department that handles addressing the risks associated with operating in a digital world, a group that can understand the risks to your business and to your customers and build a strategy to manage those risks.

In that world, cybersecurity risk is business risk, and leadership must understand and accept this. This sets the tone at the top that is critical to having a business that can put the resources and priority required on solving cybersecurity risks.

If executives understand those risks and assign them to a group (security organization), then the strategy envisioned and enacted by that organization will be aligned with understanding and mitigating risks the business cares about. Conversations about resources and priority should be simpler as you are now like everyone else, a force being utilized to ensure the success of the company.

Even companies not directly working in the digital world will still have cybersecurity risks that need addressing, and their cybersecurity teams should make sure their strategy is centered around addressing the risks the senior leadership decides are important.

What are your communication tips for interacting with executive leadership?

I'm a no-frills straight-shooter. My communication upward is entirely centered around an understanding that their time is valuable, so I ensure that I use it wisely. I aim to communicate the information my leadership needs in as direct a way as possible; however, sometimes this is difficult when converting complex technical risks into business terms and showing the complex ways they interact and influence each other. I make sure to tie the technical risks and choices we make to the influences they will have on business outcomes.

Communication between myself and my peers is often centered on helping them get ahead of risks and issues before it becomes a situation they have their leadership breathing down their necks about. It's not always successful to try to get people to proactively take action, often just on my own say-so from my own experience. When that fails and we end up being reactive, I generally try to make the conversations about how I can help.

In any conversation about dealing with the realities of a risk, clouding the issue with a deep discussion of how we got there is generally not an effective way of getting others to cooperate in solving the issue, even if it is the exact thing we talked about several months ago and they brushed off.

With conversations downward, I am as open, honest, and transparent as I can be, often more so than some of my peers. I like my people to be fully aware of what is currently going on and what might be coming down the pipe so they can make good choices.

I struggle with "toeing the company line" unless I truly believe in the decisions that were made and the reasons behind them. I have no problem delivering bad news upward or downward, as long as I am not being asked to help justify or cover up something that resulted from terrible leadership or poor decisions. People need to own their decisions, the same way I do.

How do you cultivate productive relationships with your boss, peers, direct reports, and other team members?

I believe in having regular, honest communication. This usually takes the form of one-on-ones or small team meetings. These one-on-ones are a two-way street, and I make time to not just talk about what I want to communicate to them but what they have to say that I need to hear. These are absolutely not status updates. They focus on asking and answering questions that ensure both sides of the relationship have what they need.

Trust is critical in any relationship. Through open, honest communication you build trust. I also operate on assuming good intentions from the other side of the relationship until proven wrong. I think most people are good people and want to do their jobs well and are acting in good faith. When that fails or I am not dealing with someone operating in good faith, then it's important to understand that and act accordingly. Often that is a direct conversation about what is happening, hoping to resolve it.

I let nothing sit and be left unsaid or unaddressed or create a wall. Far too often something will happen between people and, due to a fear of confrontation or healthy disagreement, they will leave things unresolved. So I practice active conflict resolution, with a healthy dose of situational awareness. You want to understand what is causing a conflict and address the root issue. I am always trying to empathize with the other party to understand what motivates, drives, or affects their decisions.

Have you encountered challenges collaborating with revenue-generating teams like sales and product development?

I have encountered some challenges when collaborating with revenue-generating teams in the past. I think it depends on the culture in your business groups and how they see security/risk. Putting risks into the terms they understand (often revenue loss or lost opportunities) can help bring them to the table to discuss things early, before it becomes a major reactive situation.

Conversations about accountability and ownership at the highest level in your revenue-generating organization can bring the right "tone at the top" and help set the culture and relationships at lower levels. If tone at the top is set correctly and we establish the accountability for risk, then culture and relationships become collaborative. Cybersecurity teams become a resource to help the organization understand and deal with certain kinds of risks early.

> If tone at the top is set correctly and we establish the accountability for risk, then culture and relationships become collaborative.

It's important to make sure it is widely understood that there is no blame associated with making a mistake. A culture of associating blame for security incidents/risks will just drive a wedge between teams that need to communicate well. Often how early a problem is caught can affect the downstream impact.

Have you encountered challenges collaborating with technology teams like information technology and software development?

I think every leader in this space has. It's traditionally been hard; we are seen as blockers to them achieving their goals. The critical problem here is that, traditionally, being secure has not been a goal of many of these technical teams. They are held accountable for uptime, velocity, or productivity. When you align accountability at the top and set the right tone so that these technical teams understand that if they build it, they are responsible for making sure it is secure, then the relationships can be far more positive.

I strongly believe that there should be one set of hands, and one direct line to accountability, for anything technically required for the business to achieve its mission. When you allow multiple sets of hands to operate something and they report to differing parts of the organization, you allow finger pointing or uncertainty about who is accountable for risks.

I view my team's role as assurance, measuring and understanding the risks associated with the technology they are implementing, and operating. Security "doing" should be embedded in the teams accountable for building products and reporting up through the same organizational structure, either by training existing people in security or by hiring people to that part of the technology organization who have significant security experience. This evolves to DevSecOps, which should just be the transition from operations teams to operations teams with a focus on delivering and operating secure products.

This is all driven by the tone at the top and an understanding of the risks posed to the business by not building and operating secure products. Solving for a top-level understanding of risks and having them set and inform tone at the top will result in much simpler relationships between those who engineer and those who inspect the engineering for new risks or resolve risks.

Do you have any favorite books to recommend for people who want to lead cybersecurity teams?

- *First, Break All the Rules: What the World's Greatest Managers Do Differently* by Marcus Buckingham
- *War and Peace and IT: Business Leadership, Technology, and Success in the Digital Age* by Mark Schwartz
- *Accelerate: The Science of Lean Software and DevOps: Building and Scaling High Performing Technology Organizations* by Nicole Forsgren PhD, Jez Humble, and Gene Kim
- *The Cisco Handbook: A Practical Guide to Securing Your Company* by Michael Gentile, Ron Collette, and Thomas D. August
- *How to Measure Anything in Cybersecurity Risk* by Douglas W. Hubbard and Richard Seiersen

I choose reading material by what others recommend, sometimes by reviews, and often by just buying a book that I think looks like it might help out with something I am working on, dealing with, or trying to improve.

I tend to like to buy hard copies of tech books, but things like *First Break All the Rules* I get on Audible.

"The biggest struggle that I have experienced as a leader is accepting that I am a leader."

Websites: www.linkedin.com/in/tashbettridge/ and www.wosecnz.com/

Tash Bettridge

7

Kia ora, I am Tash Bettridge, and I am a cybersecurity analyst working on the incident and response team at Vodafone New Zealand. I previously worked as a remote cybersecurity consultant for an organization in New Zealand. I have a bachelor's in computing systems with a focus on networking and cybersecurity. Currently, I am doing my master's with a focus on women in cybersecurity and how a support network such as the New Zealand Network for Women in Security (NZNWS) can bring together a community of women to mentor, train, and retain them in the industry.

Do you believe there is a massive shortage of career cybersecurity professionals?

This question is a bit difficult to answer from a global perspective. If I relate this back to my personal experience in New Zealand, I do believe we have a cybersecurity talent shortage. This is because many organizations prefer cybersecurity professionals with at least two years of industry experience and relevant security or networking certifications. Therefore, this becomes a huge divide for many grads who want an opportunity to enter the cybersecurity field in New Zealand.

I think one way to bridge the cybersecurity gap is for organizations to set up graduate programs that enable graduates to bring their theory and practical education into a professional environment. I believe we can bridge the gap between education and employment by giving university students the opportunity to learn and grow in an organization.

What's the most important decision you've made or action you've taken related to a business risk?

The most important decision I have made as a systems analyst for a social media startup was to make sure our team was aware of ethics surrounding the GDPR, indigenous data, data sovereignty, and Māori data sovereignty. The social media platform that we were designing and developing was targeted to communities with most of the users identifying as minority groups (indigenous people of New Zealand and the Pacific Islands).

Data sovereignty covers indigenous peoples of Canada, New Zealand, Australia, and the United States of America. Data sovereignty refers to the understanding that data is subject to the laws of the nation in which it is collected. Therefore, this includes Māori data sovereignty, which recognizes that Māori data should be subject to Māori governance.

For a startup, building processes and software targeted to a global audience can be challenging as it is. This situation was a risk for me, as I was coming from a cultural perspective and a privacy perspective on this project. This did take a while to progress due to communicating with various lawyers and indigenous data security experts; however, my perspective is if you are building an application for the majority, then keeping security in mind while developing will enhance the project.

The GDPR is now taken very seriously, but data sovereignty for indigenous people is often disregarded. I am a true believer that data sovereignty should be treated with the same respect as the GDPR.

How do you make hard decisions? Do you find yourself more often making people, process, or technology decisions?

This all comes down to context. If it has to do with people, I am someone who makes hard decisions based on cognitive and emotional reactions based on the experience of others.

If it has to do with internal processes in an organization, I guess I am someone who would make hard decisions based on mitigating various risks. If it has to do with technology, I would have a look at what we have implemented to defend our system.

What's something that you struggle with as a leader, and how do you overcome that?

The biggest struggle that I have experienced as a leader is accepting that I am a leader. I have always been someone who identifies more as a team member than a leader. I have always downplayed my achievements or leadership capabilities because I suffer from imposter syndrome.

I have always been someone who loves to help others, and when I started NZNWS in New Zealand with my cofounder, Sai Honig, I saw that I wasn't the only woman who had experienced the imposter syndrome in cybersecurity.

There have often been times when women in cybersecurity leadership wanted to drop out of their careers because they felt like they were imposters in the industry. Even though I was still new to leadership, I felt sad that women were feeling the same way I was feeling. Worst of all, I was new in the industry whereas they had years of industry experience. Therefore, this made me overcome my imposter syndrome and embrace a growth mindset.

How do you lead your team to execute and get results?

As someone who has worked with various startups, I believe that communication within the team is vital. Specifically, in startups it is already an intense environment, as you and your whole team have to wear many hats to execute and get results.

What are your communication tips for interacting with executive leadership?

I have been in situations where I have to put my integrity aside and leave myself at the door. However, now that I'm further along in my career, I believe the most important thing when it comes to communicating with executive leaders is to be open and honest with them.

It is important to be transparent with peers, and it is okay to ask for help or further training. Especially in cybersecurity, we are not perfect, and it can be intimidating for new cybersecurity professionals to step up and advise that there are issues due to fear of being targeted as being incompetent.

How do you cultivate productive relationships with your boss, peers, direct reports, and other team members?

In New Zealand there is a Māori value called *whanaungatanga*, which is the process of establishing positive and meaningful relationships. This value is vital to have a strong workplace environment that is supportive and where all members of the team are striving to reach the same goal.

Cultivating productive relationships through mentorship can help the team with personal development and professional growth.

Have you encountered challenges collaborating with technology teams like information technology and software development?

I wouldn't consider this as a challenge because communicating with members of the team is vital to delivering a product that has security measures in place. As per the data sovereignty situation with the startup I was working for, it was important to be transparent with and educate the team working on the project.

Do you have any favorite books to recommend for people who want to lead cybersecurity teams?

This is not in any order, but here are a few of my favorite books. These books are not based on leadership; some of these books are just good reads.

- *The Hacker Playbook: Practical Guide to Penetration Testing* by Peter Kim
- *Code Girls: The Untold Story of the American Women Code Breakers of World War II* by Liza Mundy
- *The Girl with the Dragon Tattoo* By Stieg Larsson
- *Breaking and Entering: The Extraordinary Story of a Hacker Called "Alien"* by Jeremy Smith

> "As leaders, we must care for team members in the best way possible, which sometimes means transitioning them to another role or even to the next stage of their career with another company."

Website: gettingsecuritydone.com

Philip Beyer

8 Philip Beyer is the vice president of security engineering for Global Payments Inc., a leading pure-play payments technology company delivering innovative software and services globally. He leads the teams that build solutions to protect customer and cardholder data.

Mr. Beyer is mission-driven to guide security leaders to higher effectiveness. His company Getting Security Done supports professionals with business communication and value creation training. He cofounded the Texas CISO Council, a regional committee that develops free strategic resources for security leaders. He holds a BS degree in physics from Trinity University, as well as the CISSP certification. Outside the office he is a martial artist and ultra-marathon runner.

Do you believe there is a massive shortage of career cybersecurity professionals?

I believe there is a dearth of effective leaders in cybersecurity. Our professional community has an abundance of technical ingenuity, innovative products, and original thoughts. We have the tools and techniques to do more to protect ourselves than we are doing today. Now more than ever, companies need leaders willing to deliver effective cybersecurity, and that means achieving results aligned with business objectives, engaging and retaining their people, improving performance over time, communicating and building relationships with peers, and making hard decisions.

There may be a shortage of skilled professionals ready to hire, but there is definitely a shortage of effective leaders in cybersecurity. Effective leadership multiplies the value of a group (a team, department, company, etc.) and can help us bridge any gap (real or perceived).

There may be a shortage of skilled professionals ready to hire, but there is definitely a shortage of effective leaders in cybersecurity.

What's the most important decision you've made or action you've taken related to a business risk?

The most important risk management decisions I've made have involved ending or eliminating some sort of project or work effort. It has been easy for me to find more work to do to protect the company. I have found it much harder to identify wasted effort and valueless activity. I'm not referring to administrative overhead (i.e., TPS reports), which we can all agree is frustrating. Rather, my *most* important risk decisions involved the responsible elimination of tools that our company was not equipped to operate. Our inefficient operation of those tools didn't protect the company, negligently increased expenses, and had detrimental side effects (stressed out team members, who had less time for more productive work). It would have been easy to maintain the status quo, but that would have counterintuitively increased risk.

There's another reason why I consider this kind of decision to be my most important: it happens regularly to every leader throughout their career. For any number of reasons and because we're human, each of us tends to find and stick to routines. In so doing, we find ourselves and our teams doing more and more, while neglecting the hard work of trimming and optimizing. As Greg McKeown has said, "If it isn't a clear yes, then it's a clear no." For more on how important this skill is and how to do it, see *Essentialism* by Greg McKeown.

How do you make hard decisions? Do you find yourself more often making people, process, or technology decisions?

Executives make decisions. Effective executives make effective decisions. This is one of the key points made by Peter F. Drucker in his classic book on self-management, *The Effective Executive*. I have struggled with decision-making throughout my career and so have devoted time to studying it. I have found Drucker's comprehensive approach to be the hardest to grasp but ultimately the most practical. Following his guidance, I surround myself with a variety of professionals to encourage "the clash of conflicting views, the dialogue between different points of view, the choice between different judgments." Commensurate with the value and impact of the decision, I involve supporters, challengers, and detractors; loud and quiet people; task-oriented and people-oriented perspectives; technical folks and the not-so-technical; stakeholders and independents. For the hard decisions, it's usually not easy to do this, but the result is worth the effort.

After the decision is made, an effective leader ensures it is put into effect, the most time-consuming step in the process. In *The Effective Executive*, Peter F. Drucker says, "Unless a decision has degenerated into work, it is not a decision; it is at best a good intention."

For more on creative thinking and novel approaches to great decision-making, see *Creating Great Choices* by Jennifer Riel and Roger L. Martin and *Questions Are the Answer* by Hal Gregersen.

People decisions are the hardest for me, so that's where I spend my time. Every minute spent on people has a resounding impact. As leaders, we must care for team members in the best way possible, which sometimes means transitioning them to another role or even to the next stage of their career with another company.

What's something that you struggle with as a leader, and how do you overcome that?

I struggle the most with having the critical, hard conversations with team members necessary to convey constructive criticism and negative feedback. That's a big problem. Effective leaders multiply the value of a group (a team, department, company, etc.) by improving performance over time, and that is best done with course-correcting guidance delivered through frequent, clear conversations. Talking about performance is a fundamental behavior of a manager. Mark Horstman presents his guidance on the subject in *The Effective Manager*. I have found his approach to be invaluable in tackling this challenge and developing this skill.

Knowing that talking about performance is important and that it's hard for me, it won't be a surprise to hear that my first management role was my most challenging. Before I became a manager, I had no training, didn't know of any resources, and assumed neither was strictly necessary. In all of my prior work experience as a contributor, I had been successful operating independently and with little oversight. My managers provided infrequent feedback, and when I did receive it, the delivery was awkward or unhelpful. I was always anxious leading up to my own annual performance reviews, not because of poor performance, but because I didn't know what to expect. When I became a manager, assuming responsibility for my team members' performance was a big change, and it's the one that still intimidates me. Thankfully, I learned practical techniques from Horstman for how to talk about performance and, more importantly, how to deliver it frequently. Now, my team members know what to expect and how to improve...and I'm pretty sure they aren't nervous about their performance reviews!

In addition to his book, Horstman and his co-founder Mike Auzenne, along with their team, provide extensive training and resources via Manager Tools. For even more on delivering constructive criticism and being an effective manager, see *Crucial Conversations* by Kerry Patterson, Joseph Grenny, Ron McMillan, and Al Switzler, and *Radical Candor* by Kim Scott.

How do you lead your team to execute and get results?
I've been experimenting with productivity systems and techniques for most of my life. I excel at starting things and suck at getting them done. After I read *Getting Things Done* by David Allen and learned how to use GTD, I adopted his approach and have used it to maintain focus in both my professional and personal life ever since. As a contributor, all I really needed was a system to provide the structure and rules for me to follow. Habitual practice then yielded results.

Maintaining team focus is much more challenging. I don't think cybersecurity is different from any other technology profession in this regard, but it sure *seems* like we have critically urgent issues interrupting our planned work *all the time*. Having seen the results of a systematic approach individually, I went on a search and experimented with a variety of productivity systems and techniques for teams. After I read *The 4 Disciplines of Execution* by Chris McChesney, Sean Covey, and Jim Huling, I knew I had found what I was looking for. I'm learning how to use 4DX and have started to adopt the approach with my teams.

For more on personal productivity, see *Free to Focus* by Michael Hyatt. For more on corporate productivity, see *Execution* by Larry Bossidy and Ram Charan.

Do you have a workforce philosophy or unique approach to talent acquisition?

I increase the talent pool available to me by increasing my participation in the cybersecurity professional community. Expanding my professional network provides more exposure to job seekers, and getting more candidates into the pipeline is the hardest part of the hiring process. I try to do more than just attend meetings or conferences. To differentiate myself from other attendees and stand out in the crowd, I share my experience or contribute to the conversation in some way to make myself both available and memorable. There are many different ways to do this, like giving a presentation, conducting a training, volunteering to help, or contributing to a book. Each method requires a nontrivial amount of time, and that effort sets you apart. The fringe benefit of this commitment is that a strong professional network is also available when you initiate your own job search.

Rather than focus on employee retention, I direct my effort to increasing engagement. The familiar attraction of cybersecurity positions with higher compensation is challenging to be sure. After I've done everything I can to raise salary ranges to their fiscally responsible limit, I recognize I have no more control over the situation. Everything left to do is set forth in Gallup's seminal work on management, *First, Break All the Rules* by Marcus Buckingham and Curt Coffman. Develop team member talent on an individual basis, build on an employee's unique strengths, and set clear expectations. Engaged employees are more productive, achieve higher customer satisfaction ratings, and stay at their companies longer.

Hiring is a discipline unto itself. I've been successful in the past, but my approach has admittedly been intuitive and nonrepeatable. I spent time this year learning more about how to do it better. For specific guidance on the hiring process I have adopted, see *The Effective Hiring Manager* by Mark Horstman.

Have you created a cohesive strategy for your information security program or business unit?
Every strategic plan I've produced has been flawed or incomplete in some significant way. I've never been proud of one. Ideas have always come easy to me, but putting them together effectively is much harder. I'm still learning how to improve in this area and don't have much practical guidance. However, I do have one piece of advice, and it is to follow Paul Smith's example and *Lead with a Story*. Explaining your strategy and persuading your audience to provide support is a perfect opportunity to employ the tool of storytelling.

What are your communication tips for interacting with executive leadership?
Communication is the primary skill a leader uses to influence others. Effective communicators know that all people have habits of communicating. The ability to recognize different natural communication styles presents an opportunity. You can become a more effective communicator by recognizing these styles and modifying the way you communicate. When you understand more of what your listener is thinking and feeling, minor changes to your delivery can upgrade your influence.

> When you understand more of what your listener is thinking and feeling, minor changes to your delivery can upgrade your influence.

Though it's not a universal truth, most executive leaders have dominant, forceful personalities. They tend to be direct, no-nonsense, and they can be perceived as aggressive. With this natural style, the cardinal rule for communication is to be brief. Get to the point as soon as possible. Under pressure, stand firm without raising your voice. When questioned, give a clear, succinct answer followed by an action plan.

If this seems like a gross oversimplification to you, then you're not wrong. I encourage you to explore the extensive training and resources on effective communication provided by Manager Tools. Understanding behavior is how I approach communication.

How do you cultivate productive relationships with your boss, peers, direct reports, and other team members?

Following on from earlier, I use effective communication strategies as often as I can to cultivate relationships. We all want to be heard and understood. As I improve in my ability to understand a person's natural communication style, it helps me understand what is important to them, how they view the world, and how they will likely react to my own communication style. Then I can adapt my style to be more like the other person, which makes it easier for them to understand me. Moving toward another person's style in this way makes it more likely that we will *click*. It's not manipulative but thoughtful. It makes this person's life easier and means we're more likely to have a successful collaboration.

These techniques can also work in the other direction to explain what you see or hear. When I understand that another person's natural communication style is assertive and task-focused, I know their one-line email wasn't sent from anger, nor was it intentionally vague. The same is true of an abrupt hallway conversation. Knowing the communication style helps me to be tolerant of different kinds of communicators in the workplace.

Again, if this brief answer leaves you wanting more, I encourage you to explore the extensive training and resources on effective communication provided by Manager Tools.

Have you encountered challenges collaborating with revenue-generating teams like sales and product development?

Growth is the key motivator for any business unit charged with generating revenue. Leaders of these teams are predominantly focused on eliminating any impediments to revenue growth. To do this, they want the freedom to act independently. Simultaneously, they want to

As cybersecurity leaders, we are technology risk managers.

do the right thing for the company, and that is common ground you share. To partner with these leaders, provide clear boundary conditions for their decisions. As cybersecurity leaders, we are technology risk managers. Describe the class of risk decision that belongs to a business unit leader as well as those that belong to others. Then get out of their way and let them make money!

Understanding motivation is how I approach partnership.

Have you encountered challenges collaborating with technology teams like information technology and software development?

The key motivator for technology teams is the drive to build. Leaders of these teams are predominantly focused on enabling the development process. Whether it's systems, networks, clouds, or code, they want to create something worthwhile. They want their creation to be resilient in the face of adversity, and that is common ground you share. To partner with these leaders, foster trust and mutual respect. As cybersecurity leaders, we are technology vulnerability experts. Describe the applicable threat model and educate them on the implications. Then get out of their way and let them build!

> Every corporate leader knows that the cybersecurity team is responsible for monitoring, testing, and validating.

Every corporate leader knows that the cybersecurity team is responsible for monitoring, testing, and validating. The most effective cybersecurity leaders find ways to make that part of their role only as prominent as it needs to be.

Do you have any favorite books to recommend for people who want to lead cybersecurity teams?

I like reading and listening to books. I thrive on ideas. Hearing the perspective and approach of others helps me to chart my own course.

In addition to the books I've already mentioned, I recommend the following for aspiring, new, and veteran leaders alike:

- *Dare to Lead* by Brené Brown
- *The Infinite Game* by Simon Sinek

For those with a thirst for more reading material on leadership and excellent professional development guidance, I recommend the monthly book club LeaderBooks.

"For me, many security decisions can be hard decisions, but if we do our homework and use the data to our advantage, we can make well-informed decisions and minimize impact."

Twitter: @kylebubp

Kyle Bubp

9

For more than a decade, Kyle Bubp has worked for enterprises, hosting providers, the FBI, the Department of Energy, and the Department of Defense to analyze and improve their security posture. As cofounder of Savage Security, he focused on cutting through fear, uncertainty, and doubt (FUD) to help make defensive strategies cheaper and easier for customers. His company was later acquired by Threatcare, where Kyle served as the director of strategic services and worked directly with the CEO. Kyle continues to develop practical defensive strategies, research security issues, and publish articles and presentations on improving the security industry. Outside of work, you'll find him hiking, riding motorcycles, hitting the gym, playing music, and exploring the globe.

Do you believe there is a massive shortage of career cybersecurity professionals?
I'm not sure how I would define a career cybersecurity professional. I think there's a shortage in realistic expectations.

Perhaps instead of a shortage of talent, we have an excess of expectations? By that I mean most of the really good cybersecurity folks were once really good Windows/Linux/network admins. They've been around the block; they understand how to configure and maintain the systems they are now entrusted to protect. They've likely written scripts to automate repetitive tasks, and they've had to work with management and cross-functional teams on projects. They don't have "security" or "cyber" in their job titles, but they would likely make excellent security practitioners.

Perhaps we should stop scouring the job sites for "security" candidates and instead think about our environments, where our risk resides, and then find folks who are experts in those systems with an interest in security, demonstrated ability to work across teams, and a continued history of education, training, and curiosity.

What's the most important decision you've made or action you've taken related to a business risk?

I don't know if it's the most important decision, but it's certainly a recent decision that could have had a massive impact on email, both to and from our organization. We recently implemented SPF and DMARC in a hard fail mode. This impacts not just inbound email but also any marketing emails that masquerade as coming from our domain. Anyone who has worked in a large environment with multiple technical teams will tell you that there is shadow IT. We did our best to do our due diligence and gather logs of who was sending as us, validating those senders, and then adding them to our SPF records. The time came for the change to go into effect that would hard fail any sender not aligned to our policies. Furthermore, we are a retail organization going into the holiday season, so any email delivery issues could really impact revenue.

I chose the path to move forward with a hard fail on our 15+ domains because I trusted in our team, the work we did to gather logs, and the risk reduction of spoofed emails. After the change, we monitored our aggregate and forensic reports, compared that data and volume to before the change, and worked with our marketing departments to ensure that there was no disruption to their services.

How do you make hard decisions? Do you find yourself more often making people, process, or technology decisions?

A lot of the decisions we make affect many aspects of the organization, so it's important that we take into account the impact not simply on cyber risk but on how it might affect processes and workflows elsewhere. For me, many security decisions can be hard decisions, but if we do our homework and use the data to our advantage, we can make well-informed decisions and minimize impact. I know that's super vague, but that's really what it comes down to. Digest the facts, weigh the risk, and make the best decision you can make at the time. Adjust as needed.

My time is mostly dedicated to technology and process decisions, which in turn affect people.

What's something that you struggle with as a leader, and how do you overcome that?

Initially I had an issue with delegation, but I also recognized this as an issue and dealt with it by being a better communicator. I took the time to first run through the process myself and document it. Then I would walk through the process with whomever I was delegating to, asking them to follow my documentation and make changes as they saw fit. This allowed me to see their process, as well as errors in my own, and gave both of us the ability to ask questions and get answers. Finally, I simply handed it off.

As the team grows, I realize I won't be able to have this one-to-one workflow with every employee, so we are focusing on building up our playbooks. I believe that empowerment and autonomy are key for engagement, so I try to foster that as much as possible.

How do you lead your team to execute and get results?

Clear and concise communication of what the results should be is step 1. If we don't know what is expected of us or what the end goal should look like, it's hard to really drive to those goals and hold ourselves and others accountable for them. We also break up large projects into small milestones and then assign those milestones to individuals. We use a Kanban board to track progress, and I review the board daily when we get there in the morning. I encourage our team members to seek advice from others, offer ideas and opinions, and get involved outside of purely technical teams.

This is similar to how I try to contribute as an individual, so I suppose I'm not too creative in that aspect.

Do you have a workforce philosophy or unique approach to talent acquisition?

I don't value degrees all that much; instead, I would like to see certifications, projects completed, and technical assessments. I look for folks who are hungry, show a passion for learning, and try to solve issues on their own before engaging others. Technical prescreens for candidates are important, and it helps save a lot of time and money in the hiring process. I also try to understand how the candidate would react in a lose-lose scenario, as those tend to happen in our industry. This helps me understand their emotional IQ.

Retaining goes back to the whole autonomy thing I mentioned earlier. Of course, our employees should also have a well-communicated career path, requirements, and milestones. I want to make sure they feel like they have support to pursue their interests, and I hope they stick around, but eventually everyone will find "the next big thing," so if we can build them up to better their lives elsewhere, so be it.

Have you created a cohesive strategy for your information security program or business unit?

This seems to be a moving target as business requirements change and new ideas are incorporated into our organization. We also have to be cognizant of regulation and legislation that is passed, and those things impact and influence our strategies.

From a technical perspective, we stay up to date on tactics, techniques, and procedures (TTPs) to ensure we are doing the right things to minimize our risk there. We support the technical decisions with documented policies and procedures so that employees know what is expected of them and how to execute.

The most difficult part is the disruption around "We've always done it this way." Whenever a new idea or process is implemented, even if it's better, there will be pushback. Humans like routine, and when our routine is changed, it causes friction. Clear and concise communication about what to expect, and why the change is being made, is important. However, empathy is also extremely important here, and I think that's what some folks miss.

What are your communication tips for interacting with executive leadership?

Never try to bullsh*t anyone, whether they are above you, a peer, or below you in the org chart. Everyone brings different life experiences to the workplace, and eventually you're going to get found out. People don't forget, and once that trust is gone, it's hard to get back.

That being said, I try to keep my communication with executives very short and concise. Their worlds are busy, so I try to feed them exactly the data points they need, what it means to them, and what I recommend we do (or inform them of what we have done). They want to keep their finger on the pulse, but they don't need the full-panel bloodwork results of the physical.

My boss gets a little more context and some more off-topic bumper conversation, but I still try to respect his time to keep things on task. My communications are concise, and I make it a point to let him know when I need his help to move a project along.

With peers and direct reports there is more of a friendly, jovial environment. I try to find opportunities to mentor folks when possible but also take time to be mentored by others.

At the end of the day, I just try to respect everyone's time, learn a little bit about them, and make them feel respected and welcomed.

How do you cultivate productive relationships with your boss, peers, direct reports, and other team members?

In a word, respect. I know that the security program is nothing without everyone's knowledge, support, and technical expertise. I try to keep that in perspective and don't shy away from acknowledgment of their efforts and appreciation of their time.

Outside of that, it's just being human: learning about your peers, finding things you have a mutual interest in, supporting each other when you can tell someone is having a bad day, and asking what you can do to help (even when you really know there's nothing you can do). Just be a good human.

Have you encountered challenges collaborating with revenue-generating teams like sales and product development?

Of course, but you have to realize that many times your goals are not their goals, and if you get in the way of their goals, it's not going to be good for them. To simplify, you have to be selfless and understand that the reason the business exists at the end of the day is because they generate revenue, not because you have the best firewall rules this side of the Mississippi. It's about communicating your goals, why they're important, how they will affect the user, and the risk of not doing it. Take time to educate, understand, and communicate, and it generally goes well. Also, expect to be the butt of a joke or two. Don't take offense; just roll with it.

Have you encountered challenges collaborating with technology teams like information technology and software development?
Yes, indeed. I'm not sure one can build a security program without encountering these challenges. I approach it the same way as the previous question. It's really important that everyone has their own priorities, and security usually isn't one of them. Thus, the communication of the risk, the impact, and what is necessary is crucial. Also, in the technical scenarios, it's important to offer to do as much of the work as possible. Many times, you will be turned down, but it's important to offer and do the work if they take you up on your offer.

Do you have any favorite books to recommend for people who want to lead cybersecurity teams?
Leading a security team and building a security program is a mix of management, social engineering, and sales. Here are a few of the books I think have made an impact on the way in which I approach things:

- *Rework* by Jason Fried
- *The Phoenix Project* by Gene Kim
- *The 21 Irrefutable Laws of Leadership* by John Maxwell
- *Drive* by Daniel Pink
- *Death by Meeting* by Patrick Lencioni
- *Let's Get Real or Let's Not Play* by Mahan Khalsa
- *Never Split the Difference* by Chris Voss
- *Louder Than Words* by Joe Navarro
- *Linchpin* by Seth Goden

"In my experience, it is almost always possible to find common ground where all sides can have their needs met in situations where the stakeholders have divergent or even competing goals."

Website: www.linkedin.com/in/joanna-burkey

Joanna Burkey

10

Joanna Burkey is the global head of Cyber Defense at Siemens. In this role, Joanna and her team have responsibility for cybersecurity defense across the IT/OT infrastructure as well as products, solutions, and services. The Cyber Defense organization includes Product CERT, Corporate CERT, and three global Cyber Defense Centers in the United States, Portugal, and China.

Joanna has a computer science/engineering background from The University of Texas at Austin and Angelo State University and has focused on cybersecurity throughout her career. She was previously the Americas CISO at Siemens, and her previous roles have included software engineering, product strategy, and security evangelism.

Do you believe there is a massive shortage of career cybersecurity professionals?

The way our industry defines "cybersecurity professional" is, in my mind, still quite limited. There is a prevalent mindset from those both within and outside of our field that the cybersecurity expert is the super-techie who was already successfully exploiting systems before their 10th birthday. But just like any domain, we need all types of career professionals! There is a space in cybersecurity for everyone from marketing to project managing to, yes, the technical experts, and I believe we can all continue to recognize and push the message that there isn't one "type" who has to work in this field.

Continuing to make it a priority to role model all of the various ways that individuals can succeed in cybersecurity is also key. Particularly during professionally formative years such as secondary and university education, all of us can look for ways to demonstrate to students how many varied opportunities and paths there are for all types of skill sets.

What's the most important decision you've made or action you've taken related to a business risk?
When I initially moved from being on the product side of cybersecurity to being on the practitioner side, one thing I noticed was that many times the business leaders accepting cybersecurity risks were not the ones who would actually face the consequences if the risks were to manifest. The first time that I directed my team to force the issue and bring the risk acceptance to the actual organization that was being exposed to increased risk due to a services change, it was a painful process for everyone involved. But I felt strongly it was the right thing to do in order for the appropriate business leader to be aware and informed of how the cybersecurity topic could truly affect their business. In the past, they had never had to deal with being confronted with it so directly and having to make a choice to accept the risk or change the service strategy.

I believe this is critical to every company both now and going forward: to understand that cybersecurity risks are real and can have tangible effects on areas of the business that they have never had to think about before.

How do you make hard decisions? Do you find yourself more often making people, process, or technology decisions?
Years ago I heard, and it stuck with me, the statement that "Good leaders make clear decisions quickly and don't hesitate to change those decisions as soon as it's needed." My experience

has validated this time and again, so I have taken it to heart. Decisions should be clear, and once made, they should not be revisited over and over again until and unless it is shown that the original choice was not the appropriate one. Leaders ultimately suffer more loss of respect by sticking with the wrong decision than by acknowledging that a change is needed to their original one.

These days I very seldom make technology decisions, though I do strive to always be informed by my team and understand the technology directions that they decide on. I more frequently find myself focusing on more strategic decisions to make sure that we are consistently following a path with our people and with our processes that supports our overall vision and how we achieve that vision.

What's something that you struggle with as a leader, and how do you overcome that?

It took me a long time to realize that I took every problem brought to me as though I personally needed to solve it. And sometimes I still find myself falling into this trap! It is not good for anyone, as it quickly would overwhelm me to solve every problem, and doesn't allow members of my leadership team to have the opportunity. So I remind myself to not just jump in but instead to listen, advise, and delegate. I can't overestimate the importance, and difficulty, of the "listening" part in that statement!

Along these lines, I really struggled with my very first people management role, as I did what so many people do at every level. I defaulted into what I knew I could succeed at when the going got tough. But what had made me succeed before management was software engineering—that's not exactly what I needed to do now as a new manager! Fortunately, I had some good mentoring to point this out to me, and I continue to believe it's one of the biggest pitfalls for new managers. So you won't be surprised to see me strongly recommend *What Got You Here Won't Get You There* by Marshall Goldsmith.

How do you lead your team to execute and get results?

Empowerment and enablement, while sounding similar, are different concepts but equally critical in their importance for successful teams. I believe that often the best ideas come from the experts in my organization, not from me as their leader. An environment where all levels of the organization are both appropriately empowered and enabled, in my opinion, is the most important foundational block for a high-performing team.

To make good decisions, a team also needs good information, thereby making clear and transparent communication a constant and vital requirement of a leader.

Do you have a workforce philosophy or unique approach to talent acquisition?

The most important quality I look for in hiring is the ability and desire to learn! Topic knowledge can be taught, but the most important qualities I look for come from inside, regardless of education level or even career background. I prioritize hiring people and teams that complement each other, bring different strengths to the table, and are unified by their desire to have a positive effect on the world by making it more secure.

It is an easy and common trap for leaders to hire people who either very strongly resemble them or who won't be too prone to rock the boat. I really value having an organization that will not be shy to challenge me and will complement me where I am not as strong. Then we can all focus on utilizing our strengths, thereby raising the performance bar across the whole organization, not just making one leader look good.

Have you created a cohesive strategy for your information security program or business unit?

If one remembers that a vision is where you're going and a strategy is how you get there, having a clearly and easily understood strategy is a must for a group at any scale. It is key that every member of a team be able to look at each decision and action through the filter of the overall strategy and therefore be able to prioritize and focus in a way to further that strategy.

And, of course, strategies should be continuously adapting. Sometimes more, sometimes less, but if any strategy goes too long without evolution, then it's likely that it isn't being referenced very much. An important requirement of leaders is that they remain aware of and linked into the intercompany relationships outside of cybersecurity to stay current on overall company direction and strategy so that the cybersecurity strategy stays complementary.

What are your communication tips for interacting with executive leadership?

Listening, while maybe the least dynamic part of communication, is the most critical for success. It is too easy to want to flood an audience with a flood of information to reassure them of our knowledge and capabilities. But by listening we can better understand what their needs are—what are they really looking for in any specific interaction? It might be information, a recommendation, or a question to be asked, and by paying attention we can receive input on how to best meet them where they need us to.

Remember also that no one ever has as much time on any topic as they would probably like. Be concise, focus on clearly communicating your points, and elaborate only if there is clearly a desire for continued information. Most execs don't have the extra time for deep diving on every nuance of a subject and therefore appreciate clearly expressed options and recommendations to help guide their decisions and way forward.

How do you cultivate productive relationships with your boss, peers, direct reports, and other team members?

We all have motivations, priorities, needs—but seldom, if ever, are those actually the same for all of us. I find it extremely helpful, when working with anyone, to keep in mind where they are coming from. What do I know about their business incentives? What have they communicated to me in the past as their challenges and their priorities? By keeping these in mind, it helps me know how to most productively work with this individual, no matter the goal or the relative working relationship or position level between us.

And, remember how important credibility is—we often trust each other by default, but it takes very little to lose that trust. Be honest, be straightforward, and be willing to acknowledge both successes and failures in a constructive way.

Have you encountered challenges collaborating with technology teams like information technology and software development?

Most of the time, cybersecurity is a cost center. And unfortunately, those of us who work in it are really good at being so focused that we forget that the statement "You have 14 vulnerabilities with CVSS scores of 9.6 or above in your newly released product" might not scare everyone the way it does us. Recognizing a few basic business truths and remembering that everyone in a company has their own priorities really helps to give us cybersecurity folks a reality check when we need to influence those outside of our area. Every organization, whether it is revenue-generating like sales or technology-focused like IT, will have a framework of working and a set of goals that may or may not easily line up with the mission of the cybersecurity group.

I see less and less of the "we set policy and we said so" approach and more understanding that cybersecurity organizations need to speak and understand a business language centered around our target audience. This is a positive trend that will help avoid the potential for irrelevance of the cybersecurity department in daily business.

In my experience, it is almost always possible to find common ground where all sides can have their needs met in situations where the stakeholders have divergent or even competing goals. One of our risks as cybersecurity organizations is not recognizing that discussion and compromise are a required part of achieving our mission. Everyone appreciates feeling that their voice is heard and valued!

Do you have any favorite books to recommend for people who want to lead cybersecurity teams?

As I've mentioned earlier, I think any topic-specific knowledge can be taught. Therefore, when I focus on leadership, I don't really think about cybersecurity-specific leadership—good leadership is good leadership! The books in the last decade that have resonated with me the most in continuing to refine my leadership style are:

- *Team of Teams: New Rules of Engagement for a Complex World* by General Stanley McChrystal
- *Turn the Ship Around!* by L. David Marquet
- *What Got You Here Won't Get You There* by Marshall Goldsmith

There is a danger in creating your own personal echo chamber by choosing only reference material that harmonizes with your already-set view of how leadership should work. I recommend challenging yourself by intentionally stretching your comfort zone. The first time I read about the idea of holacracy, I thought, "There's no way this works!" But after incorporating some of the basic concepts into select situations, I see the ways it can benefit an organization.

"I spend a fair amount of time coaching and educating folks on how to handle personal communications and deal with the quirks that make each person unique."

Bill Burns

11

Bill Burns is currently Informatica's chief information security officer and head of privacy protection, ensuring that customers can trust Informatica with their most important data.

Bill has built and grown high-scale security programs at Accenture, Netscape, Netflix, and Informatica; worked security from both IT and R&D perspectives; and shaped information security investment strategies when in venture capital. His teams have been part of digital transformations on a global scale, incorporating security, compliance, and risk into companies' corporate DNA.

Bill has two computer security patents, is an active startup adviser, and in his free time trains disaster preparedness and emergency communicators in Northern California. Bill has 25+ years of security experience and holds degrees in electrical engineering and business from Michigan Technological University.

Do you believe there is a massive shortage of career cybersecurity professionals?

I believe there's a shortfall, but I don't believe it's as massive as we read in the press. When security is held as a corporate goal and incorporated into the organization's DNA, my thesis is that untapped capacity will reduce the perceived cybersecurity skills gap and improve the overall cybersecurity posture.

I believe there is a shortage of companies that set and enforce an appropriate tone of cybersecurity expectations at a company culture level. There is a shortage of employees with cybersecurity-related goals in their annual objectives and measures, tied to tangible outcomes like bonus payouts or department funding, for example. We still need deep security expertise reserved for career cybersecurity professionals, and this need is growing, but we cannot expect that a dedicated team can be responsible for "security goals" while the rest of the business has "business goals" that are separate and distinct.

Modern business skills now need to include security aspects. A company's cultural values need to be consistent with its security and risk appetite, setting a tone of what is accepted and expected to properly run the business. Otherwise, either business decisions are made in a vacuum, outside the scope of the cybersecurity team, or the business decisions are set and then taken to the security team for sign-off afterward. In the former case, business decisions create a growing backlog of security debt, and in the latter case the security team is seen as a business inhibitor instead of a business partner because the security impact is evaluated too late in the decisioning process to have strategic impact.

What's the most important decision you've made or action you've taken related to a business risk?

We were releasing a new product on a new platform and architecture. There was considerable pressure to release this to market, and while it was a familiar product that we had deployed before, it was on an unproven platform and had very little dwell time—so there was considerable risk of operational unknowns: things we hadn't yet anticipated or experienced. In particular, we were concerned with availability risk: either technical or process snafus that could create unplanned outages while we all got more familiar with the differences in our product on the new platform. We were familiar with our old platform, but it had been a while since we launched with this much operational and process change underneath a product.

Up until that time, our typical process was to release the product to customers and let them experience it in a preview/nonproduction mode, collect feature feedback to incorporate into enhancements and adjustments, and then eventually release it to production. The alternative in this case was to not release/delay the product until it was ready: a binary decision.

As a newly combined product launch/readiness team, some of the members hadn't considered that we had a "third option": to incorporate security/risk metrics into their readiness checklist. By identifying the failure modes and risk use cases, we could tie risk metrics to readiness triggers that could add a more holistic measure of when the product was ready/good enough to release to the next level. And by setting objective, measurable metrics, we could all observe the same effects over time and make a data-informed decision. We time-boxed the measurement period so that the maximum amount of product delay was mutually agreed upon but reasonable enough to ideally capture a failure that we anticipated.

Because we positioned the problem statement and potential solution the way we did, the security/risk team wasn't seen as the "team of no." We were seen as a true business partner and aligned to the same high-level business objective of making a great product available to customers as early as practical. We also were actively engaged and part of the solutioning as well, not just pointing out potential problems or risks and leaving it to business owners to figure it out. No one on the team wanted to release an unstable product before it was ready, but everyone was eager to get the early product out to our customers for their feedback.

In the end, we finally launched the product to the customers later than originally planned, but we learned several key technical and process-related lessons during that period. Thankfully, we did experience a previously unexpected failure mode in an underlying third-party architecture. When the product was finally released, the whole team was collectively more confident in the product's operations and stability and ultimately released a more stable product to customers.

How do you make hard decisions? Do you find yourself more often making people, process, or technology decisions?

If I have the time (in other words, it's not an urgent *and* hard decision), I try to collect and consider as much perspective and feedback about the problem as I can. Getting a broad set of viewpoints about the problem helps ensure that you're solving the right problem and have considered what impact your decision will have on the stakeholders who will be impacted by the decision.

Cultural-level decisions typically have the broadest impact. Those don't (shouldn't) change often, but are most important when you're building from scratch or transforming a company. They also tend to have a lasting impact on stakeholders today and in the future, and they typically also affect downstream policy, process, and technology choices.

How I divvy up focusing on people, process, or technology changes; this is largely dependent on what stage of growth the company and department is in. In the early stages, there are a lot of architecture and technology choices to make—rapid innovation that becomes hindered by too much process, where the team needs to quickly build/test/learn/adapt/repeat. Making the right people choices at this stage are also critical: the amount of responsibility and leverage each new person on the team has is immense. In more mature phases of a company or department, the focus tends to be on efficiency and optimization. There is more emphasis on people, from a process and responsibility perspective (e.g., RACIs/DACIs). The same feedback loop happens—you're swapping out less technology and doing it less often, but you still use feedback loops with stakeholders to stay aligned.

As our programs mature, I find that my teams and I are more frequently engaged on business-process level decisions. In this feedback model, stakeholders operate in a "thrower" and a "catcher" mode—someone is producing output from one process or service, which is received by another person or team. These work units have requirements, specifications, and RACI/DACI "contracts" associated with them.

At the end of the day, I tell my teams that to be effective at business you need to focus on both results and relationships. While the program or project outcome is important, we eventually have to work with another person in our line of work. This means working with people who have personalities and backgrounds different from your own. I spend a fair amount of time coaching and educating folks on how to handle personal communications and deal with the quirks that make each person unique.

What's something that you struggle with as a leader and how do you overcome that?

I struggle with "good enough." I take a lot of pride in my work and my teams' work. I love to learn new technologies, better ways of working, and new ways to be more efficient and effective. I appreciate lean and MVP approaches, delivering "something useful" that's fit for purpose, and the endless journey to improve something if it's not quite right, especially if you're in a building/innovation phase.

I've learned to dampen perfectionism by collecting outside feedback from stakeholders, measuring value at critical milestones to help quantify when improvements or changes produce diminishing returns on investment. Even if the measurements and feedback are qualitative, the process of getting an outside-in perspective helps counter the inner dialogue to keep improving or solve all the corner cases of "What if...?" When stakeholders and/or I are sufficiently satisfied with a decision or a deliverable, it's refreshing to then get excited about working on the next idea or invention.

One of the most challenging roles in my career was when I went into a completely different industry and role than than I had experienced before, in the venture capital space. Although it was related to a domain I had deep expertise in, the skills and tools used were quite different. It was challenging in different ways, and yet very rewarding—much like I would imagine if an expert athlete trained in one sport had to cross over and become skilled at a different sport. Interestingly, as I got into my groove in the new role, I relied on many of the "soft skills" that I had built over the years and found that my professional network was incredibly helpful in the new role.

How do you lead your team to execute and get results?

Start by setting a clear vision for the high-level objective(s) and share as much context as you can about the decision to be made, the constraints that are known, and the business impact the objective(s) will have. Ask up front what resources the team needs and clear any roadblocks or prewire any conversations you anticipate will be needed.

During execution, ensure that the teams and stakeholders receive and/or provide frequent updates, especially as assumptions or parameters change, and give feedback to key members and/or solicit feedback frequently to ensure you're on course or to make any small course corrections. Afterward, capture lessons learned and share them broadly to empower others to be able to do even better for the next objective.

Do you have a workforce philosophy or unique approach to talent acquisition?

I don't think I have a unique approach, but I feel blessed to have worked alongside so many brilliant, passionate people in my career so far. While I do rely on past experience as a predictor for future performance when I'm getting to know potential candidates, when I ask them about situations they've been in previously, I'm listening for more than just achieving objectives. I'm listening to the context in their answer: what did they learn, how high is their emotional intelligence, what soft skills did they use to accomplish the task, do they have a growth mindset, how well do they handle unknowns and ambiguity, what motivates them to keep doing what they enjoy, how do they stay motivated when doing things they don't necessarily enjoy, and what causes them to move on from previous roles?

Hiring the right person for a particular job is a mix of all of these. Retaining them is also a mix of all of these and is unique to each person-role combination.

Have you created a cohesive strategy for your information security program or business unit?

I've ended up creating different strategies for each of the security teams I've built in my career. Each was at a different phase of the company's journey, each had different needs and constraints, and each had different underlying business objectives. The programs shared similar sets of core services and deliverables, but they were delivered differently because the overall corporate culture was different and/or the stakeholders interacted with the rest of the business differently. It was important in each case for the success of the security program (and the company) to be aligned and compatible with the existing cultural norms and ways of working.

Bringing a high-control, regulated security program into an innovation-driven, rapid growth–phase company would come across as "tone deaf" and ultimately not be successful. This is where it's important that your security program and leadership teams are aligned in terms of both culture and outcomes: if a new security program is designed to support a cultural change (say, from rapid innovation to high-efficiency or increased regulations), then it's important to use that context as the leadership team introduces changes throughout the company and works with stakeholders.

What are your communication tips for interacting with executive leadership?

Here's a few tips:

- To communicate effectively, use the style and method most compatible with your audience (e.g., are they a "bullet list" kind of person or a "storyteller" with lots of detail; are they qualitative or quantitative; do they prefer tables or graphs?).
- Prewire and socialize decisions ahead of time.
- Use bottom line, up front (BLUF). Put your summary up front and then get into the details. Make the summary brief and focused on the business risk and impact. Tell the receiver why you're speaking or presenting to them: are you asking for guidance, providing an update, asking for a decision among choices, providing direction, etc.?
- Don't be afraid to deliver "bad news." It's worse to withhold news that then becomes a "surprise" (hint: time delays usually don't help make matters better in those situations). It's better to share early and involve executives in the decision-making process or let them know that the situation is being worked on, is under control, and when they can expect a decision or another update. You'll also likely get quick feedback on how/when they'd like to be communicated with for similar events in the future.
- Don't provide a single "option" when asking for a decision. Show your work on how you came to your recommendation, typically from a narrow set of final potential options. This gives them a chance to share some context or experience you perhaps hadn't considered, but be prepared to defend your recommendation.
- When dealing with people I directly support or my peers, I ask a lot of questions, both to learn about the problem space but also to understand how much the person I'm talking to has done their homework and gathered the appropriate context of the situation. Actually, I do that in pretty much every conversation.

How do you cultivate productive relationships with your boss, peers, direct reports, and other team members?

Start with forming a common ground: what problem or goal do we share? Get to know the other party so that you can be of assistance with something you might have now or in the future: expertise, knowledge, resources, or someone else in your network. Understand their communications preferences and style; personal profile queues are also helpful to be more effective and efficient when interacting with them (e.g., Insights, DISC, etc.). Get to know the other person at a personal level too; you're likely going to be spending a lot of time with them throughout the work week!

Check in with your network, even when neither of you needs something specific. Even if it's a quick, touch-base meeting or a short hallway conversation/email/call—you don't want a purely transactional relationship with the folks you work with; we're all humans after all! Sometimes the best exchanges I've had have started with "Hey, I don't have anything urgent, just checking in to see how you're doing."

Have you encountered challenges collaborating with revenue-generating teams like sales and product development?

Of course, and I've also had the opportunity to be embedded in such teams in order to build and grow new programs. It's given me a new perspective on how those teams operate, what their norms are, and how to best interact with them. The best partnerships I've developed have started with building a shared context and set of goals, in many cases to act as a bit of a "translator" between our organizations and a trusted partner.

Do you have any favorite books to recommend for people who want to lead cybersecurity teams?

Off the top of my head, only one comes to mind quickly: *The Effective Manager* by Mark Horstman (and the Manager Tools podcast). While it's not technology- or security-specific, it's excellent, business-centric advice that prepares you to be effective in any leadership role. And for people interacting with leaders, it makes them more effective businesspeople because it provides a glimpse into what's most important (or should be) to the leaders they work with.

> "Being a good leader requires you to set aside your ego and fully understand the needs, strengths, and weaknesses of each of your team members."

Twitter: @hacks4pancakes • **Website:** www.linkedin.com/in/lcarhart

Lesley Carhart

12

Lesley Carhart is a principal threat analyst for the Threat Operations Center at the industrial cybersecurity company Dragos, Inc. She is recognized as a subject-matter expert in cybersecurity incident response and digital forensics, regularly speaking on the topic at conferences and universities.

She has spent the last 11 years of her 20+ year IT career specializing in information security, with a heavy focus on response to nation-state adversary attacks. Prior to joining Dragos, she was the incident response team lead at Motorola Solutions, performing digital forensics and incident handling services for both enterprise and public safety customers. In 2017, Lesley was named a "Top Woman in Cybersecurity" by CyberScoop news and received the "Women in Technology" award at Guidance Software's Enfuse Conference.

In her free time, Lesley co-organizes résumé and interview clinics at several cybersecurity conferences, blogs and tweets prolifically about InfoSec, and is a youth martial arts instructor.

Do you believe there is a massive shortage of career cybersecurity professionals?

I find the question that is routinely asked, "Is there a cybersecurity skills gap?" to be rather inherently fraught. As the field of cybersecurity has grown and become more diversified into skill sets and niches, we have continued to refer to it as a single field. In reality, there is minimal overlap in technical skills between, say, a malware reverse engineer and a risk and compliance auditor. Is there a skills gap? Yes, in specific niches that truly require years of study and (more importantly) dedicated work experience to gain. It does not take years of training and experience to be an excellent lower-tier SOC analyst. That merely takes fundamental computer knowledge and a time and financial commitment to train and educate by an employer. It does not take a college degree to train a proficient junior penetration tester—merely an apprenticeship with a good mentor. Until we start asking the right questions, it will be hard to solve the problems we have made for ourselves.

What's the most important decision you've made or action you've taken related to a business risk?

Joining a startup. I'm generally pretty cautious with financial and safety risk. I'm the first person to put on PPE when working on a hazardous hobby, and my financial advisor is probably pretty sick of my questions. I've worked at startups before, and it has absolutely never ended particularly well. I can only commend Dragos on its mission and relative success. I was something around employee 20, and we will have around 200 by publication. In the end, the corporate mission and ethics were the deciding factor. Sometimes your gut and sound personal ethics lead you down the right path, even if it is not the easiest one.

> Sometimes your gut and sound personal ethics lead you down the right path, even if it is not the easiest one.

How do you make hard decisions? Do you find yourself more often making people, process, or technology decisions?

Incident response is full of immediate and impactful decisions under pressure, and one's success as an incident responder relies entirely on the capability to make people, process, and technology decisions on the fly with limited information. Ultimately, I have found good decision-making to be reliant on excellent risk calculation and quantification skills and on a large pool of high-level knowledge about business and technical processes that together allow me to make educated and supported "gut" choices. This skill has served me well in business. In the end, the objective of almost every organization is not cybersecurity in a vacuum. Until we appreciate that and understand the key performance indicators (KPIs) and consequences our employer really cares about, we will never be truly able to influence their direction or business mindset.

> In the end, the objective of almost every organization is not cybersecurity in a vacuum.

What's something that you struggle with as a leader, and how do you overcome that?

The need to control and critique everything. I am a project manager at heart, and even my vacations are planned out in tidy, color-coded spreadsheets with alternative plans for rainy days. My personality can do a lot of good in analytical work, but it can also cause interpersonal conflict with other (more leisurely or casual) personalities. It can also cause me to take on all of the tasks rather than those I should rationally perform myself. Learning to be a participant in the larger picture and apply my skills where they are useful like every other contributor has been a tough road. Formal education in business management, team dynamic models, and project management were all massively helpful. You can't fix and lead a team until you understand how to fix yourself and how your personality is interpreted by other people. There are many valid types of leaders (country club, team, middle of the road, etc.), but it is incredibly important to understand what type you are and if it properly fits the situation. I recommend that every potential manager read up on these topics in detail.

How do you lead your team to execute and get results?

You can't lead a team simply by acting as an individual contributor, because there are so many more human concerns within human interpersonal relationships. Being a good leader requires you to set aside your ego and fully understand the needs, strengths, and weaknesses of each of your team members. People are not machines, and they cannot function long-term as such. If your team member is struggling, you must recognize internal or external factors that are causing this and work on finding a solution. This requires empathy as well as savvy project management skills. People getting into management or leadership rarely understand what a huge commitment this really is (particularly for introverted and analytical people).

You don't need to know every personal detail about your employees, but you need to know enough about their current and past lives, personalities, and capabilities to understand what motivates and hinders them. Do they have a kid in daycare they need to pick up every day at 4 p.m.? Are they struggling with a personal situation that is causing them to work inattentively? Can you do something to adapt their work environment to their current needs?

Do you have a workforce philosophy or unique approach to talent acquisition?
Hire for essential fundamental knowledge, a willingness to continue to learn, and a positive personality first. You may not have the capacity to train somebody without a basic level of essential technical understanding, you cannot teach somebody who is not willing to put in some effort to learn, and there is absolutely no way to fix somebody who is hostile or perpetually offensive to your team. Everything else can be dealt with. You can almost always provide further formal or internal training to an otherwise great candidate.

> You can almost always provide further formal or internal training to an otherwise great candidate.

I'm never a fan of hiring a "10x" engineer who is cruel to or dismissive of their teammates. I would much rather hire a motivated person with less technical skill who is kind and willing to share their knowledge.

What are your communication tips for interacting with executive leadership?
Present everything in terms of firm numerical figures. Consequences in terms of money is best. Know your

organization's mission statement and extrapolate business consequences that are most critical to the board, shareholders, and leadership. Then relay your concerns and needs in terms of these business interests and potential consequences. Security breaches alone mean little to executives unless you can clearly convey the probability of something negative happening during a breach versus the capital and ongoing expense of mitigating them.

Narratives are also your friend when dealing with executives. The human mind is wired for storytelling, and a good story can reach listeners on an emotional level. Combining both good narratives and solid KPIs and risk data is a solid tactic for successful interaction.

Have you encountered challenges collaborating with revenue-generating teams like sales and product development?
A key part of being a good manager is shielding your team from negative outside interactions. These interactions may be distractions during high-pressure projects or incident response, lack of needed resources, undue pressure or consequences, or inappropriate work assignments. Sales teams can certainly unintentionally cause all of these disruptions, and it is your responsibility as a manager to prevent this by delegating or acting as a first point of contact and by providing firm guidelines of what is and is not acceptable.

> A key part of being a good manager is shielding your team from negative outside interactions.

For example, understand that a salesperson's first responsibility is building business relationships and revenue for the organization. That may mean saying "yes" to customer requests outside the expected scope. Understand that the sales team reps have different priorities than security personnel, so you must make decisions that confine their requests to the possible and reasonable for the sake of your team. Sometimes this decision may be pushing your team to meet an unusual demand. Other times, it may mean compromising or clearly saying "no" and providing clear and diplomatic reasoning to all stakeholders.

"Without a doubt, leadership training makes one a better communicator and better prepared for typical situations, but at the end of the day, I try to be the leader I would want to follow."

Christopher Caruso

13

Chris has been in the civilian IT infrastructure and IT/OT cybersecurity industry for more than 30 years. He has held several certifications over the years, most recently a CISSP, and has completed 65 hours of OT cybersecurity training with DHS ICS-CERT through NCCIC. Over his professional career, Chris has worked with 4 of the top 10 companies in the United States with various facilities on almost every continent and in 45 countries as an IT/OT/cyber managing staff member.

He has IT/OT cybersecurity management experience with teams, budgets, projects, policies, back office and data center, cloud operations, custom web and financial applications, databases, local and wide area networks, telecom, and business continuity. He has managed teams ranging from 3 to 24 staff members with opex budgets as large as $2 million per year.

He currently works for 1337 Defense out of Austin and also has his own cybersecurity firm, Houston Auditing and Compliance, based in Houston, which performs cybersecurity compliance audits, provides written reports, and manages implementation teams and projects.

Most recently he has worked with law enforcement to help better understand, document and provide training into the cybersecurity tactics criminals use to evade law enforcement and disperse and hide digital evidence. Chris also served in the United States Army and currently serves in the Texas State Guard. SGT Caruso's military background includes 3 years in the CTARNG HHB 2/192FA, Signal Corps, working with secure encrypted communications and when not in the field, for Charlie Battery as their S1. He joined the TXSG in April of 2018 accompanied by a letter of recommendation from a U.S. Congressman and provides his expertise with Cybersecurity compliance, assessments, and blue team operations. Chris holds a degree in Engineering, but believes that nothing beats keeping abreast of both new technology and emerging threats.

What's the most important decision you've made or action you've taken to enable a business risk?

Virtually every choice comes with some inherent business risk, but rarely is putting someone's life in peril in an IT/OT/cyber corporate environment an expected part of business risk. I have had to make choices about putting VPN connections in less-than-friendly nation-states and sending resources out into the field in nations where they have had to be escorted by armed guards at all times to perform their tasks. Knowingly asking someone to travel somewhere that will put them in physical danger or mortal peril for business reasons and not national security is the hardest decision I have had to make. Ensuring that we can do everything possible to protect them and get them back to their families is one of the most important decisions that I have made. Life and limb come before all else.

> With very few exceptions, almost all businesses have some physical process or relationship with a key critical resource or development environment or legacy technology that puts them at risk every moment they remain married to it.

How do you make hard decisions? Do you find yourself more often making people, process, or technology decisions?

Every time we have to acknowledge that a particular business process is at a particular state of maturity that artificially limits our ability to reduce risk, and we have to make the choice to accept the risk and move on, is very difficult. With very few exceptions, almost all businesses have some physical process or relationship with a key critical resource or development environment or legacy technology that puts them at risk every moment they remain married to it. The best we can do is help them understand the potential impact, limit the fallout, and be prepared in the event the worst does come to pass.

What's something that you struggle with as a leader, and how do you overcome that?

The most difficult part of my current role is when I complete a vulnerability assessment and prepare to communicate the findings to an organization. At times the findings can be grim and the path forward rocky and steep. Presenting what we find in the context of the framework we are assessing against, with an honest explanation of the vulnerabilities and risks they pose, in such a way that is both illuminating and directional for the client is often hardest.

Each situation is unique, although the findings themselves, with few exceptions, are usually typical. But we have to communicate what we find in the arena of that particular corporate culture and environment in such a way that it is heard, understood, acknowledged, and used as the basis for remediation going forward. That is a challenge, and you have to develop your own skills that no business class or cyber training can prepare you for.

How do you lead your team to execute and get results?

I am fortunate enough to have both professional and military leadership training, as well as great mentors and leaders to emulate, while working in many different countries and types of environments. For me, the most important traits in a leader are honesty and integrity. I expect the leader to be honest with me about what I am doing right and how I can improve, and

In building trust, I build loyalty, and because of that my team is more motivated and self-confident and will typically outperform statistics in a way that seems natural and easy, even when the challenges are tough.

to understand that I have my own career and personal goals while helping the company achieve its goals and mission.

I strive to be what I expect others to be, and I have taken cues from those leaders who are most successful and respected while avoiding behaviors that make leaders less effective. Without a doubt, leadership training makes one a better communicator and better prepared for typical situations, but at the end of the day, I try to be the leader I would want to follow. In building trust, I build loyalty, and because of that my team is more motivated and self-confident and will typically outperform statistics in a way that seems natural and easy, even when the challenges are tough.

Do you have a workforce philosophy or unique approach to talent acquisition?

The most important features I look for in people that I ask to come work with me are integrity and discipline. Absolutely they have to possess the education, experience, and ability to organize and think for themselves, but what we do takes a dedication to our craft. We do what we do not just for the client but also as a line of defense against threat actors worldwide.

When we engage with a client, we are often defending them against much more than even they realize. Often they are worried about compliance or being able to show artifacts for due diligence, and we recognize their primary concerns, but while fines and lost contracts are important, ensuring that the data they manage is as secure as possible against threat actors is what cybersecurity is all about. We also understand that we can't eliminate all risk, but we can help them do everything reasonably possible and financially feasible to reduce risk to the most tolerable level. Because we are helping guide their actions and oftentimes their new corporate philosophy, we have to hold ourselves to a higher standard to live up to that responsibility.

Have you created a cohesive strategy for your information security program or business unit?

As a consultant, this is precisely what I do for every client. The answer to this question for me is a key word in the question, *cohesive*. The coefficient of internal cohesion is the mathematical representation of the physical property that holds things like concrete aggregate together. The higher the C, the more weight the member can support without crumbling.

Security programs are also aggregates. They are colloids of people, processes, and tools. They form a single solution, but each part is distinct and unique. My career has been about coming into various organizations with less than preferable states of IT/OT/cybersecurity and helping them create an appropriate and cost-effective security program that addresses their unique risks and business models.

Falling back on a concrete analogy, relying solely on compliance is comparable to strong concrete with no re-bar. Re-bar holds concrete together under stresses it would not natively support, like tension. Going beyond compliance and building a strong security strategy that addresses compliance natively is a preferred strategy. To achieve that, I have to understand what is at risk and how well the organization understands the risks and is prepared to mitigate them as effectively as appropriately possible.

While we strive to ensure compliance, we also understand the old saying that "just because you're compliant doesn't mean you're secure," so we go further and address details that compliance usually misses in order to help the organization achieve compliance through good security that best protects life, data, intellectual property, and brand integrity.

What are your communication tips for interacting with executive leadership?

Be factual, be 100 percent sure in what you are conveying, and be confident. Speak from a position of sound information. When speaking with a board, they often care more about the message than the messenger, so the message has to be clear, concise, appropriate, and correct. Understand what their agenda is, how they will "hear" what you have to say, and understand how to use proper language and tone for the target audience. When I am speaking with executives, it must be succinct and strategic, as follows:

Finding > Impact > Recommended Course of Action > Time, Money, and Human Resources

With a direct supervisor, it can be much the same but more conversational, allowing either one of us to be a devil's advocate as we consider paths forward. A boss is also constantly reassessing your character and skills as part of your cumulative evaluation, so your personal integrity and character come more

> Be factual, be 100 percent sure in what you are conveying, and be confident.

into play. With direct reports, I listen to their complaints, their suggestions, and about themselves. As a leader, I rely on them, so I give them the greatest amount of my face time.

How do you cultivate productive relationships with your boss, peers, direct reports, and other team members?
Cultivating relationships is about finding connection. That starts with the work relationship and will always be founded upon the work relationship, but as humans we have developed personalities to help us interact with one another effectively and efficiently. The role someone plays in your orbit will determine the basis of the interpersonal relationship. A boss, for example, will expect you to be appropriately dressed, be on time, be well organized, and complete your tasks correctly, promptly, and efficiently. Doing all of that will certainly make someone a good staff member, but the following is more important: how well you interface with your peers, whether you are a team player and a mentor, and whether you have a good attitude and believe in the brand and mission. There is also the fact that most of your waking hours are spent with co-workers. You have to be someone they can not only rely upon and work well with but enjoy being around. As a consultant, I don't have the advantage of being able to develop long-lasting interpersonal relationships over many consecutive workdays; consultants have to come in and be what is needed, become someone that the client wants to have around. We have our choice in vendors, and we have to always keep that foremost in our thoughts during interactions.

Have you encountered challenges collaborating with revenue-generating teams like sales and product development?
The first step is understanding that "security gets in the way." Often we are going to be introducing change, and changes mean challenge and frustration to them and not just the other way around. Years ago, I would have perhaps characterized interacting with various silos as challenging, but now I make it a point to better understand their position and their unique needs and attempt to weave that into a more effective relationship-building strategy.

Building strong interpersonal/ interdepartmental relationships is key to implementing an effective security strategy.

Building strong interpersonal/interdepartmental relationships is key to implementing an effective security strategy. The key players can be told what to do from the top down, but if they feel like we understand what their needs are, how they will be impacted by our solutions, and how we can reduce the amount of friction on their sails, then we are already building strong partnerships and strong alliances.

Have you encountered challenges collaborating with technology teams like information technology and software development?
As a consultant, I generally have almost complete buy-in from the executives because they know compliance means fewer fines, greater likelihood that they will successfully collect insurance in the event of a cyber incident or disaster, and better defense in the event of a lawsuit. Legal, too, wants to ensure compliance for all of the same reasons. But the devil is in the details, and the details are in the implementation and the maintenance.

So then, interestingly, our closest cousins, IT and development, are typically the most resistant to security. IT's focus is on availability. Development's focus is on the next development cycle. For infrastructure, it seems like there just isn't enough time or human resources to test every hardware, OS, and application patch that comes along. Even if they could, if they deploy a patch and it brings down production, they know it's on them to fix what security broke. Telling people in IT they have to comply with policy, procedure, and help desk logs; use different accounts for different tasks; and maintain a segregation of duties slows them down. IT is that group that generally bears the greatest burden and inconvenience with respect to cybersecurity, so it is understandable that when you address them the moans start and the eyes roll. These are generally individuals whose head count is calculated as a factor of the number of personnel they or their department supports, and they will scream the loudest when it comes to the cybersecurity folks telling them that the latest vulnerability scans revealed a need for 473 patches on the customer-facing production equipment.

DevOps, on the other hand, tends to take their coding very personally. Like *Phantom of the Opera*, we often hear that it is perfect as it is and you can't rewrite what's perfect, even though we've just shown that it's susceptible to SQL injection or that DIME/DARE isn't maintained and the PII is highly susceptible to intercept.

While the examples I gave are entirely fictitious, they aren't atypical across virtually every industry. So when it comes to IT and DevOps, working with them to create a strong, cohesive partnership for security becomes paramount. Every technique I have mentioned for building interpersonal and interdepartmental relationships and being a leader comes into play. Executives can mandate that security objectives be implemented, but it is much better to have people with the direct expertise in the systems help guide vendor selection and solution implementation, because at the end of the day, it is they who will likely be doing much of the heavy lifting during deployment.

Do you have any favorite books to recommend for people who want to lead cybersecurity teams?
While I do enjoy literature about my extracurricular hobbies, most, if not all, of my reading material is career enhancing. We live in a time when information is available via many different portals and formats. There are books, physical and ebooks, podcasts, websites, newsletters, and webinars, just to name a few, so I like to remind fellow industry colleagues that books are important, but they shouldn't ignore the other portals.

I also strongly recommend keeping up to date on a daily/weekly basis with industry periodical newsletters, such as subscribing to the CISA newsletters on cybersecurity. Align the newsletter choices with your area of expertise, such as general, election, operation technology, and so on. Check out websites like C4ISR and Fifth Domain and make them part of your morning coffee/news routine along with your favorite Internet news sources. Whenever possible, keep up to date with industry webinars from Microsoft or other major vendors. As for actual books, I recommend what I call the basic standards for anyone in cybersecurity.

- Anything from the Tribe of Hackers series
- *BTFM Blue Team Field Manual* by Alan J. White and Ben Clark
- *RTFM Red Team Field Manual* by Ben Clark
- *The Art of Deception and the Art of Intrusion* by Kevin D. Mitnick and William L. Simon
- *Intrusion Detection* by Rebecca Gurley Bace—an older book but a great basis on which to build a foundation
- *The Official ISC2 CISSP CBK* if you are studying for your CISSP
- *CEH Certified Ethical Hacker Bundle* by Matt Walker, if you are studying for your CEH

"Security leaders need to think of themselves as business leaders who specialize in cybersecurity rather than cybersecurity specialists who happen to work in a particular business."

Twitter: @mchapple • **Websites:** certmike.com and www.linkedin.com/in/mikechapple

Mike Chapple

Mike Chapple is associate teaching professor of information technology, analytics and operations at the University of Notre Dame's Mendoza College of Business. Mike is a security certification expert who has written over 50 cybersecurity books and video courses. Mike began his career as a cybersecurity researcher with the National Security Agency and has run cybersecurity programs at Notre Dame and in the private sector.

14

Do you believe there is a massive shortage of career cybersecurity professionals?

The cybersecurity skills gap is real, but I wouldn't classify it as a crisis in the same way that we often see it framed in the cybersecurity media. Instead, I see it as an opportunity. The IT skills market is like any other and subject to the influences of supply and demand. As the need increases for a particular skill area, salaries rise due to market competition, and those increased salaries draw talent willing to develop those skills. We've seen this happen countless times in different technology disciplines over the years—remember how valuable a database administrator was in the 1990s?

These market forces also work within the subdisciplines of security. As organizations move to the cloud, we've seen a strong increase in the demand for cloud security specialists and an increase in compensation as well. It's no coincidence that thousands of cybersecurity professionals are developing cloud security skills and pursuing cloud security certifications. They're future-proofing their careers by following the money.

What's the most important decision you've made or action you've taken related to a business risk?
In 2012, I led an effort to shift Notre Dame to a cloud-first strategy. At the time, this was really going out on a limb. While many technology companies were cloud-native, most traditional enterprises still operated their own data centers and were only testing the waters of cloud computing. We saw the potential to increase our agility, reduce our costs, and dramatically improve the service provided to our students, faculty, and staff by embracing this trend early.

We went all in by setting a goal to move 80 percent of our workloads from traditional data centers to the cloud within three years and actually wound up exceeding that goal. Today, we no longer operate data centers on our campus, and almost all of our computing takes place in SaaS, PaaS, or IaaS services.

Setting that goal was one of the most important tools that we used to drive the change within our team. Having that concrete goal in front of us set the tone of our work far more than a general statement about prioritizing the cloud possibly could have done. Setting clear and aggressive targets creates a burning platform and motivates performance.

How do you make hard decisions? Do you find yourself more often making people, process, or technology decisions?
The most difficult decisions that I've had to make in my career all center around a single topic: cutting ties with employees

who repeatedly fail to live up to expectations. Firing someone is a complicated human and emotional decision. You've already invested a large amount of time and energy in that person's success, and admitting that it just isn't going to work out often feels like a personal failure.

That said, when it's time to part ways, there's no greater relief than finally resolving the situation—and the feeling is often mutual. A termination decision should never come as a surprise to the employee, and chances are that they've been dreading that moment for weeks or months. Cutting ties allows everyone to finally move on and find a better situation.

What's something that you struggle with as a leader and how do you overcome that?

I'm a technologist at heart, and I love to roll up my sleeves and dive into the technology. Nothing excites me more than the prospect of a day of uninterrupted coding. However, leaders don't have the luxury of spending their time focused on technical work because they have other demands on their time. More importantly, diving too deeply into the technical work often sends an unintended message to the team that you don't trust them to do their own jobs properly.

> Nothing excites me more than the prospect of a day of uninterrupted coding. However, leaders don't have the luxury of spending their time focused on technical work because they have other demands on their time.

These days, I'm a professor, and I do have the opportunity to spend my days doing technical work when I'd like, but that wasn't always the case. When I was leading security teams, I scratched my technical itch by working on side projects that served the business but weren't part of our core function. Nobody was depending upon me to deliver results on schedule, so I had the flexibility to work on them as time permitted. Doing this type of work was great because it not only satisfied my intellectual curiosity but also reminded the teams that I worked with that I was still a "real" technologist!

How do you lead your team to execute and get results?
In his book *Drive*, Daniel Pink outlines three forces that motivate individuals: autonomy, mastery, and purpose. I believe wholeheartedly that these factors far outweigh carrot-and-stick approaches to management in building high-performing teams. People thrive when they have the autonomy to achieve their objectives in the manner they choose, the room to grow and develop mastery of their field, and a sense of purpose that their work makes a meaningful contribution to society.

Do you have a workforce philosophy or unique approach to talent acquisition?
I believe strongly in hiring people who have a track record of excellence and intellectual curiosity, rather than seeking out specific technical skills. Hiring star performers almost always results in success, as they will acquire whatever technical skills they need to get the job done.

I also believe in hiring people with a strong foundation in computer science and information technology. Security professionals need the ability to work and think up and down the stack, and a broad foundation is crucial to doing that successfully.

Have you created a cohesive strategy for your information security program or business unit?
Security programs need a strategic plan to thrive. Each time I've led a team, I've set out both short-term and long-term plans for its success. The short-term plan focuses on a combination of addressing critical risks and resolving points of friction with the business, while the long-term plan focuses on maturing the organization's security function. This approach doesn't necessarily imply that the security function is immature, but there are always pain points to address and strategic initiatives to implement.

I like to illustrate strategic plans with a one-page bubble chart showing the progress of initiatives over time. For example, here's the strategic plan that we put together when I took over leadership of the information security program at Notre Dame in 2006. The project examples are dated, but we clearly set out our priorities and built a sequence of projects designed to achieve our security objectives.

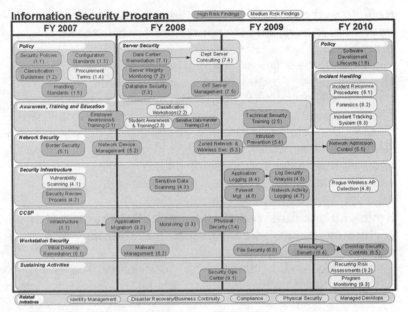

Image courtesy of Mike Chapple

The use of a one-page plan like this one facilitates clear communication within the technology organization and provides a quick glimpse of the program for leadership. I used a similar approach when I led the university's cloud transformation effort from 2012 through 2017.

What are your communication tips for interacting with executive leadership?

Keep the jargon at home! Technology leaders and managers are far too often prone to bringing an overwhelming amount of technical detail into conversations with executives. Understand the mindset of a leader and their level of technical knowledge, and craft your message accordingly. It's far more productive to deliver a clear and succinct message that is tied to business objectives than to give a lengthy talk full of technical detail that's not necessary from a leadership perspective.

> It's far more productive to deliver a clear and succinct message that is tied to business objectives than to give a lengthy talk full of technical detail that's not necessary from a leadership perspective.

How do you cultivate productive relationships with your boss, peers, direct reports, and other team members?

In my mind, the single most important thing you can do to develop strong relationships at work is to spend time meaningfully present with people. Whether it's your direct reports or your boss, take the time to disconnect from the buzz around you and get to know people on a personal level. Understand their ambitions, fears, and motivations, and you'll find that productive relationships naturally follow. It's easy to work with people you respect and understand.

Have you encountered challenges collaborating with technology teams like information technology and software development?

It's natural for security teams to have conflicts with other business and technology functions. The key to navigating those situations is having an established base of credibility and strong relationships. Security leaders need to think of themselves as business leaders who specialize in cybersecurity rather than cybersecurity specialists who happen to work in a particular business. When other leaders understand that you share the same priorities, they're more willing to work with you when difficult situations arise.

> It's natural for security teams to have conflicts with other business and technology functions. The key to navigating those situations is having an established base of credibility and strong relationships.

Do you have any favorite books to recommend for people who want to lead cybersecurity teams?

Reading is one of the most important ways that you can keep your skills sharp and broaden your horizons. I try to read a broad mix of technical, business, and leisure books and find myself surprised at the places where I find inspiration.

Here are five titles that I'd recommend to any leader:

- *Essentialism* by Greg McKeown. Leaders have more potential work on their plates than they could ever reasonably accomplish. McKeown's book provides great

advice on how to identify work that is truly important and
focus on the things that really matter.

- *Getting Things Done* by David Allen. This book is much more
  tactical than *Essentialism* and provides a system for managing
  your work. I've adapted my own style from this book and used
  it to manage my own work for more than 15 years.

- *Good to Great* by Jim Collins. This book is now almost two
  decades old, but the management lessons it teaches are just
  as important today as they were when Collins wrote the book
  in 2001.

- *The First 90 Days* by Michael Watkins. I often give this book
  as a gift to new leaders or leaders moving into new roles.
  I've re-read it myself each time I've started a new role. It's an
  important road map for navigating a new role and making
  an impact from the start.

- *How Charts Lie* by Alberto Cairo. I'm a big fan of Cairo's work.
  Leaders must be able to clearly communicate data in an
  impactful way, and this book uses counterexamples to
  point out ways to tell impactful stories with data.

"The industry needs to figure out how to bring in less experienced people with great potential who can level up with the right training and support."

Twitter: @sushidude

Steve Christey Coley

15 Steve Christey Coley is a principal InfoSec engineer at the MITRE Corporation. He was the cofounder and technical lead of CVE and chair of its editorial board from 1999 to 2015. He co-authored the "Responsible Vulnerability Disclosure Process" IETF draft and contributed to CVSS v2. He is the technical lead for the Common Weakness Enumeration (CWE), including the SANS/CWE Top 25 from 2009–2011. He supports the FDA on medical device security, including vulnerability handling, risk assessment, and policy development. He seeks to make the cybersecurity profession more inclusive, diverse, and accessible to everybody who seeks a place in it.

Do you believe there is a massive shortage of career cybersecurity professionals?
There is probably a shortage, but we don't really know how bad it is since many people are trying to break into InfoSec and can't find a job. Many new professionals struggle to break in at the junior level, although some of them might be targeting only

the more famous companies and missing out on more fulfilling opportunities at lesser known, less glamorous companies. But at the same time, many organizations have unrealistic expectations in their job listings. They'll advertise a job with a long laundry list of a wide variety of required skills that no human can have. The best match for a job might have only half of the skills being asked for and might not even apply. For example, many women and autistic people will not apply to a job listing unless they meet all the requirements. The industry needs to figure out how to bring in less experienced people with great potential who can level up with the right training and support. Companies should also consider mid- and late-career prospects who are transitioning into InfoSec from other careers. NIST's NICE program might be helpful, but it's not easy to use at first glance and may be too much of a firehose.

What's the most important decision you've made or action you've taken related to a business risk?

In my particular position, I haven't had to make many high-stakes decisions that may put a project's existence at risk, and/or I've consulted with team members and managers to achieve consensus. I make sure that the team knows that I'll take responsibility if things go awry. For the biggest risk, one time, my personal choice to leave a major project introduced some business risk. I tried to manage the risk with plenty of lead time and controlled experiments (e.g., vacations without contact), but in retrospect, I focused more on the tech transfer of a legacy system than on sharing and teaching what I learned about community engagement and developing solutions in a vastly multistakeholder environment.

> I make sure that the team knows that I'll take responsibility if things go awry.

How do you make hard decisions? Do you find yourself more often making people, process, or technology decisions?

I am generally deliberate and cautious with hard decisions. I try to take all perspectives and outcomes into account, as well as the different risks that could occur with any approach and the possible benefits. I try to be careful with identifying my assumptions and considering what could happen if my assumptions are wrong.

The potential impact on people—co-workers and our users—is paramount to me. Input from colleagues is essential, as they will see things that I won't. It requires being humble and egoless, not assuming that I know all the answers.

What's something that you struggle with as a leader, and how do you overcome that?

At this level of my career, having worked at the same company for so long, I struggle with knowledge transfer: translating my knowledge and experience, including the decision-making process I follow in technical leadership. Getting thoughts "out of my brain" is easier said than done. I think that's a common challenge with certain kinds of expertise, especially knowledge work.

I generally have low risk tolerance and sometimes prioritize high quality over other important business considerations, so it helps to have a peer or understanding manager who is more aggressive in terms of goals. I'm lucky that I've had multiple colleagues like this, but it takes a long time to build the mutual trust and understanding that's necessary.

How do you lead your team to execute and get results?

It's a consistent challenge to balance giving people enough guidance so they don't get lost at the beginning of a task with leaving them the freedom to make their own decisions. In earlier years, I used to care a lot about many things, and I've grown to mostly let those go. I've noticed that at least with technical people, the early stages of a project can be the most important, as they do not yet have a well-defined process to follow. Helping to define such processes in the early stages can reduce frustration and help with focus.

> It's a consistent challenge to balance giving people enough guidance so they don't get lost at the beginning of a task with leaving them the freedom to make their own decisions.

Do you have a workforce philosophy or unique approach to talent acquisition?

The only unusual philosophy I have is that I think many people prioritize "passion" when hiring. But people can be passionate but not necessarily productive, and quiet people may have significant passion even if they don't demonstrate it outwardly. Being a dispassionate person who's reliable and does solid, steady work can be critical to the success of a project even if they're not a "rock star."

What are your communication tips for interacting with executive leadership?
Let the leaders' questions guide what you need to say, and watch for potential misunderstandings or assumptions. Avoid details, which took a while for me to learn because of my desire to always be accurate and not mislead somebody about small risks. Try not to pretend you know everything or give the impression that you think you do.

How do you cultivate productive relationships with your boss, peers, direct reports, and other team members?
Transparency is key, including delivering bad news, apologizing, recognizing my own weaknesses, and admitting when I don't understand something. Careful listening is essential, too—looking beyond just what somebody says. Also:

> Transparency is key, including delivering bad news, apologizing, recognizing my own weaknesses, and admitting when I don't understand something.

- Making sure people know that their inputs are considered and explaining why a decision is made that conflicts with the inputs
- Ensuring that everybody's voice is heard and asking if needed
- Seeking the best-quality result while acknowledging that perfection is not achievable
- Giving recognition to others' contributions regularly

Do you have any favorite books to recommend for people who want to lead cybersecurity teams?
Unfortunately, I don't read books as often as I used to due to time and environment, but there are many articles and blog posts that are out there and easy to find. For technical leads, I suggest the books by Camille Fournier (*The Manager's Path: A Guide for Tech Leaders Navigating Growth and Change*) and Patrick Kua (*Talking with Tech Leads: From Novices to Practitioners*).

"I always looked at my last promotion as more than likely my last promotion. That gave me the freedom to always do what was right and what was best for the overall mission and our country, not what was best for my career."

Jim Christy

16 Jim Christy is a retired special agent who specialized in cybercrime investigations and digital forensics for more than 32 years with the Air Force Office of Special Investigations and the Department of Defense Cyber Crime Center (DC3). He served as a senate investigator for the U.S. Senate, Permanent Subcommittee on Investigations (1996), and was selected as the DoD Representative to the President's Infrastructure Protection Task Force (1997) and created the DoD Computer Forensics Lab and the DC3.

In 2013 he retired after 42 years of public service and started his own consulting firm, The Christy Group, LLC. Most recently he has been the cyber lead for the D.B. Cooper Cold Case Team, the only unsolved skyjacking in U.S. history.

Do you believe there is a massive shortage of career cybersecurity professionals?
I would say there is a massive shortage of qualified and quality career cybersecurity professionals today. It seems everyone

is now a cybersecurity professional. Everyone with an IT background is now hanging out their cybersecurity shingle because it's a hot topic. The demand has grown so dramatically that it left a significant void that has been filled by anyone who can spell cyber with a C.

Certifications and references are a good way to start to cull the crowd. The military has some of the very best training, but colleges and universities are still woefully behind. As for primary and secondary education, they really need to step up to the plate and start kids out with the basics at a much younger age and build cyber and cybersecurity into the next generation's DNA.

I wrote a blog that was published on March 30, 2017, for Cymmetria entitled *Cyber Education: Why Not Start Early?* My point was how shocked and disappointed I was that there was no cybersecurity program in the Anne Arundel County Public School System here in Maryland, where I live.

Anne Arundel County is literally the cybersecurity capital of the free world. It is home to the National Security Agency (NSA), U.S. Cyber Command (USCYBERCOM), Defense Information Systems Agency (DISA), the DOD Cyber Crime Center (DC3), the Naval Academy, and literally hundreds of government contractors employing tens of thousands of employees to support these agencies.

Three months after the blog, I received an email from the deputy superintendent of the Anne Arundel County Public Schools, asking me to meet her for lunch with the Chair of the Education Committee of the Ft. Meade Alliance. They wanted to discuss my blog. I was pleasantly surprised that someone had actually read what I had written. It didn't happen much when I was in the government.

The deputy superintendent gave me the background for calling the meeting. Someone from Anne Arundel Economic Development Corporation had contacted her office regarding my blog. She then started to list everything Anne Arundel County Public Schools was doing related to cybersecurity.

When she finished, I respectfully told them that there was obviously a major disconnect between what she thought was going on and the reality of what was really going on at the school level. I informed her that I had been working directly with three different high schools in the county for 12 years, trying to create programs to no avail. As recently as two months prior, I had discussed possibilities with the principal and faculty of one school where I coached the JV baseball team and offered my suggestions and availability to help. I never heard back from them. I gave them several other specific examples. They looked at one another and just shook their heads.

I was told they weren't surprised. The deputy superintendent said the roadblock was the nine teacher unions. They refused to take on anything new without additional compensation. She said they had to deal with this all the time.

They asked if they could have some time to put together a plan. They would get back to me in three weeks. I was excited.

Three months later they got back to me with their proposal. It was for me to look at the curriculum of 3 of the 12 county high schools and find spots where cyber might be relevant, and they would coordinate with those schools to provide an invitation for me to come in and talk to teachers, students, and school administrators. They were quick to point out that this would be as a volunteer, and they couldn't pay me unless I had a bachelor's degree in education.

I had more than two dozen meetings over the next nine months with the faculties at the three schools and met with only resistance and apathy. The public schools need to do better to prepare kids today for a much different and constantly evolving cyber world. Teachers must also open their minds up to the new world of cyber.

> Teachers must also open their minds up to the new world of cyber.

What's the most important decision you've made or action you've taken related to a business risk?

My path as a criminal investigator started in 1986 with the Air Force Office of Special Investigations (OSI) and was very challenging from the start. My bosses had all become very successful investigators and had been promoted to leadership positions without ever being involved in a cybercrime investigation.

Despite that, OSI was still the first law enforcement agency anywhere in the world to create a computer crime unit. They did it back in 1978 because the Air Force has always been a leader in technology and has always been a target and a victim of cybercrime. Since we were the first computer crime unit, I had to spend most of my time trying to educate and persuade my bosses to fund my program during the massive DoD budget cuts created by the "Peace Dividend" when the Berlin Wall came down.

They were cutting everything in DoD, and they wanted to cut our computer crime program as well, despite the tremendous growth in cybercrimes and vulnerabilities. A reporter once asked me how I usually spent my day. My answer was 95 percent of my day was fighting off the good guys, not fighting the bad guys. I spent almost all of my time defending the budget I had and trying to expand the program to meet the demands cyber was creating. It wasn't what I signed up for.

Since my bosses didn't get it, I had to devise a strategy of enlisting the support of our customers, the Air Force and DoD victims I supported, to let my bosses know what a critical computer crime program OSI had. I had commanders from all over the world writing letters to my bosses letting them know how valuable we were to the Air Force and DoD missions, so they just couldn't cut my budget. These other Air Force commanders also gave us positions/billets, people, equipment, and resources that I couldn't get from my own organization. My program was protected by senior Air Force leadership from outside my organization. I burned a lot of bridges along the way with this strategy, but the program grew and was by far the best in the world. Unfortunately, my own organization didn't know it.

How do you make hard decisions? Do you find yourself more often making people, process, or technology decisions?

I generally make my hard decisions based on my initial gut feelings. I have come to trust my gut over the years, and it doesn't let me down very often. As far as making decisions, I would prioritize my decisions by having people first and process second. Technology is definitely third and can enhance and support the people and the processes, but technology without the right people or process is going to be a failure and very expensive.

Too many folks in the IT community try to solve

> Too many folks in the IT community try to solve all of their problems with technology when common-sense nontechnological solutions could solve the problem more effectively and inexpensively.

all of their problems with technology when common-sense nontechnological solutions could solve the problem more effectively and inexpensively. For my IT friends, I would say if all you have is a hammer, everything looks like a nail. Be the carpenter, not the hammer.

I always looked at my last promotion as more than likely my last promotion. That gave me the freedom to always do what was right and what was best for the overall mission and our country, not what was best for my career. Again, truth to power, chips fall where they may.

What's something that you struggle with as a leader and how do you overcome that?

I'm not a college graduate and was not considered for jobs or promotions because I didn't have a degree. Through the years, I have had many doctors, lawyers, professors, and PhDs work for me but never felt inferior to them because I didn't have a degree. I've had many very well educated staff who were not very effective.

In 1971, I had to drop out of college after my second year to support my parents and lost my student deferment. I immediately got my draft notice (only lottery I ever won), so I enlisted in the Air Force. They made me a computer systems administrator. It was the Air Force technical schools that gave me direction and a career. I separated after my four-year enlistment and immediately came back to the Air Force as a civil servant, GS6. I did four more years on midnight shift at the Pentagon as a systems administrator and then took a downgrade from a GS9 to GS7 to get into programming and systems analysis, which I did for seven more years before being accepted and trained by OSI.

Treating each promotion as my last served me well. I was moved up the ranks slowly but reached the equivalent of a general officer. For that reason, I've always given people without higher education opportunities as well, and they were tremendously effective and productive. I think too much emphasis has been put on education and not enough on training and experience.

How do you lead your team to execute and get results?

I've always tried to lead by example, getting my hands dirty when I could or when it was needed. I remember where I came from and try to give people opportunities that other managers might not give them.

I also wasn't afraid to jettison the deadwood.

Do you have a workforce philosophy or unique approach to talent acquisition?

Many of the shops I managed started out with only one or two people, so to grow, I would take the rejects from other offices—folks who weren't working out for whatever reason. We used to joke that we were a leper colony. With guidance and support, the majority of these folks became stars once we gave them a chance.

My philosophy has always been, be creative, work hard, play hard, and have some fun in the process. In our spare time, I would organize team-building opportunities and competitions.

Have you created a cohesive strategy for your information security program or business unit?

I think in almost everything we do, we should set and try to achieve goals that are objective and measurable. Setting goals gives you long-term vision and short-term motivation, but they must be aligned with the overall organization's goals.

But be creative! Get everyone's thoughts, ideas, and buy-in. Improve the processes. You don't have to do things the way they have always been done. Think outside of the box and push the envelope. Push your bosses a little out of their comfort zones regularly. Dare to fail!

What are your communication tips for interacting with executive leadership?

I've always been a "speak truth to power" kind of guy. It's very hard to do in these days of political correctness. Tell the truth and cut to the chase quickly and respectfully. Perfect your 15-second elevator speech for the seniors and be ready for any opportunity you get to spend time with your leadership to expand on those ideas. Plant the seeds whenever you can.

For my staff, I would have stand-ups and staff meetings regularly. I wanted to know how they were progressing and if they had any challenges the rest of the team could help them with.

I also wanted their ideas. I wanted to tap the creativity of the folks who thought outside the box and push everyone out of their comfort zones.

How do you cultivate productive relationships with your boss, peers, direct reports, and other team members?

For me, folks always fell into two categories: those who loved me and those who hated me. If you were honest, worked hard, showed creativity and passion, you probably loved me. If you just did what you had to do to get by, I probably pushed you out of your comfort zone to be better and you ended up either being more successful or hating me. There was probably no middle ground.

We were paid by the taxpayer, not the government or some corporate entity, and I believe that we needed to get the best bang for their hard-earned buck. And time is always of the essence because time is money.

Always give your boss and your team visibility and credit for your successes.

Have you encountered challenges collaborating with revenue-generating teams like sales and product development?

One of the most significant organizational challenges I encountered was between the Air Force Computer Emergency Response Team (AFCERT) and OSI back in the early 1990s. When we had an intrusion of an AF system, the victim organization was required by regulation to notify the AFCERT. Unfortunately, to maintain sole control of the incident, the AFCERT refused to notify OSI.

This created a significant problem. We had AFCERT guys running their own investigations without the necessary authorities, tools, and expertise and in many cases exceeding their authorities and violating laws themselves.

But the services CERTs were required to notify the DOD CERT at the Defense Information Systems Agency (DISA) of any intrusion within 24 hours. Since AFCERT refused to notify or contact us, I developed a tremendous relationship with DISA, and they would immediately notify me of every intrusion incident that affected AF and DoD systems so that we could get involved.

I had to force our way into the fight. We needed a team approach and certainly needed the technical expertise that the AFCERT provided, but we also had to do things the legal way.

After several successful intrusion investigations, I was able to negotiate the placement of one of my best intrusion agents into the AFCERT so we could succeed as a team. Once we started working as a team, we were even more successful and a model for everyone else.

Have you encountered challenges collaborating with technology teams like information technology and software development?

In 1998, I was working for the Assistant Secretary of Defense for C3I (Command, Control, Communication, and Intelligence) when I came up with the idea for a DoD Cyber Crime Conference; cybercrime and digital forensics were still not mainstream yet. People were just starting to recognize the cybersecurity discipline, so the first year of the conference, I required each military installation to send a three-person team comprised of a criminal/counterintelligence agent, plus the installation cybersecurity expert and a staff judge advocate general (JAG). The IT guys were not familiar with the laws and regulations that governed them, and the agents and the lawyers didn't know anything about the technology and cybercrime. Everyone had to learn their roles in an investigation and a little about each other's disciplines. They needed to know their responsibilities and when to hand off to the other and work together as a team.

In most cases, they had never even met one another until they arrived at the conference. I even created team-building games and opportunities in the evenings that were fun so they could get to know one another on a personal level and develop a working relationship. I believe you need to have a multidisciplinary team to address cybercrime.

Do you have any favorite books to recommend for people who want to lead cybersecurity teams?

- *The Starfish and the Spider: The Unstoppable Power of Leaderless Organization* by Ori Brafman and Rod Beckstrom
- *Leadership and the New Science: Learning about Organization from an Orderly Universe* by Margaret Wheatley
- *Leadership for Smart People: Book 1: The Five Truths* by Warren Blank
- *Organizing Genius: The Secrets of Creative Collaboration* by Warren Bennis and Patricia Ward Biederman

"Whether I inherit a team or build one, I take my team through an exercise to find our purpose and set a foundation for our team identity. This not only puts the entire team on the same page, it also instills a sense of mission for each of the members."

Website: www.linkedin.com/in/chriscochrancyber

Chris Cochran

17

Chris Cochran is a former active-duty U.S. Marine Intelligence analyst. He currently leads threat intelligence at Netflix. Chris has dedicated his career to building advanced cybersecurity and intelligence capabilities for government and private-sector organizations. Chris has made it his personal mission to motivate and empower cybersecurity professionals and teams through coaching, speaking engagements, and his podcast, Hacker Valley Studio. His concern for the ever-growing cyber skills gap serves as a motivator for his desire to inspire the next generation of cyber warriors to take the helm.

Do you believe there is a massive shortage of career cybersecurity professionals?

There is a current shortage, and it is currently forecasted to worsen over the next few years. While it is an issue that many people are working to address, I see it as an opportunity to get more individuals from diverse backgrounds, cultures, and mind-sets into this field that I love. Diversity isn't a buzzword. It is an advantageous characteristic of effective teams and organizations.

To bridge the gap, we must inspire cybersecurity leaders and professionals to reach out into varied communities and convey the mutually beneficial nature of cybersecurity. This outreach does not have to be grandiose. The advantage of our increasingly interconnected world is that we can reach communities from the comfort of our homes. People have started podcasts, blogs, and social media to expose our world to the aspirational or uninitiated.

How do you make hard decisions? Do you find yourself more often making people, process, or technology decisions?

The right data can make a tough decision a no-brainer. I have known teams that cultivate a data-first approach to cybersecurity operations. They believe if there is no data to support a decision, a decision cannot be made. While I think the answer is a bit more complex, I think the sentiment is a powerful one. If you expect supporting data from your teams on decisions they make and hold yourself to the same standard, progress is inevitable.

It seems as individuals progress through their careers and ascend to higher levels of leadership, the weight distribution between people, processes, and technology changes. Early in my career, technical decisions commanded the majority of my attention, with some focus on people and processes. When I lead multiple functions, I tend to look at the processes developed between the teams more heavily to ensure effectiveness and optimization.

At the leader of leaders level, it is one's direct reports who are the focus to ensure organizational health. At this level, one's ability to empower people is the most critical, in my opinion. Empowerment is important at all levels, but at this level it can make or break a cybersecurity team.

What's something that you struggle with as a leader and how do you overcome that?

One area I struggled with early in my career was giving feedback. I am much better now but still have plenty of room to grow. I wish it could always be high-fives and stellar evaluations. However, this wish is not grounded in reality. There will be individuals who struggle. There will be projects that are not running optimally. There will be things that a leader desires from their team that are nonexistent at times. Feedback is the initiator of change.

The mindset I have adopted to make giving difficult feedback a bit easier is knowing that the individual, project, or team will be better for it. There tends to be the concern that the delivery of feedback will result in a degradation of the relationship. This usually isn't the case. In fact, it can improve a relationship and enhance trust.

Historically, I have noticed that my difficulty in handling feedback grows with the number of direct reports. I had an unusually large team when I was a young leader. I was not able to spend as much time with each of my direct reports. This led me to have fragmented images of who I thought these people were and caused me to have doubts about whether my feedback was warranted. This could happen to any leader in their career. To combat this, give feedback often and do not wait until annual evaluations. Give your people a chance to grow.

How do you lead your team to execute and get results?
In my experience, one of the best ways to motivate a leader's team is to develop a strong team identity. This is something I borrow from my time in the United States Marine Corps. Most of the teams I belonged to in the Marine Corps were high-functioning. I began to notice that the stronger the team identity, the more individuals were willing to go above and beyond for the sake of the team.

There is a book by Simon Sinek called *Start with Why* that focuses on finding purpose for the individual. But these concepts map exceptionally well for teams also. Whether I inherit a team or build one, I take my team through an exercise to find our purpose and set a foundation for our team identity. This not only puts the entire team on the same page, it also instills a sense of mission for each of the members.

Do you have a workforce philosophy or unique approach to talent acquisition?
Be open-minded. I have green-lit hires who could be considered head-scratchers by some of my colleagues. While work history is important, this is not the most critical consideration from my perspective. I tend to weigh mindset and critical thinking very heavily. Being open-minded prevents one from being overly myopic. Don't miss out on greatness because of a preconceived notion.

I often share the story of an individual I was interviewing who had a plant science background. While he might not have had the experience of some of the other candidates, it was his passion for learning, problem-solving ability, and unique perspective on systems that intrigued me. He is still in cybersecurity to this day, and I consider him one of my closest friends.

How do you cultivate productive relationships with your boss, peers, direct reports, and other team members?
Another concept I carry with me from my time in the military is "One team, one fight." This saying means we are all working toward a common goal together. Teams that are plagued with politics or ego issues need more of this mentality. When the question "What can I do for the team?" overshadows "What can I do for myself?" that is an environment supportive of cohesion and productivity.

On a more practical front, one should develop and nurture these relationships on a consistent basis. Schedule one-on-one meetings to understand the people you work with.

Here are things to consider:
- What are their current or impending pain points?
- What terms do they use often in reference to operations, and what meanings do they append to them?
- What are some high-leverage collaboration nexuses that exist?
- How do they want to interact with you on a normal day, and is that preference different in times of crisis?

Do you have any favorite books to recommend for people who want to lead cybersecurity teams?
I am fortunate to have a circle of friends who are all voracious readers. We recommend books for each other based on how groundbreaking they are or how applicable they are to an issue or situation.

The following list consists of books I have either read numerous times or whose concepts I have used to lead cybersecurity programs and teams:
- *Extreme Ownership* by Jocko Willink
- *Principles* by Ray Dalio
- *Leaders Eat Last* by Simon Sinek
- *How to Win Friends and Influence People* by Dale Carnegie
- *Ego is the Enemy* by Ryan Holiday

> "One of my biggest challenges as a leader is letting go of good talent."

Twitter: @CISOEdwardC • **Website:** www.linkedin.com/in/cisoedwardc

Edward Contreras

18

A security and risk transformation leader with more than 25 years' experience focused on knowledge sharing and risk leadership, I have guided companies through breaches, risk transformations, and complete security implementations and rebuilds while embracing "next-gen" security frameworks.

Do you believe there is a massive shortage of career cybersecurity professionals?

I believe we have a shortage of "tenured" professionals based on the expectations and level of expertise we as leaders have placed on the roles. The top of the funnel is massive if we are willing to train laterally and bring in those coming out of school. This would definitely bridge the gap and build a workforce for years to come.

What's the most important decision you've made or action you've taken related to a business risk?

One of the more important decisions I have made is allowing business units to make "risk-based" decisions based on their "risk appetite." This means that I have to be willing to accept some level of risk, knowing that the business is well informed and that we both live jointly with those decisions.

How do you make hard decisions? Do you find yourself more often making people, process, or technology decisions?

I find myself taking slightly longer to make informed decisions that bring me comfort when the decisions are not popular. I lean on facts that help remove emotion and get those people impacted by the decision much more comfortable with the results, whether they are popular or not.

What's something that you struggle with as a leader and how do you overcome that?

One of my biggest challenges as a leader is letting go of good talent. I have to be willing to train leaders and know at some point they will outgrow me based on their financial and professional needs. My goal is to provide them proper training, resources, and the ability to be relevant to keep them as long as possible, but also give them the guidance to reach higher.

How do you lead your team to execute and get results?

I make sure they see the big picture but also stop, recognize, and celebrate the milestones along the way. While some efforts take months or years, recognizing their hard work through the process also gives them a sense of accomplishment while delivering to a larger cause.

Do you have a workforce philosophy or unique approach to talent acquisition?

I focus on hiring for culture over experience. I want people who are passionate and willing to learn, as opposed to experts who have challenges listening.

Have you created a cohesive strategy for your information security program or business unit?

Absolutely! I believe security must partner with the lines of business in order to help them deliver to their needs in the most risk-aware environment. Absent a strategy, a security team is stuck plugging never-ending holes with no recognition from leadership for their involvement in customer success. Security should be embedded in the DNA of a company and be second nature and not stand-alone.

What are your communication tips for interacting with executive leadership?
My style with executives is to learn the business and talk their language. A good CISO understands that other executives are not here to learn security; they are here to drive company performance, and my job is to enable their progress with embedded security that does not feel and look intrusive.

How do you cultivate productive relationships with your boss, peers, direct reports, and other team members?
It's all about constant personal investment, transparency, honesty, and assuming innocence. I do not take bad news to heart and assume that no matter how difficult a meeting or conversation is, we are all steering in the same direction. There is no wrong way to San Diego, but there are different paths, and I have to recognize that each person has their preference and understand why that is.

Have you encountered challenges collaborating with revenue-generating teams like sales and product development?
Innovation and goal reaching are healthy dialogue with friendly friction points. I try to understand the end state of their goals to help them achieve them. At times, I find myself acting more like a chief marketing officer than a chief security officer to other stakeholders to help them understand the need so we can provide a joint solution.

Have you encountered challenges collaborating with technology teams like information technology and software development?
I usually find these conversations to be some of the more rewarding discussions. Technology and software development teams have a challenge to meet the needs of their customers through interpreting "cutting edge" with current technology "limitations." This really puts a weight on the discussions but also allows innovators to take risks when they traditionally would not, so being there during these times is absolutely worth it.

Do you have any favorite books to recommend for people who want to lead cybersecurity teams?
I would recommend *The Speed of Trust* by Stephen M. R. Covey as an amazing leadership book, *CISO Compass* by Todd Fitzgerald as a great security book, and *Who Moved My Cheese* by Spencer Johnson as a great way to understand that change is constant and unavoidable.

"Effort is important, and it is something to appreciate, but success is what needs to get highlighted and rewarded."

Twitter: @danielcornell • **Website:** www.linkedin.com/in/dancornell

Dan Cornell

A globally recognized application security expert, Dan Cornell has more than 15 years of experience architecting, developing, and securing web-based software systems. As chief technology officer and principal at Denim Group, Ltd., he leads the technology team to help Fortune 500 companies and government organizations integrate security throughout the development process.

19

Cornell is an active member of the development community and a sought-after speaker on topics of web application security, speaking at international conferences including the RSA Security Conference, OWASP AppSec USA, and EU and Black Hat Arsenal.

Do you believe there is a massive shortage of career cybersecurity professionals?

I believe there is a shortage but that company hiring practices make the shortage worse than it has to be. We certainly need more people in the cybersecurity industry, but we also need to make better use of the people we have in the industry. Automation is crucial—how can we keep our human

Automation is crucial—how can we keep our human professionals focused on the things that only humans can do and let automation handle the other stuff in the background? professionals focused on the things that only humans can do and let automation handle the other stuff in the background? We also need to better develop talent. I see too many job postings looking for "unicorn" candidates with many years of experience across multiple domains and tools. That's unrealistic. I think companies need to do a better job of hiring folks and developing them over time.

In addition, to bridge the gap, we need to make sure the industry is truly open to more people. When I hear the experiences of some women and minorities in the security industry, I can see how there is work to be done to make the cybersecurity industry more welcoming to folks.

What's the most important decision you've made or action you've taken related to a business risk?
The most important business risk decision I made was to start my own company when finishing up my undergraduate degree rather than going to work for someone else. I had a couple of offers from big, stable companies that were really attractive, but I decided to do my own thing instead. My thinking was that I was young—21 at the time—and didn't really have any money and that I'd know if the company was going to be successful within a couple of years. In my mind, 21 and broke was pretty similar to 24 and broke, and I didn't figure that having experience as an entrepreneur would hurt me if I ended up needing to get a job down the road. This terrified my family—their thinking was that I needed to get a "real" job and get some experience before doing anything crazy. But I looked at the potential risks and weighed them against the potential benefits and made what ended up being the most critical decision of my career. And it seems as though that has turned out pretty well in the scheme of things.

How do you make hard decisions? Do you find yourself more often making people, process, or technology decisions?
I like to gather a lot of information—preferably from different perspectives or thought processes—so I can pull it all together

and evaluate it in a structured manner. I'd rather read three books on a subject rather than one so I can see how the different authors handled the material and look for where the narratives agree with one another and where they differ because I think that helps to provide a better perspective on issues.

I'm most comfortable with technology decisions, process decisions, and people decisions—in that order. And obviously I'm tempted to funnel my decision-making toward areas where I'm most comfortable. That has its advantages, because I think my comfort leads to greater competence, but I always have to be careful to make sure I'm not making a technology decision because I'm uncomfortable approaching the question as a people or process decision, which might be more appropriate.

What's something that you struggle with as a leader and how do you overcome that?
Taking accountability for my failures and the failures of people on my team is really challenging. When things go wrong, my instinct is to find a justification for why things turned out the way they did, and I am incredibly adept at crafting plausible excuses. Unfortunately, that approach doesn't lead to any problems getting solved. This is especially difficult when there are opportunities to blame folks on my team. "This wasn't *my* fault—it was the team member who screwed up."

> When things go wrong, my instinct is to find a justification for why things turned out the way they did, and I am incredibly adept at crafting plausible excuses. Unfortunately, that approach doesn't lead to any problems getting solved.

But if you really want to be an effective leader, you need to take accountability for your whole team—the bad and the good. Until you can do that, you leave yourself too many opportunities to make excuses.

One of our core values at Denim Group is "Get the job done," and it is a tough one to live by. When you see people who are smart and people who put in a lot of effort but who ultimately find themselves unsuccessful at certain things, there is a tendency to celebrate all the "effort" that they put forth. Effort is important, and it is something to appreciate, but success is what needs to get highlighted and rewarded. From a leadership standpoint, accepting that everything in your team rolls up to you is a tough lesson to internalize, but I've found that when I can really embrace that perspective it puts me in a far better position to be successful.

How do you lead your team to execute and get results?
I try to provide goals and direction while avoiding micromanaging. That's tough—how do you communicate your intent and leave the specifics to the individuals working to accomplish the goal? Sometimes when I think I've been clear about a "why" and have provided good suggestions on a "what" and avoided being too prescriptive on the "how," I will find out down the road that I was either too vague about the overall intent or too detailed about the specifics. It is a delicate balancing act, and different team members do better with different degrees of freedom.

> I also strive to provide praise in public, and feedback and corrections in private.

I also strive to provide praise in public, and feedback and corrections in private. Public praise is great for the whole team because we can celebrate our successes together. Public corrections are a nightmare—they put the entire team on edge and put the person being corrected immediately on the defensive in public where they have an even higher drive to save face. Not good. It is hard enough for folks to hear feedback in private—doing it in public just creates a bunch of additional dynamics that muddy waters. That's something I've seen a lot of other so-called leaders get wrong, and it has a corrosive effect on the team.

Do you have a workforce philosophy or unique approach to talent acquisition?
I have had a lot more success hiring people with potential and helping them grow rather than hiring people with specific skills. That said, I figured out a long time ago that I need to avoid just hiring people that I "like" during the interview process, so we have set up standard written assessments for all our major positions. This helps us to get an "apples to apples" view of candidates that we can then use to drive

decisions. If everyone has been through the same set of technical exercises and has been presented with the same "Tell me about a time when you..." questions, you have a set of information you can use to compare candidates, and you can be explicit about what you liked and what you didn't like. I have found that standardizing the information you have to make those hiring decisions helps me to avoid just following along with folks who are easy for me to talk with, and that has helped me to avoid making certain bad hiring decisions. I certainly still have biases, but with a consistent set of responses from each candidate, it at least gives me a fighting chance to overcome them.

For retaining people, there are a couple of things I have found to be important. You have to pay people fairly and carefully craft bonuses and incentives because you will get what you reward, which may not be what you wanted. Once that is sorted, people have to believe that their work matters and that they are doing something cool and important, and they want to feel like they have control over their own destiny. Also, I'm coming to appreciate the value of having weekly one-on-one meetings with all my direct reports—making sure there is time set aside to talk through my goals, their goals, and other issues of mutual importance. This is a pretty standard management technique, but I consider myself to be kind of a crappy manager, so I need all the help I can get.

Have you created a cohesive strategy for your information security program or business unit?
Thankfully, I'm not specifically responsible for that in my organization, but we have worked overtime to better understand our threat model and make sure we have the process and technical controls in place that we need to keep out of trouble. As a smaller organization—around 100 employees—but also as one that handles a lot of sensitive data, this is a challenging area to address. Fortunately, we have a lot of smart—and opinionated—folks on our team who contribute their thoughts, and we take great advantage of external providers who provide and manage a lot of our security technologies. We've focused on getting the basics squared away and then incrementally locking things down as we get a better perspective on our threats and security posture.

What are your communication tips for interacting with executive leadership?

Effective communication—whether to executive leadership or some other group—comes from speaking to your targets in terms they understand and about issues that concern them. For executives this is going to be high-level stuff—revenues, profits, margins, regulatory risk, brand management, and competition. Also, communications in an organization have to be like an funnel—at the bottom are lots of details and technical items, and these must get filtered, summarized, and simplified as they move to the top. Especially at the executive level, nobody wants to hear the details, and they don't want to wade into the technology.

Preparation is key as well—you need to know what you want to say and how you want to characterize things, but you also need to be able to peel back the onion a layer or two for all the issues you're discussing in situations where executives do want to dive into some details. If you can manage this, I have found that engenders trust, and trust makes communication and the actions that follow much easier.

How do you cultivate productive relationships with your boss, peers, direct reports, and other team members?

Treat everyone with respect. Embrace accountability. Build trust.

Have you encountered challenges collaborating with revenue-generating teams like sales and product development?

Well, I *am* on the product development side trying to generate revenue, so I always push on the folks who are trying to be measured and slow things down. I suspect that's part of the reason why security is so hard—because even people like me who know better are still pushing for more features, faster.

That said, I think we have a good dynamic in our product team that balances the push for new features with an understanding that we have a responsibility to our customers to keep their data safe. We've made tough calls to delay releases to address potential issues we've found through our internal testing program. I *hate* to delay releases, but as a team building a security product, we have to be able to stand up in front of our customers and say we practice what we preach. It is hard, and we don't always get it right, but it is an area where we are always pushing to do better.

Have you encountered challenges collaborating with technology teams like information technology and software development?
I'm a technologist by background, so interacting with these teams is natural for me. However, as my role has become more external-facing, I have to make sure to remind myself of the realities of being a developer. Anything looks easy if you're not the person who has to do it, so I have to constantly try to stay grounded and maintain an appropriate perspective on what it takes to develop and deliver software. That's probably my biggest challenge—I know just enough to be dangerous, so I have to keep my worst instincts in check and not push too hard.

Do you have any favorite books to recommend for people who want to lead cybersecurity teams?
Extreme Ownership by Jocko Willinck and Leif Babin is the best leadership book I've ever read. Their core tenet—that as a leader you "own" everything in your purview—is the critical leadership lesson and one that I continue to struggle with. Taking ownership of the failures of people on your team is really hard, but I really believe that until you do you will leave yourself blind spots and make excuses that lead to failure.

The Hard Thing About Hard Things is the best business book I've ever read. I'm mangling this as I rephrase it, but that book talks about how there are a million books that will tell you how to write your strategic vision, but none of them want to talk about what you have to do when that strategic vision fails and you have to lay off half the company. *The Hard Thing About Hard Things* is that book. Having been an entrepreneur for my entire career, I've had plenty of "hard things" that I've needed to get through, and the perspective I gained from this book has helped.

I read a lot—across a number of disciplines. It is just something I enjoy doing and also something that has definitely helped me during my career. Actually, experiencing things takes a long time when compared to reading about what other people think and what other people have experienced, so reading is a great way to scale your perspective.

Certainly, the lessons you learn through experience have a much greater impact than something you have just read about, but reading has allowed me to get a more comprehensive view of the world. It hasn't stopped me from making mistakes, but I like to think that extensive reading helps me make more innovative and interesting mistakes.

"Going back to a job where my core integrity was valued meant everything to me."

Twitter: @heenaluwahine

Mary Ann Davidson

20

Mary Ann Davidson is the chief security officer at Oracle, responsible for Oracle software security assurance. She serves on the international board of the Information Systems Security Association (ISSA). Davidson has testified on cybersecurity to the U.S. House of Representatives (Energy and Commerce Committee, Armed Services Committee) and the U.S. Senate Committee on commerce, science, and technology.

Davidson has a BS in mechanical engineering from the University of Virginia and an MBA from the Wharton School of the University of Pennsylvania. She has also served as a commissioned officer in the U.S. Navy Civil Engineer Corps.

Do you believe there is a massive shortage of career cybersecurity professionals?

Ninety percent of life is solving the right problem. There is clearly a shortage of cybersecurity professionals. However, before we discuss how to bridge the gap, let's step back and look at *why* we have such a great need.

Unfortunately, technology (specifically, internet-connected technology) continues to appear in places where it arguably doesn't solve any useful problems. This has the potential for creating *systemic* risk—that by definition cannot be mitigated but needs to be avoided. For example, connecting your refrigerator to the internet (so you can use your cell phone to check whether you are out of eggs) does nothing except enable your fridge to be co-opted into a botnet. (It also may allow a hacker to see that nothing in your fridge has moved in a week, and thus yours is a good house to break into since, clearly, you are not home.) Another issue is that too many people designing internet-connected systems and devices have no background or education in security, which is the equivalent of graduating civil engineers who don't understand structures: you will have a lot of bridge and building failures.

This is, unfortunately, the state of the union in cybersecurity. There are too many people designing and building systems—or dreaming up new ways to use technology—who don't think about the risks or who believe the answer to technology-induced problems is...more technology.

Changing the educational system to teach the limits of technology and reinforce that security must be "built in from the get-go" would diminish some of our need for quite so many people to solve security issues.

What's the most important decision you've made or action you've taken related to a business risk?

One of the most important decisions I made was a personal one with a business impact, but it goes to the importance of integrity and "calling it like you see it." I was working for a startup, and they wanted me to take the personal identification number (PIN) off smart cards because "a customer thinks it is too much trouble to enter a PIN." At the time, smart cards were not really used in the United States, and of course training the customer base that the cards have no value (or you wouldn't need a PIN to secure them) was just an incredibly short-sighted thing to do. I raised my concerns with my employer and ultimately made the decision to return to a previous company who valued employees willing to fight for security. Not only was this a pivotal career move, but going back to a job where my core integrity was valued meant everything to me.

Of course, there was a huge business risk to taking PINs off smart cards—it was an insane thing to do. But I felt that the personal cost to me would have been worse: "For what shall it profit a man, if he shall gain the whole world, and lose his own soul?" Indeed.

How do you make hard decisions? Do you find yourself more often making people, process, or technology decisions?

> # Whether it is a hard decision or an easy decision, you need enough information to make a good decision.

Whether it is a hard decision or an easy decision, you need enough information to make a good decision. That doesn't mean you need all information, but you need to look at decisions objectively and consider the *value* of more information. It is also important to make decisions based on what is good for your business and not based on personal likes and dislikes.

Security problems are not just "solved" by technology. Security is fundamentally a *cultural* value: every organization needs to have a culture of security. Everyone does not have the same responsibility for security, but all have some responsibility. If you don't have a security culture, you are never going to have enough resources to fix the problem *ex post facto*. You cannot hire enough people to look over the shoulder of every developer writing code; developers have to be trained on how to write secure code (and given the tools and processes to do that).

I don't think that any one class of problem (people, process, or technology) dominates my decision-making. Frequently, they are interwoven. If you make a process unnecessarily complex, for example, you will have people trying to bypass it. Technology isn't necessarily helpful if it is too complex to be used effectively. It is easy to blame users, but when technology makes what should be easy really complex, you shouldn't be surprised at unintended and unfortunate results.

What's something that you struggle with as a leader and how do you overcome that?
Given my deep passion for my work, keeping my emotions in check is something I consciously work on. I continuously make an effort to "dial myself back" when I find my voice rising or feel myself getting (unnecessarily) agitated about something. It is

easier to engage with others (and not lose your audience) if you can remain unemotional during business discussions. That doesn't mean you can't be passionate about good security—and I am—just that when you are discussing something, you should try to retain a professional demeanor. It also helps you remain objective. If people think you are going to get emotional or angry during a discussion, they may be less willing to bring problems to your attention or express an opinion different from yours.

How do you lead your team to execute and get results?

Part of being a good manager is understanding that in most cases, you should not tell a subordinate exactly *how* to do something: "That's not how I would do it." If you insist on everything being done exactly the way you would do it, you lose sight of the fact that one of your colleagues may be able to build a better mousetrap than you can— cheaper and faster, too. Worse, you lose the opportunity to learn from people who work for you, noting that you are only as good as the people willing to work with you and for you.

I also don't micromanage work priorities for people, within limits. On occasion, there are urgent security issues that necessitate "all hands on deck." In general, I try to set team goals (incorporating feedback from my senior managers), review them, and enlist people to help deliver on them. It also helps to break projects into smaller chunks (it helps make tangible progress) and differentiate between "important but not urgent" (e.g., investments in long-term improvements) and "urgent but not important."

Do you have a workforce philosophy or unique approach to talent acquisition?

Many organizations emphasize diversity and inclusion. I believe the diversity that matters the most is talent and viewpoint.

- Talent, because it takes a lot of different skills to make a successful team (and noting that as a hiring manager you should welcome talent in whatever form it takes and ignore anything irrelevant to someone's ability to do the job).
- Viewpoint, because as a manager you make better decisions when people not only have different perspectives but have the freedom to voice them. If you hire clones of yourself, you will magnify your own worst tendencies.

Another key to hiring great people is considering the value of transferable skills. Alas, too many hiring managers want to hire someone who has done the exact same job already, preferably for 20 years. Or, they allow "keyword searches" to select candidates without considering the value of transferable skills. For example, some of the most valuable people I have on my team are not experts in any one area, but they have the ability to turn weaknesses into strengths by challenging themselves in particular areas or by taking on projects that nobody else wants to do and "getting it done." Those particular skills are incredibly valuable and often overlooked.

Have you created a cohesive strategy for your information security program or business unit?

I feel very fortunate in that executive management understands and "gets" security and has since the company's inception (we built the first commercial relational database for a large government agency). My position was created to ensure that we engineer security into all products and services, and that is what my team focuses on. In that respect, I have an easy job because I have the full support of my management chain. Security is important because all our customers expect (and depend upon) our software and services to be secure and because we run the company on our own products and services.

Alas, many peers at other companies who (for example) have the title "chief information security officer" find themselves in a challenging position: their employers want someone to hold accountable if there is a data breach but won't listen to advice up front about how to lessen that risk. Your best bet in that situation is to find another job, since "responsibility without authority equals frustration."

What are your communication tips for interacting with executive leadership?

Not everyone in an organization is a security expert or needs to be. One of the tools I use to explain geeky security issues is analogies. For example, the ethical hackers who work for me are far more technically astute than I am, and when they explain a security issue to me, I try to use an analogy ("So, this is like that, correct?") to demonstrate that I understand the issue. I also use analogies to explain the issue to others. Let's face it, hardly anybody can make a business case by saying, "We need a secure frabistat protocol. It's really important to have a secure frabistat protocol." That doesn't answer the questions, "What is a secure frabistat protocol, why do I need it, what does it do, and why does it matter to our business?" Much less, "Explain this to me in a way I can understand that doesn't devolve into bits and bytes unless it really has to."

Another tool I use a lot is separating the wheat from the chaff. Specifically, if you are going to raise an issue to an executive for a decision, you should put together an executive summary: what's the issue, what are the options, what are you recommending (and why), and what do you want from the executive (approval, support, funding, headcount, or other). You can put all the gory details in a "discussion" section. This makes it easy for someone whose time is really valuable (and equally limited) to get to the point faster and more easily. It's respectful of their time and much more likely to lead to fast approval (or disapproval) than a 70-slide PowerPoint.

How do you cultivate productive relationships with your boss, peers, direct reports, and other team members?

A lot of fostering productive relationships boils down to "do unto others as you would have them do unto you." Treat people with respect, listen to their views, don't make disagreements over business issues into personal disagreements, and make sure that your management knows about the good work the people who work for you do (i.e., give them direct credit instead of saying "me" or "my team").

As far as your boss, I always try to resolve issues at the lowest level I can. If something cannot be resolved, then I may pursue escalation to a higher level of management. Last but not least, if I think something is going to "blow up," I try to give my boss a heads up so he is not unpleasantly surprised by, for example, receiving a cold call.

Have you encountered challenges collaborating with revenue-generating teams like sales and product development?

There are always challenges dealing with others, no matter what your role—or theirs—may be. To me, focusing on the business is key, and that includes the long-term implications of business decisions.

For example, a customer may want us to commit to something in the security realm that is not our standard business practice. Sales may (understandably) want my team to approve those nonstandard terms to close a deal. However, there is a big difference between making a business *decision* to do X—including weighing the costs and benefits of X—and doing X to close a single deal. In my experience, there are no "one-deal deals"; if you agree to X for a customer, you may end up having to agree to that on every subsequent contract with the customer. So, how to resolve it? You can explain to the customer why X isn't feasible or desirable and offer an alternative you can both live with. You can also help educate sales on your security practices so they understand and can advocate for them. You should also consider whether general business practices or market expectations have changed, in which case there may be a business case for changing your security practices. At that point, deciding to agree to X is an informed business decision, and not a one-off agreement, done under duress, that may have long-term unintended consequences.

For example, one customer wanted a commitment to fix any security issue *they* deemed critical in three days. Note that the "criticality" was not based on something objective, like a Common Vulnerability Scoring System (CVSS) score, and it also did not consider the increased use of third-party code (in which case, a vendor cannot commit to fix things in three days because it is not their code but the third party's). This commitment would also mean that the entire algorithm for fixing security issues would be based on what a single customer wanted. The solution, in this case, was to explain how we attempt to a) proactively find security issues in our own code; b) CVSS score the security issues; and then, c) prioritize the worst issues first, all of which optimizes the use of scarce resources to protect the most customers in the most timely fashion from the most severe issues.

Have you encountered challenges collaborating with technology teams like information technology and software development?

My team's responsibility is assurance—making sure we engineer security into everything we build. Therefore, we must have a productive working relationship with development. In fact, we have "deputized" individuals across all development teams (and consulting) to implement our assurance program, including appointing security leads (who are architect-level individuals on large development teams) and security points of contact (who are responsible for the security of smaller development groups under the security leads).

One of the ways we encourage cooperation is by treating the security leads and security points of contact as "customers" of our assurance program. To that end, we have created an advisory council (as we do for customers of our products and services) to give us feedback on our program: what works, what doesn't, what could be made better. "Building security in" requires a team effort: we need teams to "own their code," and for our part, we need to make it as easy as we can for development to do the right thing in a cost-effective manner. Working with the people implementing your program to seek feedback—and offering some flexibility in terms of exactly *how* they can meet the core security requirement—is key to building relationships and providing a pathway to success.

Do you have any favorite books to recommend for people who want to lead cybersecurity teams?

While I think it's important to "remain current" and I try to read at least one meaty cybersecurity article a day, I have a different take on this question. I try to read broadly: e.g., history (especially military history), biology, and economics, not only because "code is ephemeral" and much of the knowledge we amass in tech is obsolete relatively quickly, but because there are lessons one can learn from these nontech areas that can enhance your ability to think differently (or more constructively) about a cybersecurity problem.

For example, one of the ways I think about resource allocation is cost avoidance or opportunity cost (a concept from economics). I once used a lesson from military history to convince an executive to invest in a particular product area. The executive had served in the Marine Corps, and my example was "How did the Marines hold Guadalcanal?" Answer: they took and held Henderson Field, which was strategic to holding the entire island. And the analogy was that investing in technology X was strategic to our entire business. The executive "got it" immediately.

"I encourage others in leadership roles to welcome honest and frank discussions from all colleagues, regardless of position. Living in an echo chamber surrounded by folks who agree with you isn't providing value to you or your company."

Twitter: @mzbat • **Website:** StabOps.com

Kimber Dowsett

21

Kimber Dowsett is the director of security engineering at Truss and is passionate about privacy, encryption, and building user-driven technology for the public. She joined Truss after serving at 18F, an office of federal employees that collaborates with other agencies to improve how government serves the public through technology. She also served six years as a mission information specialist at NASA Goddard Space Flight Center securing instrument and ground systems in complex laboratory environments.

In her spare time, Kimber developed and maintains the framework for Mock Interview and Resume Review (MIRR) Workshop, a project that partners mentors with mentees from underrepresented communities who are un/underemployed in tech and seeking opportunities for professional development. She also enjoys designing and building PCB-based electronic projects. Kimber is an avid admirer of Chiroptera, comic books, and video games.

Do you believe there is a massive shortage of career cybersecurity professionals?

Forbes published an article in 2018 highlighting a shortage of cybersecurity professionals predicted to peak at 3.5 million unfilled positions by 2021. There are tons of folks out there looking for roles in security, and this industry has a pipeline problem. While we've made some progress seeking out and hiring the best and brightest, we still have a long way to go. A lot of companies are missing out on great talent by using the same tired, old recruiting networks. Additionally, unrealistic requirements in position descriptions and poor company culture discourage folks, particularly those from underrepresented communities, from applying for open roles. We can't fix the pipeline overnight, but I think focusing on expanding recruiting networks, developing realistic position descriptions, and focusing on improving company culture are great places to start.

How do you make hard decisions? Do you find yourself more often making people, process, or technology decisions?

Every tough decision starts with data. Lots of data. I'm fortunate enough to be surrounded by smart humans on whom I rely to "give it to me straight." I have an experienced mentor who offered this guidance: "Whether it's a people, process, or tech decision, the question is always, 'What problem are we trying to solve?'" I ask that question at least a dozen times a week, and the answer is rarely aligned with the proposed solution. Taking a step back to ask more questions, although laborious, yields the best decision. I don't always make the right call, but I strive to make the best one I can, relying on information available at the time.

What's something that you struggle with as a leader, and how do you overcome that?

I have a tough time identifying my own measures of success. My current position is, by far, the most challenging role I've had. I'm very fortunate to have the trust of my employers to "do the right thing," but I often struggle to prioritize. Years with the Feds conditioned me to see everything as a low priority or "Oh, no! It's on fire!" Look, things aren't great across the security industry, but everything isn't on fire. If we keep holding on to that notion, priorities won't matter; it'll be a self-fulfilling prophecy. These days, I'm trying to focus on wins and think of success as taking baby steps without falling on my face, rather than viewing it as this monumental (unattainable) thing. YMMV.

How do you lead your team to execute and get results?

I strive to place people over product. I truly care about the folks who work for me, so I spend a lot of time thinking about team culture, goal setting, and staffing projects appropriately. I don't want to manage people; I want my team to have a solid understanding of our deliverables so we can work together to deploy something great. At Truss, we call this strategy "laying down a beat," and having our teams—regardless of practice area—align on a desired outcome yields pretty awesome results.

Do you have a workforce philosophy or unique approach to talent acquisition?

Protecting team culture has to be a top priority, particularly when bringing in new talent. The wrong person can wreck a team or project in a short time, leading to trust issues with leadership and negatively impacting the business at large. Behavioral interviews are becoming more common, as they should be. In my current practice, applicants aren't moved ahead to submit a work sample or complete a technical interview until they've successfully made it through the behavioral round. From initial screen to final interview, the process can take up to eight hours of an applicant's time, twice that on our end, but the goal is to hire folks who share our core values and have a desire to be part of, and protect, our culture. A strong emphasis is placed on professional development, mentorship, and work-life balance. I'm fortunate to have a low attrition rate, but I acknowledge there's always room for improvement.

Have you created a cohesive strategy for your information security program or business unit?

My approach to strategy is organic; I know where I want our program to land, but I accept that security is a rapidly changing industry, and goals aligned with corporate strategy may need to be periodically re-evaluated to ensure they continue to satisfy the requirements of the security program. One of my top priorities while building our security program was to tear down some silos. Security has to coordinate with other practices (infrastructure, engineering, research, design, etc.) if we want to deliver the best—and most secure—product we can.

What are your communication tips for interacting with executive leadership?

As a member of the executive team, I value honesty and radical candor. I report to founders who expect the same from me. Leadership sets the communication tone for the entire organization. Transparency is the path to trust, and trust is the path to honest feedback. That's not to say honest feedback has to be harsh or insensitive. Respectful and thoughtful delivery of information takes practice. I encourage others in leadership roles to welcome honest and frank discussions from all colleagues, regardless of position. Living in an echo chamber surrounded by folks who agree with you isn't providing value to you or your company.

How do you cultivate productive relationships with your boss, peers, direct reports, and other team members?

Empathy. Full stop. At the end of the day, no one wants to work with—or for—a jerk. One-on-ones, sanity checks, and active listening are the best ways to build trust. Teams are made up of people with different backgrounds, experiences, and training. I've worked for employers who didn't understand how important cultivating positive relationships can be to the success of a project. I certainly get frustrated, but I try to approach my colleagues with an open heart and positive attitude. Knowledge is power. Learning not to take things personally will change your life. I encourage everyone, particularly in the high-stress world of security, to read up on emotional intelligence (EQ) and adversity quotient (AQ) and practice techniques to develop skills using both.

Do you have any favorite books to recommend for people who want to lead cybersecurity teams?

I once read that people leave managers, not jobs. Great communication skills play a huge role in the success of leaders, teams, and projects. Self-care is critical to survival and sets the tone for team culture. I've found these resources to be very useful in my day-to-day life, both at work and at home:

- *Own It* by Sallie Krawcheck
- *The Five Dysfunctions of a Team* by Patrick Lencioni
- *Crucial Conversations* by Kerry Patterson, Joseph Grenny, Ron McMillan, and Al Switzler
- *Daring Greatly* by Brené Brown
- *Radical Candor* by Kim Scott

"Providing space for team members to learn and grow into their positions is one of the most important aspects of leading anyone."

Twitter: @JediMammoth • **Website:** jedimammoth.io

David Evenden

22

David is the founder of StandardUser Cyber Security, an educational security firm dedicated to bringing work to freelance hackers and bringing top-tier industry-standard information security certification training to the university classroom.

David is an experienced offensive security operator with experience working in the U.S. intelligence community (IC). He learned Persian Farsi, worked at NSA Red Team, and was a member of an elite international team operating in conjunction with coalition forces to aid in the ongoing efforts in the Middle East.

He is currently focused on working with DHS to aid in the efforts to enhance the bidirectional sharing relationship between the U.S. government and commercial entities and to track foreign intelligence activity in U.S.-based commercial critical infrastructure.

Do you believe there is a massive shortage of career cybersecurity professionals?

I've learned over time that perception is reality. If everyone perceives something to be true, then it will be widely accepted as true. Because of that I believe we do have a shortage of career cybersecurity professionals and think there is a three-part approach to bridging that gap, and it will require effort from all sides.

To begin, I believe the corporate world defines professionalism differently than the cybersecurity community does. The corporate community defines professionalism traditionally with words like *accountability*, *respectful behavior*, and *submission to authority*. The cybersecurity community cringes at the sound of some of those words. We generally define a cybersecurity professional as someone who is highly skilled technically at their job but doesn't always feel comfortable submitting to authority or showing bidirectional mutual respect. Because of that, the corporate community views a large portion of the cybersecurity community as unhireable. To bridge this gap, the corporate community will need to increase its willingness to accept additional risks, and the cybersecurity community will need to remember that someone pays their bills, and they are responsible and accountable to someone else.

The second approach will be for organizations to recalibrate job postings, listings, and descriptions to better represent the personnel needed for specific tasks. I personally believe stacked job requirements are created in order to close the corporate gap defining professionalism. Companies believe if they list jobs with unrealistic stacked requirements, they'll get someone who has been in the industry for a while and is more suitable for a "professional" environment. Calibrating job requirements and roles and responsibilities will open job listings to the vast number of cybersecurity professionals who need their first foot in the door.

> Calibrating job requirements and roles and responsibilities will open job listings to the vast number of cybersecurity professionals who need their first foot in the door.

Additionally, aspiring cybersecurity professionals may not always meet all the requirements of a job posting, but they can still get the job done well. There is a shortage of career cybersecurity professionals because many in the cybersecurity workforce don't apply for jobs when they may not feel qualified. I would encourage all cybersecurity professionals to apply for jobs they know they can do well, even if they don't meet all the requirements posted, because there are lots of managers who will give them their first chance.

What's the most important decision you've made or action you've taken related to a business risk?

The most important decision related to business risk I've made in my career was to leave a company that wasn't taking the risk of cybersecurity seriously enough.

If you have a high-tier security role but your cybersecurity recommendations aren't being seriously considered, you're not the security person; you're the fall person.

How do you make hard decisions? Do you find yourself more often making people, process, or technology decisions?

To be honest, making hard decisions is difficult for me, while making dumb decisions comes easily to me. Knowing the difference isn't always clear.

When I can see the potential outcomes and know they're hard decisions, I make hard decisions by being overly methodical, taking into consideration various scenarios and outcomes. These days I find myself making process decisions more often than other types of decisions.

What's something that you struggle with as a leader and how do you overcome that?

As a leader, I struggle with imposter syndrome. Even after being in this industry for more than 10 years, having led small and large teams, started a small company, and become a subject-matter expert in a specific cyber field, I'm still constantly learning and always feel like I'm just getting started.

How do you lead your team to execute and get results?

Until recently words like *gentleness* and *kindness* were not generally associated with my ability to lead teams. Coming out of the military and being raised in a military family all over the world, I've always been a very assertive and demanding team leader. I set high expectations for myself, and I always expect those same high expectations to be shared across my team members without excuse.

That's not how you lead effective teams.

Providing space for team members to learn and grow into their positions is one of the most important aspects of leading anyone. Having said that, providing space for team members to grow works only if the team leader sets realistic and clear expectations and practices effective communication. Being an effective leader who begets results requires effective communication.

Do you have a workforce philosophy or unique approach to talent acquisition?
Yes. Hire for attitude and aptitude...then believe in and speak life into people. People will generally live up to or down to your expectations of them. Regardless of what you think, their view of your expectations of them is directly proportional to how you speak to and treat them.

Raise up, encourage, and support fellow team members because if you do, they will nearly always unimaginably exceed the requirements of the position they fill.

> Raise up, encourage, and support fellow team members because if you do, they will nearly always unimaginably exceed the requirements of the position they fill.

What are your communication tips for interacting with executive leadership?
Focusing your conversation to adapt to your target audience is a key tip for effective communication with executive leadership. If they started talking about market growth strategies, regional sales cycles, and international channel partners, you might not know what they were talking about; the same applies to them but with regard to cyber initiatives.

Put things in context that allow them to develop a basic understanding of corporate risk and discuss the proportional business impact that the risk could lead to. Without showing impact, risk is often meaningless to executive leadership.

How do you cultivate productive relationships with your boss, peers, direct reports, and other team members?
Listen. Listen. Listen.

I'm a devout Christian, which has nothing to do with the question, but I love having the opportunity to pray for the needs of people. As I listen, I learn more about their lives and their struggles, and I have the opportunity to build a relationship with them I could not have otherwise.

Cultivating productive relationships starts with listening and caring, and remember, don't confuse hearing with listening.

Have you encountered challenges collaborating with revenue-generating teams like sales and product development?
Yes. I nearly always run into the problem of revenue-generating teams over-promising features and overextending SLAs. However, after learning more about revenue-generating teams, I've come to understand that this type of behavior is more of a cultural problem than a misunderstanding of capabilities.

Revenue-generating teams often have to meet quotas and will regularly over-promise to produce results.

It is difficult to shift cultural change from the outside, so this issue will likely not change overnight. However, I've found it's easier to influence the direction of individual revenue-generating team members by helping them understand the impact of over-promising or over-extending SLAs and how that can affect the rest of the team, potentially completely reducing the bandwidth for new clients.

So far conversations like these have been met with understanding and mutual respect.

Do you have any favorite books to recommend for people who want to lead cybersecurity teams?

- *Principles* by Ray Dalio
- *On Becoming a Leader* by Warren Bennis
- *Leadership and Self-Deception* by The Arbinger Institute
- *The Anatomy of Peace* by The Arbinger Institute

> "I do not believe that groups of people make decisions—people make decisions."

Twitter: @armorguy • **Website:** www.linkedin.com/in/martinjfisher

Martin Fisher

Martin Fisher is a 20-year information security veteran who has worked in the commercial aviation, finance, and healthcare delivery industries. He was a founding host of the award-winning Southern Fried Security Podcast for 10 years, has appeared on NPR's "Science Friday with Ira Fladow," and has spoken internationally on a variety of information security topics. He has led a variety of teams through significant transformations and helped create high-performing teams of engaged and effective security professionals.

23

Do you believe there is a massive shortage of career cybersecurity professionals?

Yes, there is.

That said, I don't think cranking out 60,000+ new CISSPs is going to fix the real underlying problem. That problem is that our current generation of security technologies hasn't matured to the point where we can reliably automate responses across all environments. I think the current focus on creating mills where we turn people into "security professionals" is an almost decent bandage to the problem, but we're ignoring the fact that we need to better integrate security into all aspects of IT operations. Let's be honest—security operations is a subset of IT operations, and the sooner we realize that and develop/adopt the kinds of automation and processes that make IT operations (like DevOps) a practical reality, we will always be behind the curve.

What's the most important decision you've made or action you've taken related to a business risk?
What comes to mind immediately may seem small, but it changed the way I think about risk.

As the CISO for a hospital, we once got a frantic call from a presurgery unit because one of the devices monitoring a patient was showing a malware infection. The screen that had the data for the patient was being overlaid by a warning from the endpoint security tool. The tool wanted to do a reboot, but that had a chance of creating a patient safety issue.

What do you do? Do you protect all of the other devices on the network, reboot and clean the device, and have the clinical team monitor the patient differently? Do you quarantine the device?

What I decided to do was remotely remove the endpoint software from the device so it wouldn't alarm during the rest of the procedure. Then, and only then, we cleaned the device. We also started monitoring the rest of the environment closely to see if the malware was spreading. Thankfully, the patient had a great outcome, the malware didn't move, and we got everything cleaned up.

I've told this story before, and I almost always see one of two reactions. The first is "Wow, that makes sense," and the second is a mix of bewilderment and dismay that I somehow allowed the Bad Guy to win. The lesson here is that the point of information security is to support the goals and objectives of the organization. At a hospital, that's "we heal people—we do not harm people," so that decision was the right one.

How do you make hard decisions? Do you find yourself more often making people, process, or technology decisions?
I look for what data is available to inform the choices. I have a small cadre of trusted staff who have very different

viewpoints than I do, and we discuss options, outcomes, and pitfalls. We try to come up with different responses and what the likely results will be for each. We have Plan A, Plan B, Plan C, and so on.

Then *I* decide. I do not believe that groups of people make decisions—people make decisions. I value the input of my team immensely, but, at the end of the day, I am responsible. If the decision was the correct one, I will let the plaudits fall on my team, as they are usually the ones doing the actual work. If the decision was faulty, that is my responsibility alone.

That is what leaders do.

What's something that you struggle with as a leader, and how do you overcome that?

I'm entering a stage of life where many times I am the oldest person in the room. It's easy to use the "I have experience" or "How could you, Young Person, possibly have insight on this?" crutches to control conversations and drive decisions. Some/many/most people wouldn't even realize I was doing that.

However, as Admiral Akbar tells us, "It's a trap!" I do have experience. I have seen a lot. But the younger folks on my team have a different set of experiences and (even more importantly) a totally different world view than me. If I dismiss their ideas, their experiences, or their perspective out of hand, I have wasted a valuable resource that the organization pays a lot of money to make available to me.

How do you lead your team to execute and get results?

Most everything I do in this arena is built on what I learned as a young officer in the United States Army. You lead your team by example. You set high expectations, provide resources and support, and then get out of the way. I am routinely stunned at how much my folks do with what they have to a level of quality that exceeds my wildest expectations. What's even more, they usually do it in a way that bears little resemblance to the way I thought it could be done.

As an individual contributor (and yes, leaders are also individual contributors), I always alter my style to fit into what my leaders want/need/expect. Not every boss I've had uses the same methods I do. In fact, some of the best bosses I've had had wildly different leadership styles that I was able to adapt to and succeed.

Do you have a workforce philosophy or unique approach to talent acquisition?

I have to give a lot of credit to Michael Auzenne and Mark Horstmann of Manager Tools (www.manager-tools.com) and their "Effective Hiring" series of podcasts in shaping how I currently hire people. By focusing on reasons to say "no" about a candidate versus looking for a "yes" radically shifts how you evaluate candidates for a complete fit and minimizes the chances of the dreaded Bad Hire.

Retention is a function of creating challenging work environments and decent work/life balance and supporting the career growth of your folks. Sometimes that means changing their roles. Sometimes that means helping them find a role outside of your organization. It always means creating a team culture that knows the leader cares about the team individually as career professionals.

Have you created a cohesive strategy for your information security program or business unit?

Yes-ish, because the strategy is always evolving and is never fully set in stone because the strategy of the business is always evolving and never fully set in stone.

We ensure that our program is aligned by always gut-checking ourselves with our corporate values. I'm a CISO for a hospital system. Patient safety is always the highest priority. Ensuring quality of care comes second. Protecting sensitive data comes after that. Looking at our program through that lens ensures that we are aligned with every other department in the organization. Those departments know we're aligned, and that makes collaboration with them to resolve difficult problems easier than the traditional adversarial relationship security had with other groups.

What are your communication tips for interacting with executive leadership?

Know what your executive leadership cares about. They probably are not interested in how many malware infections your endpoint security system squashed last quarter. They probably do care that outbreaks were identified, contained, and eradicated; that your cost projections were accurate; and that you didn't cause operation impacts.

Speak the language of executive leadership. The days of impressing C-levels using "security speak" are long over. You need to know how your organization makes money and be able to speak in those terms. As a hospital CISO, I need to be able to use the language of safety and quality to describe what we do and how we do it.

Listen more than you talk. I'm shocked how many people believe that the five minutes they get with a CEO/CFO/COO needs to be a mini-TED talk versus realizing that listening for four minutes about what that executive really wants is insanely valuable.

When your team did well, use the pronoun "we." When your team screwed up, use the pronoun "I." Never should you ever do the reverse. Executives see through that and (rightly) judge harshly.

How do you cultivate productive relationships with your boss, peers, direct reports, and other team members?

The hospital term is *rounding*. I go and visit people on a regular basis to talk to them. I keep my commitments to them. I work to understand what is important to them, and they understand what is important to me. Professional courtesy is a thing that's super helpful and too often neglected up, down, and laterally in business relationships.

Have you encountered challenges collaborating with revenue-generating teams like sales and product development?

Of course! Revenue generation is what keeps businesses alive. If you build positive relationships in advance of the challenge, they know you want to protect them and that you realize the value of what they are trying to do. We call this "Don't say no. Say 'not like that'" on my team. We must help revenue generation teams generate revenue safely. Otherwise, we have negative value.

Have you encountered challenges collaborating with technology teams like information technology and software development?

These are some of the hardest challenges to handle. Technology teams are desperately trying to accomplish

Technology teams are desperately trying to accomplish their goals, be they reliability, deployment, innovation, and so forth.

their goals, be they reliability, deployment, innovation, and so forth. They get so laser focused on that goal that they perceive any delay or obstacle as true evil and will sometimes do crazy things to get around it.

The most effective solution I have is in the other key phrase we use on my team: "Guardrails, not speed bumps." Think of it this way: speed bumps really don't accomplish much other than damage the undercarriage of your beloved low-slung car. Guardrails, on the other hand, will let you drive as fast as you can and, should you lose control, prevent you from crashing to the bottom of the rock-filled canyon. Your car will be damaged, but you will not die.

The extension here is that our security program creates baselines, expectations, and guidelines but doesn't judge a solution. We will collaborate through the life cycle of the project and warn the project team when we feel they are getting too close to a guardrail. Should the team hit the guardrail, we will help pick up the pieces. The team has control of their fate. That empowerment builds the best relationships.

Do you have any favorite books to recommend for people who want to lead cybersecurity teams?
So many.

- *The Unicorn Project* by Gene Kim,
- *Excellence Wins* by Horst Schulze,
- Field Manual 22-100, "Military Leadership," by the United States Army (1990), armyoe.files.wordpress .com/2018/03/1990-fm-22-100.pdf
- The Interdependency Series by John Scalzi

I look for books that have compelling characters who face challenges and lead through them, be they fictional or biographical. I also look for books that suggest actionable behaviors I can emulate or help develop thought processes I can use.

"I would say the biggest risk I have taken in my career is to hire people who are new to the field and pour my heart and soul into teaching them everything I know and everything I am."

Twitter: @humanhacker • **Website:** www.linkedin.com/in/christopherhadnagy

Chris Hadnagy

Christopher Hadnagy is the founder and CEO of Social-Engineer, LLC, and the CEO of the nonprofit Innocent Lives Foundation. Chris possesses more than 17 years of experience as a practitioner and researcher in the security field. His efforts in training, education, and awareness have helped to expose social engineering as the top threat to the security of organizations today.

24

Chris established the world's first social engineering penetration testing framework at www.social-engineer.org, providing an invaluable repository of information for security professionals and enthusiasts. That site grew into a dynamic web resource, including a podcast and a newsletter, which have become staples in the security industry and are referenced by large organizations around the world. Chris also created the first hands-on social engineering training course and certification, Advanced Practical Social Engineering, attended by law enforcement, military, and private-sector professionals.

In 2017, he started an InfoSec community initiative nonprofit called The Innocent Lives Foundation. He gathered experts from the field in OSINT, investigation, and other areas to help assist law enforcement in tracing, tracking, and unmasking child predators who try to hide online. More information can be found at www.innocentlivesfoundation.org.

Do you believe there is a massive shortage of career cybersecurity professionals?

This is an interesting question because on one hand there are more courses in universities that teach cybersecurity skills, which is great to see. But on the other hand, I feel there are fewer people motivated by passion for the field. When I was starting up, there was no expectation to make 60, 70, 100, 200K a year doing this work. We did it because we loved it, we had a passion to learn and understand, and we wanted to see the world be safer. I don't see that same passion in a large majority of younger ones today.

Bridging that gap is easy to talk about and hard to do. The reason it was easy for me and others in my generation to have passion is we could "play" in the field easily without destruction and without problems. Now you either have malicious hackers, hacktivists, or college kids who don't have the resources to really play in the field. To bridge that gap, we need to step away from focusing so much on degrees and focus more on the skill that is needed to understand the real problems in the world of hacking.

> To bridge that gap, we need to step away from focusing so much on degrees and focus more on the skill that is needed to understand the real problems in the world of hacking.

What's the most important decision you've made or action you've taken related to a business risk?

I love this question. Recently I gave a speech at the final DerbyCon about what I learned from risk as a business owner. I talked about what I learned from the risk I took by starting a social engineering–only company when *no one* else on Earth was doing that. I talked about the risk of focusing on trying to leave everyone I met better for having met me, even though I am hacking them. But on top of it all, I would say the biggest risk I have taken in my career is to hire people who are new to the field and pour my heart and soul into teaching them everything I know and everything I am.

I chose this path because I felt it was the best way to get people to help me make my company and this industry amazing. For the largest majority, it paid off; I have a team of some of the most amazing people on Earth. I really do. But there have been times that it backfired on me, and people have left the company—even stolen the things I taught them to try to compete or turned a deaf ear to our mantra.

With that said, I would not change much about what I did with that risk, because the end result is to have some of the best people I have ever met at my side, making this company and industry a better place to be.

How do you make hard decisions? Do you find yourself more often making people, process, or technology decisions?

Social-Engineer, LLC, my company, is focused on the people side of security. So, more often than not I am making decisions about people and processes—people I hire and work with, as well as the best way to train, educate, and work with people to make them more secure.

It is much like dieting and working out, which I need to do more of: there is so much benefit, but the changes are slow at first. Sometimes that slowness can make all of us impatient, and then we want to take the easy route.

So, I find myself trying new methods, trying new processes, and trying new ways of testing, training, and auditing the human side until I find one that works.

What's something that you struggle with as a leader, and how do you overcome that?

The "should" statement. That is my biggest struggle as a leader. I work hard to make sure my small company can provide the best environment for people. As a small company we have great salaries, full health benefits, dental, eye, life, 401K, unlimited PTO, and paid holidays as well as annual bonuses and raises as the company remains profitable. All of that has made me at times say, "Well, I offer all of these amazing things to people, so they *should* be loyal to me." Or I found myself saying, "Because I gave this person a chance when they had no experience and brought them up in the community, they *should* be grateful to me."

I have found that these *should* statements are really damaging. There is no causal link between my giving them all those benefits and that person being honest, hardworking, and loyal. A loyal, hardworking, and honest person, like my friend Ryan who works for me, will be that way despite the benefits that come his way because it is who he is, not because he *should* be that way due to my actions.

This was challenging for me to learn, and I learned it the hard way, through a lot of disappointment. But I can say that lesson taught me a lot and helped me realize that those two things are not linked at all. I can be a great boss, or I can be a terrible boss; either way none of that *should* lead to any expected results. My job as CEO is to take care of my people the best way I know how and can afford, and their job is to do the job I hired them for. Any loyalty or friendship that comes is extra icing on the cake of success.

> I can be a great boss, or I can be a terrible boss; either way none of that *should* lead to any expected results.

Once I learned that, I found much more happiness in my amazing team of wonderful people I have now.

How do you lead your team to execute and get results?

I found that for me what works is not expecting my people to do anything I would not do. I work as hard as I want them to work, I spend more time than I want them to spend, I put in as much effort as I want them to put in. In the end, it is my example that allows me to demand excellence from them. But I also learned that I have to take the lead in taking a break. They need to see me unplug, stop working, and go completely off the grid throughout the year, so they feel it is okay to do the same.

As an individual, I try my hardest to have a relationship with every employee. Granted, some are closer or deeper than others, but I try to have a relationship with each.

Do you have a workforce philosophy or unique approach to talent acquisition?

We use a communication profiling tool called DISC. It helps us see how a person likes to communicate and how they communicate with others. When we need a new employee, we decide what type of communicator fits the best in that role. When we get down to our top five candidates, we then give them the DISC test and use that to choose our top candidate.

That is not foolproof, but it does help. Once we get that person inside, we try to keep them motivated and challenged as well as rewarded to ensure that they love their job and the team they get to work with.

Have you created a cohesive strategy for your information security program or business unit?

Each and every day we are working with some of the world's largest companies on their security programs; this helps my company and me to really be constantly thinking about how we apply these same principles. Some recent (in the last two to three years) amazing hires have also enhanced our internal security infrastructure to help us become an even better company.

We are big believers in the human firewall as well as technology to help us stay secure.

> We are big believers in the human firewall as well as technology to help us stay secure.

What are your communication tips for interacting with executive leadership?

Again back to DISC. When a new employee is hired, we post the results of their DISC test on our intranet for all to see. The results describe how this person likes to communicate, how they like to be managed, their strengths, and their weaknesses in communication. Every employee, including me as the CEO, has their profile on the intranet. This gives each person the chance to really learn how to properly communicate with anyone else in our company.

I will read each person's profile before employee reviews so I can learn how to best motivate that person and effect change. I have found that those who read my profile tend to communicate with me the best too.

How do you cultivate productive relationships with your boss, peers, direct reports, and other team members?
By having an open and fun environment to work in and by making an environment where every employee can express their feelings without problems. I strongly feel that you can have any emotion you want, positive or negative, whether it is right or wrong. The only thing I ask is that we express that emotion in a way that is not attacking.

No one is perfect at this—I am definitely not—but by keeping this attitude fresh for myself and all employees, we can work on problems and learn to communicate more openly.

> I strongly feel that you can have any emotion you want, positive or negative, whether it is right or wrong. The only thing I ask is that we express that emotion in a way that is not attacking.

Have you encountered challenges collaborating with revenue-generating teams like sales and product development?
Not at all. My sales and biz dev teams are like best friends. And my interaction with them is a joy. I can see they truly love their jobs and love working together and with me. That makes collaboration really easy.

Do you have any favorite books to recommend for people who want to lead cybersecurity teams?
This is self-serving, but my book *Unmasking the Social Engineer* is a great book on how to communicate more efficiently using nonverbals.

Besides that, I love these books:
- *Presence* by Amy Cuddy
- *What Everybody Is Saying* by Joe Navarro
- *Emotions Revealed* by Dr. Paul Ekman
- *It's Not All About You...* by Robin Dreeke

Twitter: @andrewsmhay • **Website:** www.linkedin.com/in/andrewhay

Andrew Hay

"I'm an analytical person, so I tend to rely on hard data as opposed to 'gut feelings'."

Andrew Hay is a veteran cybersecurity executive, strategist, industry analyst, data scientist, threat and vulnerability researcher, and international public speaker with close to 25 years of cybersecurity experience across multiple domains. He prides himself on his ability to execute the security strategy of the company with which he works without neglecting business objectives and the needs of its customers. Andrew is the author of multiple books on advanced security topics and is frequently approached to provide expert commentary on industry developments. He has been featured in publications such as *Forbes*, *Bloomberg*, *Wired*, *USA Today*, and *CSO Magazine*.

25

Do you believe there is a massive shortage of career cybersecurity professionals?
Yes and no. I believe that there is a shortage of entry-level cybersecurity professionals who are unable or unwilling to accept an entry-level role to start off in a particular company. Everyone wants to work on the cutting edge of technology and

be compensated for it, but few people want to put in the work to start at the ground floor.

What's the most important decision you've made or action you've taken related to a business risk?

Knowing when to walk away. Whenever you're presented with a challenge, you can either fight it or walk away. As a leader, however, you must be able to recognize an unwinnable situation that could adversely affect your career, your team, or the business itself. You can't always save the business from itself, especially if the business chooses to ignore or accept the risks presented.

How do you make hard decisions? Do you find yourself more often making people, process, or technology decisions?

I'm an analytical person, so I tend to rely on hard data as opposed to "gut feelings." I truly believe that if an individual or team is armed with the proper data, you can make a more educated decision on the course of action that you're looking to take. I like to think I spend 90 percent of my time making people decisions, but, unfortunately, that's not the case in most startups. Instead, I'm spending a lot of time developing processes to guide the use of technology to remove roadblocks for the people. At some point, I truly believe my role will shift to people decisions.

What's something that you struggle with as a leader, and how do you overcome that?

Coming from a military family, I was raised in a "command-and-control" leadership environment. That, however, doesn't always mesh with how individuals or teams work. The biggest challenge I continue to work on is moving away from the command-and-control mentality to more of a coaching model. In the coaching model, I'm giving people the tools and skills to succeed and telling them what the end result is. I'm not giving them the "Andrew's way it should be done" speech. Instead, I'm letting them be creative within the constraints of the project.

How do you lead your team to execute and get results?

I was once told that the sole job of a leader is to remove the roadblocks impacting their team. This is something I still believe in, and it has served me well over the years. If I can remove the roadblocks to success and the team is aware of the final objective, I can get out of the way and let them reach the goal. That's not to say that I take my hands completely off the wheel. If I notice struggles or additional challenges (e.g., wrapping things up in a timely manner), I can step in to help move the process along.

Do you have a workforce philosophy or unique approach to talent acquisition?

I hire hungry people. I want people who not only want the job that they're applying for but want to better themselves through formal education, personal learning, and elevation within the company. I've worked hard to get to where I am in my career, and I want to lead people just as motivated—if not more motivated—than myself. To retain top talent, I rely on sports coaching methodologies. I see myself as a coach whose job it is to develop the top players in the field, and I want to give them every opportunity to improve and rise to the next level of their career.

Have you created a cohesive strategy for your information security program or business unit?

Many security professionals tend to think security first, business second. Unfortunately, this isn't usually why the business exists. To develop a cohesive strategy, you must think of developing a security program that aligns with the overall objectives of the business. It's a compromise that few people understand until the role is thrust upon them. One of the best things you can do is to forge relationships with your peers in other teams to learn what they care about most. From there, you can align the security program so that it embraces the business objectives.

What are your communication tips for interacting with executive leadership?

Always align the communication objectives with the needs of the business in the language of business. The executive team will not care how many vulnerabilities you're finding on a weekly basis. They care about how you are removing those vulnerabilities from the books and reducing the overall risk profile of the organization. With any type of interaction, you need to know your audience and adjust your communication style accordingly.

How do you cultivate productive relationships with your boss, peers, direct reports, and other team members?

Figure out what they need and determine how to get it to them without compromising the objectives of the information security program. There's a time to give in and a time to stand firm. Neither should get in the way of forging productive relationships with others in the organization. If you can determine a need or want, deliver on it, and not compromise your personal or program beliefs, the relationships will materialize.

Have you encountered challenges collaborating with revenue-generating teams like sales and product development?

Always. Ultimately you have to put yourself in their shoes and empathize with them. A sales team exists to sell, and a product management team needs to translate customer requirements into a product or service. Security cannot get in the way of either of those by implementing a "my way or the highway" stance. Rather, you must figure out ways to weave security into their hierarchy of needs so that they see your contribution as a seamless component of their deliverable or, even better, as a way to increase the velocity or quality that they're delivering.

Have you encountered challenges collaborating with technology teams like information technology and software development?

Where there are different teams, there will always be challenges in collaboration. The best way that I know of to approach partnerships is to determine how you can help that team do their job in a better or more efficient manner that makes their lives easier. This doesn't mean running over and telling them that the way they're doing something is wrong but rather to suggest tips or tricks that will help them get more of their free time back. This will win you points as a collaborator that you can cash in later when you need their help.

Do you have any favorite books to recommend for people who want to lead cybersecurity teams?

Honestly, the best books cybersecurity leaders can read are those related to conducting negotiations and interacting with people from different cultures and backgrounds. For negotiations, *Negotiation* by Luecke and Harvard Business School Press is still a valuable source as it shows that you don't have to win every negotiation for there to be a positive outcome.

For interacting with people from different cultures and backgrounds, I always recommend *Kiss, Bow, or Shake Hands* by Morrison and Conaway. It will give any leader a view into how to conduct business with an international audience, taking culture, customs, and norms into account. It's something every leader needs to understand.

Twitter: @markofu • **Website:** www.linkedin.com/in/hillick

"It's incredibly rewarding watching others grow."

Mark Hillick

Mark Hillick is currently the director of security at Riot Games, where he leads the security department from a tech and product perspective. Their goal is to enable Rioters to securely ship fun player experiences and games with high integrity. Mark has been involved in InfoSec for almost 20 years and has run CTFs, done more certs and incident responses than he can remember, and presented at conferences such as BruCon and AWS Re:Invent.

26

Do you believe there is a massive shortage of career cybersecurity professionals?
Not to turn the question around, but I believe it's a shortage of "good" security professionals versus a shortage of people (interested) in cybersecurity.

I think we need to be more open about hiring from other disciplines, and I don't necessarily mean networking, DevOps/sysadm, or software development, but even outside of technology altogether. People like Charles Munger, David

Epstein, and Nasim Taleb talk about a multidisciplinary approach in their writings about their various fields, and I think we (in InfoSec) need to take a leaf out of that thinking.

I also believe our field could do with becoming a little bit more approachable. Although more "rock stars" have been called out in recent years, the industry still has a tendency to overanalyze, look inward, and focus on the technical problem, when many of the actual real problems with risk are anything but uber technical. In general, cybersecurity is based on risk and mostly processes around people.

How do you make hard decisions? Do you find yourself more often making people, process, or technology decisions?
Over the last seven years, I've typically worn three hats in my role across people, product, and technology, with process going across all three. Product and technology are typically the most enjoyable; however, working with people is the most rewarding.

In previous years, the split was probably fairly equal in three ways, but over the last few years as my role has expanded in terms of seven teams from a product and technology perspective, in addition to a greater role across the company, it currently looks like 60 percent people, 20 percent product, and 20 percent technology.

I set some of the technology direction for the company; however, I always involve those closer to the problem space, be they members of security or folks from other teams, because I will always have knowledge gaps and blind spots. Despite setting product direction for the overall security department, I provide the what (i.e., the direction of where we should go in order to support the company in securely achieving its objectives) in collaboration with the team leads, who then work with their own teams to work out the how and if it's reasonable. Feedback flows upward, downward, and across with everyone having the desire to achieve the common goal.

> Feedback flows upward, downward, and across with everyone having the desire to achieve the common goal.

What's something that you struggle with as a leader, and how do you overcome that?

I've many blind spots, and as someone who is fairly methodical, I'm a huge believer in receiving feedback so I can improve; however, I have realized that when I receive feedback, then is not the time to start trying to clarify and understand. It is usually quite hard for someone to deliver feedback, so it's best to leave some time before asking further clarifying questions because that can often come across as challenging the feedback, thus decreasing the likelihood for that person to give you feedback again.

I've overcome it by reading about the topic and listening to those who pointed it out to me, so I am now very self-aware of it and don't do it.

Many leaders are promoted because they were good at their previous, more technical job, and, as a result, in the position of leadership they can no longer do that job. However, watching someone more junior than you make mistakes and take longer on a task can be difficult, especially when there are deadlines. As you grow in leadership, you realize a few things:

- People learn better through making mistakes.
- Five or ten people will do much more as a team than you ever could as the single SME.
- Trying to advise too much or even do too much shows a lack of trust and is disrespectful.
- It's incredibly rewarding watching others grow.

How do you lead your team to execute and get results?

I delegate as much as possible, but when I delegate, I do not abdicate; I ensure I'm fully supportive, emotionally and technically.

I modify my approach per team and individuals, as not everyone is the same. I also ensure people on my teams understand how I work and what my weak areas are, asking them to help me improve.

Do you have a workforce philosophy or unique approach to talent acquisition?

I don't think there's anything unique here. When we hire people, we are part of ensuring they succeed; if they don't, it's on us. Failure and success on everything here are shared.

> When we hire people, we are part of ensuring they succeed; if they don't, it's on us.

Have you created a cohesive strategy for your information security program or business unit?

This can probably be summarized as collaborative but with me being held accountable for the execution of the strategy.

There are seven teams within security at Riot. I set the overall product and technical direction for the department. Our vision and mission are tied to the overall company strategy, and I am part of the senior leader group, which enables me to have a detailed holistic view into strategies across the company.

I work closely with my team leads in defining our mission, ensuring it aligns with the company strategy, and then we align on the commitments that we will make for the coming six to twelve months so that the company achieves its goals in as secure a fashion as possible. The team leads break down the what into the how (i.e., individual projects), which they then present with myself in the investor role.

Over the past 18 months, we have begun to measure a lot more, everything from standard uptime metrics to security issues to "work," but more specifically what results that work achieves and what the objective of it is (i.e., using objectives and key results [OKRs]).

What are your communication tips for interacting with executive leadership?

- Understand the company strategy and vision.
- Discover what executive leadership thinks the purpose and objective of having a security team is. (I think many folks in security will find their leadership has a different perspective of what a security team should actually do.)
- Know what risks executive leadership feels the company has (what keeps them up at night).
- Challenge and ask questions, but do it constructively, judging each scenario/environment independently.
- Don't use jargon; speak in their terms.
- An example could be quantifying and measuring much more qualitatively, such as in money versus high/medium/low.

How do you cultivate productive relationships with your boss, peers, direct reports, and other team members?

As I've become more senior, I have realized that my words carry an increasing amount of weight, so it's become necessary

> As I've become more senior, I have realized that my words carry an increasing amount of weight, so it's become necessary to establish productive relationships with full transparency and honesty.

to establish productive relationships with full transparency and honesty. Furthermore, this progression has meant I've moved further away from the problem space, so I try to always ensure that when I'm asking questions or seeking clarification I am trying to understand and learn, not question or judge (though I sometimes fail at this).

I use a multitude of methods to build relationships, altering the approach depending on the person because everyone is different and we all process information differently, depending on our personalities, background, and how we slept the night before.

I have regular one-on-ones (mostly in informal settings away from the team space to encourage conversation) with all of the above. I strive to ensure that my reports understand they "own" these one-on-ones, so the agenda is theirs, but I am always prepared to initiate, and I am keen to discuss topics that are outside of the professional world (as appropriate) so that I can learn more and support my colleagues better.

From a road map and direction perspective, I err on the side of sharing too much and seeking too much collaboration from leads of the individual teams within and outside of security because I want people to feel involved and that they have the capability to question or challenge, as opposed to the direction being top-down, dictatorial. A major learning for me has been that I should provide context prior to those questions, acknowledging that they have more depth in the subject matter, but given the greater holistic awareness I have across the organization, there's some things they may not be aware of, so we can mutually benefit each other and come to a better solution by listening to each other and learning.

Additionally, I've used the README template to provide a quick introduction to new hires or new team members, mostly as an icebreaker but also to quickly describe the following:

- What I do on a daily basis
- How I work
- How to contact me

and to encourage people to give me feedback. (I've found simply telling people I want feedback to be an effective first step in establishing an open, transparent relationship with colleagues.)

Finally, a recent learning on my behalf has been that it's important to provide explicit clarity (with context) on what I and leadership *care* about so that others understand focus areas, when to escalate, and *why* certain questions may be asked.

Have you encountered challenges collaborating with technology teams like information technology and software development?

Yes, because many people believe that the security team is a group of people who will say "no" or block teams (like the security person in Gene Kim's book *The Phoenix Project*). Since I joined my current company, I have worked hard to change that belief and build a culture where the security team is seen as collaborative, knowledgeable, approachable, and supportive, but equally prepared to say "no" if the risk is too large or systemic.

Overall, I take a consistent approach across all teams regardless of their revenue generation or product capabilities. I first seek to build a collaborative relationship of equals where I strive to ensure that the nonsecurity team understands we are here to help, are open to feedback, and have the same goals as them (e.g., to deliver the product to players). I try to understand where they're coming from and what's important to them, ensure that they understand the risk, and work out how security can help them securely achieve their goals.

Do you have any favorite books to recommend for people who want to lead cybersecurity teams?

I genuinely think this list could be limitless, and it's difficult to be concise, especially when each team is unique in itself, but let's give it a try.

- *High Output Management* by Andrew S. Grove: This is the management bible in many ways. It's a truly fantastic book that describes how to lead and manage your team(s) and how to best spend your time on what's important. It's survived the test of time, being published first in 1983, and although this is more than 30 years later, this book is still highly relevant and educational.

- *Principles*: In this book, Ray Dalio (founder of Bridgewater) concisely describes his principles, providing examples of successes and failures in a humble manner. Through these principles, he explains his decision-making and shares the tools that he uses, while also detailing that he encourages "thoughtful disagreement."
- *Radical Candor* by Kim Scott: This book is one of the best leadership/management books that I've read. There were many great takeaways and tidbits of practical advice that have helped me have tough conversations in a more constructive and caring way while still ensuring the message is clearly received.
- *Thanks for the Feedback* by Douglas Stone and Sheila Heen: Although much of the advice is common sense, *Thanks* was thoroughly enjoyable and very educational for me. The book will remind you of some awkward conversations from your past, but it is valuable because it actually explains the how of giving and receiving constructive and actionable feedback.
- *Work Rules:* This is a great book from Laszlo Bock as he describes what worked and what didn't work as he built the HR side of Google. Key takeaways:
  - The author recommends separating performance reviews from compensation discussions.
  - He described various stories on "nudges" (e.g., checklists to prevent mistakes) and how beneficial they can be to driving change. Driving change is necessary for any security team (read *Switch* by Chip Heath and Dan Heath if you want to learn about some tricks to driving big cultural changes) and checklists are hugely beneficial in this (*Checklist Manifesto* by Atul Gawande talks about this in more detail).
  - He helped revamp the hiring process at Google to be less about brain teasers and more about identifying the right candidates.
  - He encourages the "spread of teaching" among employees because "teaching gives purpose" and fosters both growth and mentorship.

- *The Five Dysfunctions of a Team* by Patrick Lencioni: For me, this book succinctly described the key issues that lead to a team failing. So many of us simply avoid the hard issues and difficult conversations, which ultimately results in teams falling apart with a resulting back-stabbing culture pretty much inevitable.
- *The Five Dysfunctions of a Team: A Leadership Fable* by Patrick Lencioni: The concept of *First Team* was fairly new to me and has definitely encouraged me to think differently in terms of who my team is, which becomes more nebulous as you progress through the ranks and/or begin to manage multiple teams.
- *Quiet* by Susan Cain: Not a leadership book per se, but in this world of extroverts, it's important to realize that those with the best ideas are rarely going to be shouting from the rooftops. This book will make you think about those you lead who you may not be encouraging to speak and share.
- *Extreme Ownership* by Jocko Willink and Leif Babin: The book emphasizes the extremely high level of "ownership and accountability" that a leader should exhibit. The authors are ex–Navy Seals, and throughout the book, they provide intense examples of leadership from their experiences in Iraq and then provide a correlating example from the business world. There are several key takeaways:
  - Discipline equals freedom.
  - There are no bad teams, just bad leaders.
  - Simplicity, not complexity.
  - Take ownership of everything.

In terms of choosing worthwhile reading material, it's a mix of things really.

- Recommendations from friends
- New books from authors I like
- Reading material/references for books that I've found to be educational and enjoyable
- Recommendations that I stumble across when researching a particular topic

"Because I'm a CISO, the decisions I make, either good or bad, can affect all aspects of the business."

Twitter: @tjackson78 • **Website:** www.linkedin.com/in/terencejackson

Terence Jackson

Terence Jackson is currently the chief information security officer at Thycotic Software. His responsibilities include protecting the organization's information assets and managing the risk and information technology programs. Terence is an industry-acknowledged expert and public speaker and is regularly invited to speak and share his insights by some of the largest and most respected organizations in the world, including Forbes, Dark Reading, BrightTalk, Cloud Security Alliance, SC Magazine, InfoSec Magazine, Tech News World, The Guardian Hedge Fund Monthly, and Spectrum News. When not working, he enjoys spending time with his wife and two children.

27

Do you believe there is a massive shortage of career cybersecurity professionals?
I don't believe the skills gap is as wide as reported. With the ability for remote work, there are many qualified candidates, but if you are trying to source to one geographic region, then yes, the talent may be limited. In addition, with the shortage of skills, there has been an uptick in organizations that focus on learning

and certifying for cyber skills and pulling candidates from other parts of the business.

What's the most important decision you've made or action you've taken related to a business risk?

I chose to exclusively use a quantitative approach to measuring risk using the FAIR model. As a CISO, I'm the chief revenue protection officer, and to do that I had to quantify risk and speak the language of the board.

How do you make hard decisions? Do you find yourself more often making people, process, or technology decisions?

Each day is different and so is each decision. More often than not, the toughest decisions that are made are in regard to processes. Too many processes can prevent business operations from occurring, but too few can also prevent business from occurring.

What's something that you struggle with as a leader, and how do you overcome that?

Making the right decision. As a CISO, the decisions I make can affect all aspects of the business either good or bad. So sometimes I can fall into analysis paralysis. I identified this as an area of improvement and implemented strategies to become more decisive—to make a decision and make the decision right.

How do you lead your team to execute and get results?

First, I trust them to be the experts I hired; second, we collaborate on projects, and I respect their opinions. Ultimately, we make the best business decision.

Do you have a workforce philosophy or unique approach to talent acquisition?

A résumé will get you noticed, experience will get you an interview, but passion will propel you.

Have you created a cohesive strategy for your information security program or business unit?

Yes, I used ISO 27001 and the NIST CSF to build our information security program. These are both fundamental frameworks for building a robust information security program that can be tailored to the business to support its overall mission.

What are your communication tips for interacting with executive leadership?

In daily interactions with different levels of the organization, you should be aware of their communication styles and their preferred styles. Some are into details, some just want the short truth, but ultimately effective communication starts with conscious, active listening and observing and then tailoring your message to fit that person's communication style. The DISC assessment has been key to helping me discern these different styles.

How do you cultivate productive relationships with your boss, peers, direct reports, and other team members?

I spend time with them outside of the four walls of work; we discuss our families or vacations. In short, we have *real* conversations.

Have you encountered challenges collaborating with revenue-generating teams like sales and product development?

I have not because I understand the function of the business, and it is not solely security. Security is a function that supports the business and business units. For too long security has been seen as a blocker. I like to believe that security can be an enabler and competitive differentiator if approached and implemented correctly.

Have you encountered challenges collaborating with technology teams like information technology and software development?

In my current role as CISO, both information security and IT report to me. This has allowed a much more collaborative approach. As far as software development teams, there is always some give and take, but for me it's choosing a secure collaborative approach to a mutual win.

Do you have any favorite books to recommend for people who want to lead cybersecurity teams?

How to Win Friends and Influence People by Dale Carnegie and *Ego Is the Enemy* by Ryan Holiday. Both of these will help you be a more effective leader by taking the spotlight off of you and putting it on others, which is key to effective leadership in any arena.

> "It took me a long time to realize that managers are not always leaders, and leaders are not always managers."

Twitter: @shehackspurple • **Website:** SheHacksPurple.dev

Tanya Janca

28

Tanya Janca, aka SheHacksPurple, is an independent security consultant. Her obsession with securing software runs deep, from running her OWASP chapter for four years and founding the OWASP DevSlop open source and education project. With her countless blog articles, workshops, and talks, her focus is clear. Tanya is also an advocate for diversity and inclusion, cofounding the international women's organization WoSEC, starting the online #MentoringMonday initiative, and personally mentoring, advocating for, and enabling countless other women in her field. As a professional computer geek of 20+ years, she is a person who is truly fascinated by the "science" of computer science.

Do you believe there is a massive shortage of career cybersecurity professionals?

Yes, I believe there is a shortage of technology professionals who are adequately trained in information security. Not only do I believe we don't have enough people working in roles whose main responsibility is to ensure the security of our systems and data, but I also believe that many people who are in IT roles are not given enough training to perform the duties of their jobs in a secure manner, which is part of why we are currently having so many problems ensuring the confidentiality, reliability, and availability (CIA; the mandate of every IT security team) of the systems and data that we create and maintain as an industry.

I believe the second part of this problem is with academia. Most colleges and universities do not currently have programs that create information security professionals, and at the same time they are graduating IT professionals in other specialties (programming, network admins, etc.) without adequate training to build security into the software, networks, and other systems that they create and maintain. Our current industry is made up of people who are self-taught or who have learned on the job, meaning we have no standards and it is very hard to know who you should hire. Expecting adults to take multiple years of their lives to self-train (and self-fund) with no guaranteed job after is a huge demand to put on newcomers to our field, especially when there is no clear career path once they have trained themselves. This situation does not make our field very attractive to potential new candidates.

To solve this problem, I feel we must make changes on multiple levels; we need to create post-secondary programs that graduate industry-ready information security professionals, we must adjust our current post-secondary programs to ensure that students learn how to do their IT jobs securely, as an industry we must make a commitment to training our employees in security and to hiring junior folks and training them to be security professionals, and lastly, industry professionals need to give back by mentoring junior members and newcomers to our industry to ensure that the junior professionals of today become the senior professionals of tomorrow.

Earlier this year I started the #MentoringMonday online initiative on Twitter to match InfoSec professionals with people who want to join our industry or to switch within the IT industry into security. The community response and support have been absolutely overwhelming. It is clear we care and want people to join us; we've matched hundreds of people, and we do it every Monday.

What's the most important decision you've made or action you've taken related to a business risk?

When I first started managing incidents, I started holding postmortem meetings after each one, even if it was just an event so that we could improve. Very quickly, I saw huge payoffs, as we streamlined our processes, had better communication, and solved the issues faster. After the big event that we had worked toward, I took all of my findings, analyzed them, and figured out that we had five different causes for our security events and incidents and that four of them were preventable. I looked at the cost of prevention versus the cost of continuing to allow the issues to happen, and it was clear that prevention was cheaper (and less embarrassing for our company). I used this data to talk management into letting me launch my first application security program, which completely changed my career path, and I would consider that the most important decision I've made in my career.

Making business and career decisions based on data is never a mistake.

How do you make hard decisions? Do you find yourself more often making people, process, or technology decisions?

I make hard decisions by weighing the pros and cons and then re-evaluating based on what is "right" and "wrong." Sometimes a business decision might seem logical, but when we evaluate it from an ethical standpoint, the pendulum tips the other way. If we always make business decisions that align with our personal ethics, we never have to fear being humiliated or embarrassed if something were to be leaked or exposed. More than once I have said in large meetings that I was actively voting against a policy or project specifically because I was unwilling to break my own moral code for a paycheck, and I have resigned from one position because of what I viewed as a conflict that I could not live with.

Technology decisions are a delight. Processes are fun. People decisions are always the most difficult decisions, because feelings are involved. If all decisions were made purely on logic, life would be much, much easier.

What's something that you struggle with as a leader, and how do you overcome that?

It took me a long time to realize that managers are not always leaders, and leaders are not always managers. As it turns out, I am a great leader, but I find it incredibly emotionally draining to manage people. I was promoted to management several times in my career and have stepped down each time. I have always struggled with the idea that you should not become too emotionally involved with your employees, as I tend to have "too much" empathy, making managing people difficult for me as a person.

How do you lead your team to execute and get results?

Whenever making a large decision for my team, I always ask everyone's opinions; we have several smart people on the team, not just one, so why would I make large decisions alone? Having the entire team be heard tends to result in buy-in from all members. If we made the decision together, I'm not "telling them to do something"; we are following the plan that we all made together. I also always try to create an environment of trust so that my team knows they can come to me with a problem or mistake and that we will fix it together. No finger pointing, no blame—let's just fix it and move on.

As an individual, I usually try to support our boss's vision. I have found that most managers do not try to reach a consensus as I do; that would be the main difference I see.

Do you have a workforce philosophy or unique approach to talent acquisition?

I prefer to hire a junior person if I can afford it (in regard to time commitment) and train them into the security professional I want to have on my team. If you are the person who teaches someone everything, I find they are very loyal. I also find that if you talk to your employees and ask where they want their careers to go and then ensure that they are on their way to reaching their goals, they will want to stick with you as long as possible. Also, take their complaints seriously. Your best advertisement for your workplace is the employees who already work for you. If they are happy, satisfied, and wanting to stay, they will tell all of their friends.

What are your communication tips for interacting with executive leadership?

My first time leading a security team I had a meeting with several executives; I told them about a serious problem, but I couldn't get buy-in. I told them the sky was falling, but it fell on deaf ears. After the meeting I complained to my boss, and he said that everyone in that room was extremely bright, and if they didn't understand the risk, it's because I needed to work on my communication skills. He said I can't just tell them it will "be really bad." I need to explain the exact things that will or could happen and the resulting damage to us from a business perspective. The next meeting, I came back with data, detailed explanations of the risk, examples of how it could negatively affect our customers, what the likelihood was of it happening, and how much effort it would be for a malicious actor to launch such an attack. They were sold, immediately, and I had approval to start on solving the problem the moment I left the room. I have used this tactic from then on.

In another situation, I was being dismissed by the managers of other teams, and they were refusing to implement security fixes that I had approval for. They removed the changes from their sprints, marked things as "fixed" that were not, and other things that went on for a few months. I created a "risk acceptance document" (which was entirely my own invention) and detailed each of the issues and the business risk involved and then sent it to the heads of both departments, asking them to formally "accept the risk." I immediately received a call asking me, "What is this bull****?" I explained that the managers below had been blocking me and telling me it wasn't important. I was immediately given approval to tell them the fixes were approved by the department head, and they were to take place *now*. My "risk acceptance document" has been helpful in several workplaces since.

How do you cultivate productive relationships with your boss, peers, direct reports, and other team members?

Honesty, respect, transparency, integrity. All those words that companies put in value statements but often ignore. It turns out that stuff actually works.

Have you encountered challenges collaborating with revenue-generating teams like sales and product development?

I have worked most of my security career in the Canadian government or as a consultant, meaning I never had to fight those battles. As a consultant, you just do the work and leave; you are not invested in the outcome. As a government employee, there is no revenue to generate, but of course we had other types of battles.

Have you encountered challenges collaborating with technology teams like information technology and software development?
Yes, I have had challenges with management or development team leads who didn't feel their team had time for my security patches/upgrades/features/requests/requirements. For those situations I asked for management buy-in via my made-up "risk acceptance document" or tried hard to communicate the risks more clearly to make sure they understood the importance of what I was asking. I also always try really hard to see their side of the equation and have found myself suggesting that we "accept the risk" of quite a few of the items found when doing security testing; it depends on the situation, and I try to be flexible and reasonable.

More often than not, I have found that problem situations are caused by egos and insecurity; there are some people in our industry with limited social skills who belittle others when they feel threatened. Personally, I try to leave my ego at home when I go to work; I don't find that it adds value in very many situations. When confronted with people like this, I try to approach them in a nonthreatening way, asking questions and speaking from a place of empathy, to try to get to the answer or result that I am looking for. It works quite often. If it doesn't, I tend to excuse myself and ask management to handle it; there's only so much crap a person can put up with. I don't work in a daycare on purpose, and if someone is acting like I child, I have better things to do.

Do you have any favorite books to recommend for people who want to lead cybersecurity teams?
- *The DevOps Handbook* by Gene Kim, Jez Humble, Patrick Debois, and John Willis
- *The Phoenix Project* by Gene Kim, Kevin Behr, and George Spafford
- *The Unicorn Project* by Gene Kim
- Shameless Self Promotion: *Alice and Bob Learn Application Security and written* by the contributor Tanya Janca

For reading material, I usually ask friends for recommendations. I also buy quite a few audiobooks based on reviews and the subject and then just return them if I don't like them. If I see a talk by someone I really like, I often ask which books they would suggest.

"Keeping people happy, making sure the culture is right, and believing that anyone is teachable are some of the main areas of focus for me."

Twitter: @HackingDave

David Kennedy

29 David Kennedy is the founder of two organizations: TrustedSec and Binary Defense Systems (BD). David is an avid gamer and father of three, and he is passionate about coding, hacking, and red teaming. David previously was a chief security officer (CSO) for a Fortune 1000 company with offices in more than 77 countries. Considered a forward thinker in the security field, he is a keynote speaker at some of the nation's largest conferences and a guest on several national news organizations. He also worked on cyber warfare for the U.S. Marine Corps (USMC) and on forensics for the intelligence community, including two tours in Iraq.

Do you believe there is a massive shortage of career cybersecurity professionals?

I don't believe that the gap is as great as it's made out to be. The main problem we see is that most organizations are requiring pretty extensive career experience even for junior positions. It's difficult to come out of college or high school and immediately start a job in cybersecurity. One of the things that we've been doing at TrustedSec is selecting two to three interns per year to go through, and so far, each of the interns we've had have completely come on full-time. I think having organizations that focus on teaching people and growing them from a professional development standpoint can make a huge difference. I also think that the college programs are starting to get much better at teaching fundamentals and foundation. Although I do not believe a degree is necessary and hiring should be purely on talent, passion, motivation, and drive, leveraging a college degree may help provide an additional mechanism to bridge the requirements for joining a company early on.

What's the most important decision you've made or action you've taken related to a business risk?

Running multiple companies isn't the easiest job in the world. You have to balance company growth with culture and the desire to ensure that everyone believes in the mission you are trying to accomplish. My goal has always been "to make the world a better place," and I'm a huge fan of David Logan's *Tribal Leadership*. When you are looking at business risk specifically, you have to consider not just the risk it poses to your business but also the impact it will have on people. One of the most important decisions that I've made from a business risk perspective was probably the investment into our research division over at TrustedSec. Our team noticed that it was getting more difficult to compromise organizations and that we would need higher capabilities to maintain a high level of quality. Investment into R&D is a tough one because it requires you to have direct expenses that you cannot equate to a return. Going back to the company, it was absolutely the right decision and one that has benefited us substantially as we scale and grow.

How do you make hard decisions? Do you find yourself more often making people, process, or technology decisions?

When making hard decisions, there are a lot of things that can happen. First, emotions are the worst factor for making hard decisions. If you are making a quick decision without first understanding the facts or understanding the situation completely, it can make for a disastrous decision that was wrong. Calming down, relaxing, and recognizing that there are multiple data points that need to be derived first is important. Second, how a decision will impact a customer or the people who work for you is equally as important. When

I'm making a tough decision, I try to gather as many facts as possible as well as try to identify as many viewpoints as possible to make a decision. Many times, with my leadership team, I bounce ideas off of them and try to understand other viewpoints or alternatives to what my opinion is. Having a team that will challenge you is also extremely important; the team needs to feel empowered that if they do not agree with my decision, they can express that and provide context as to why.

Early on in my career, I was part of a company that had a very toxic culture. The executive at the time was overpowering and would use intimidation, fear, and politics to get a desired outcome. No one on the leadership team would ever question his decision even if it was terrible, and ultimately that company failed. In fact, what it caused was for the leadership team to turn on one another to deflect blame when things were being thrown at them by the executive. I learned early on in my career that this type of leadership is destined to fail every single time. You need to surround yourself with people who can challenge your decisions and provide you with different perspectives on things.

What's something that you struggle with as a leader, and how do you overcome that?

The biggest single challenge that I face is the balance between company, community, family, and travel. If anyone knows me, they know that I'm always on the road speaking at a conference or at a customer site and that I'm rarely in the office. It's not that I don't want to be in the office, but I have a tough time saying no to people who ask me to help them. For me, I would prefer to not travel nearly as much as I am now and focus on communication with my companies and with growing the companies. There's a shift that has to occur when running a company or leading people. The focus cannot be on you as an individual but as a team collective. When I first started TrustedSec, it was out of the basement of my house. I was in charge of sales, marketing, consulting, delivery, reporting, and running the business. As we grew, my responsibilities never seemed to shrink, just focused in different areas. The biggest challenge for me is finding a balance between traveling and spreading the word of TrustedSec and Binary Defense and being there to help the company grow in the right direction. I've taken some steps to speak less over the next year and really focus on spending more time at the office and with everyone at the company.

How do you lead your team to execute and get results?

Being a leader is not about directing people to do things. Being a leader is recognizing that you have a specific role in motivating people and ensuring that you are in line with the objectives put in front of you that everyone works toward and believes in. To be an effective leader, there are a number of ways to lead a team. The most effective are positivity, selflessness, and compassion, as well as being willing to help on a moment's notice and get your hands dirty. Being a leader also means being consistent and not changing the direction continuously and focusing on the mission at hand but also looking forward. For me, I usually try to keep meetings to a half-hour max. Most of the time it's five to ten minutes. There is a great book that Chris Nickerson recommended to me called *Rework* by the creators of 37signals (now Basecamp). In that book, something I remember every day is that when you have a meeting, include only the people who are absolutely needed to make decisions and execute. Keep the meetings short and focus on keeping on track. That's how you get results, and that's how you keep everyone's attention.

Do you have a workforce philosophy or unique approach to talent acquisition?

I've always been a person who looks to hire people not necessarily with the experience but with the passion and drive to want to learn. You can tell when you interview someone if they have that spark you are looking for that you can mold into someone who can eventually complete the work. I also believe that people shouldn't be held to a 9 to 5 job—that people can come in whenever they want and leave whenever they want as long as they get the job done. Keeping people happy, making sure the culture is right, and believing that anyone is teachable are some of the main areas of focus for me.

Have you created a cohesive strategy for your information security program or business unit?

When you go into an organization, changing the strategy or direction is difficult. Most organizations are set in their ways, and if it was easy to implement an information security program, everyone would be doing it well. When I first joined as the chief security officer over at Diebold, one of the biggest challenges was management buy-in for support and changing the way IT did things. Historically security was looked upon as the naysayers, and there wasn't a lot of trust with security and the IT groups. While I was asking the executive team for support, one of the most important things that I did was establish a good working relationship with IT. We helped them out wherever we could even if it wasn't our responsibility and bought them pizza and drinks when they had to work late. To have a strategy that works for everyone, you need to have relationships with everyone first. From there everything else falls in line. Having a relationship with executives also establishes trust and the ability to have direct support when you need it. Also, listen carefully to what their expectations are. I think some of the biggest challenges we have in security result from not understanding the corporate strategy or living in a vacuum without listening to everyone's perspectives.

What are your communication tips for interacting with executive leadership?
Executives have only a basic to minimal understanding of what information security is talking about. Developing a relationship and spending time with executives is first and foremost. They need to have the trust in your leadership that you will implement their vision. Most people fear pushing back on executive leadership for fear of retaliation. It's actually the opposite; most executive leaders recognize that they understand the corporate strategy the best but not how to implement a cybersecurity program. Providing them with facts and your opinions and marrying that with the corporate strategy makes most executive leaders' decisions fairly easy. Also, talking in a language that they can understand becomes extremely important. What I find is that you can provide additional notes and material for them if they want to dive into additional subjects, but you should keep your communications short and to the point and let them know of any struggles or hurdles you are having.

How do you cultivate productive relationships with your boss, peers, direct reports, and other team members?
Relationships are so critical—in my belief the most critical. It's important to understand everyone's perspectives on things and to be a listener. Most people fail in spending time to develop these relationships, and that's where issues and misunderstandings can occur. Most people have the best intentions when they make decisions but don't have the right amount of information. Having the right people in place, keeping in constant communication, and getting other people's perspectives makes relationships much easier. I find that if there is a roadblock, I need to work with the individual involved

to expand that relationship and understand their perspective. Conflict can happen; however, working through issues and ensuring that they don't ruin a relationship can be crucial.

Have you encountered challenges collaborating with revenue-generating teams like sales and product development?

The priorities and perspectives of others can be difficult to understand; dealing with revenue-generating groups especially can be difficult as their motives are very different. This applies to other departments too that might not be revenue generating but have specific timelines that have to be met in order to support the operations of the company. It's important to understand their perspectives but also to be assertive and aligned when certain things that may introduce substantial risk to your company need to be addressed or communicated. There should be escalation paths that you focus on in the company in order to provide the business with a way to identify and communicate certain risks to your company.

Have you encountered challenges collaborating with technology teams like information technology and software development?

There are always challenges dealing with different teams as their priorities aren't usually yours. That's why having a governance structure with executive buy-in as well as relationships are the recipe for a successful information security program. It's all about how you present the priority to other organizations that do not see that priority. For me, it was important to have security not be a roadblock but an enabler of the groups to be successful. For software development, having champions in those groups that knew more security-related items and whose job descriptions included them had a substantial amount of success. Collaborating with other groups means working with them and understanding their difficulties and helping them change their process to include yours because they believe in the mission and the guidance that fits the corporate strategy.

Do you have any favorite books to recommend for people who want to lead cybersecurity teams?

- *Rework* by Jason Fried and David Heinemeier Hansson, founders of 37signals
- *Tribal Leadership* by David Logan
- *Extreme Ownership* by Jocko Willink and Leif Babin

"I'm quick to do favors when reasonable, with no expectation of reciprocation, and tend to be the one people want to share their problems with."

Twitter: @joe_krull • **Website:** www.linkedin.com/in/jokrull

Joe Krull

30

Joe Krull, CISSP, CISA, IAM, CRISC, CIPP, is a senior analyst at Aite Group. He splits his time between San Antonio, Texas, and Tel Aviv, Israel. He has 45 years of security and privacy experience, has worked in 115 countries, and has advised large enterprises on four continents. Previously, Joe was a member of Accenture's security strategy and risk practice, a security leader at a Big Four, an executive at an application security vendor, and a leader at his own company assessing risks to telecommunications companies. Prior to consulting, Joe was the chief information security officer at three Global 1000 companies, and he served as an operations officer and military attaché at seven U.S. embassies. Joe is a graduate of the University of the State of New York and the United States Foreign Service Institute. He is multilingual/multicultural in English, French, German, and Hebrew.

Do you believe there is a massive shortage of career cybersecurity professionals?

I do believe that we have a skills shortage today. It is a perfect storm that started about 20 years ago when the internet hit critical mass and we saw e-commerce applications proliferate. At that time, we should have predicted that we needed to ramp up security curricula at our universities and technical colleges. That did not happen, and we also made no substantive efforts to expose students and youth to the possibilities of rewarding careers in information/cybersecurity. When cyber degree programs finally came online, the curricula were very theoretical and based on already outdated trends. We also saw that soft skills like presentation delivery and negotiation—critical for security professionals—were not emphasized. In my opinion, the professors at that time were simply ill equipped to teach as they did not have real-world experience.

Skills shortages were also exacerbated by other factors. One factor was inflexible human resource policies at midsize and large enterprises that mandated four year degrees or computer science concentrations for all IT candidates. I led very large teams, and some of my best cyber practitioners did not have degrees—and they were highly effective. One of my best cyber-defense operators was a widely acclaimed musician with a high school diploma. Another factor that made recruiting cyber talent problematic was ill-conceived company salary surveys that tried to lump cyber roles into general IT lists and did not factor in the complexity and uniqueness of these jobs. Finally, career counselors did not promote cyber to students, mostly because we did a poor job exposing the counselors to what we do.

To bridge the gap, we need to overcome two decades of poor planning and execution. Some things I've done and highly recommend include expansion and corporate support of the National Collegiate Cyber Defense Competition and the CyberPatriot Program at the high school level. These programs identify talent early as well as people who have already seen the potential of a cyber career.

I also recommend internal recruiting of systems administrators, network technicians, and other IT practitioners based on a flex work program where they can be exposed to the cyber team a few hours each week and apply for open roles. One sysadmin that I gave a shot to in 2005 is now leading incident response for a multibillion-dollar international company.

I've been very impressed by HP's support of Girl Scouts of America, where the scouts can earn merit badges based on cyber studies and projects. We need more of these initiatives. I have been involved in the development of immersive and entertaining computer games with cyber offensive and defensive scenarios and believe that these will further promote our career field to future generations.

What's the most important decision you've made or action you've taken related to a business risk?
More than 20 years ago I was the senior security executive for one of the world's largest electronics products companies. We had an opportunity to develop a new type of mobile phone that would allow a large mobile operator to rapidly enter the lucrative business of prepaid cellular. Rather than an expensive and slow network upgrade, we designed a solution that allowed for storage of credit, e.g., money, in the handset. This was a risky and bold approach, but one that would serve as a stopgap measure in conjunction with the operator's network upgrade. At that time, the operator wanted assurances in the contract that the solution was impervious to hacking. I was heavily pressured by the sales and engineering teams to sign off on the section in the contract but would not. Instead, I inserted a clause that essentially said that anything built by a person could be broken by a person with the right resources. The deal was delayed and almost scrapped, and several executives recommended my dismissal, but I stuck to my decision and convinced company leadership that the client's proposed clause was a huge risk. Ultimately, the handset was launched and was wildly successful but risky, as the encryption solution was embedded in the phone. We regularly advised the operator to quickly launch their new network and phase out these handsets. About a year into the program, the handsets were reverse engineered by a group of students using a university supercomputer, and their published paper allowed hackers to modify the phones to essentially make free calls on the network. The hack was widely covered in the international press, and the operator sought relief from our company for losses and brand damage. Had I signed off on the contract

clause, it would have cost us millions of dollars in damages, but ultimately, we were protected.

Slowing down or objecting to a big commercial deal is a risky career move for a security professional, but I kept company leadership informed every step of the way while managing the operator's expectations. Ultimately, it would have been a decision that could have been overruled by management, but in this case, I kept everyone from running with scissors.

How do you make hard decisions? Do you find yourself more often making people, process, or technology decisions?

I really like to be collaborative when I make hard decisions—up to a point. I give my team members and stakeholders outside of security a chance to weigh in, and I carefully consider their input. But I expect them to state their points of view quickly. We are not in a business where we have the luxury of weeks of analysis or for me to chase people down for multiple follow-ups. I give an opportunity to provide input and will ultimately make the decision if I don't hear back after a few days. They had their chance to be heard.

Most of the decisions I've made have been process related as opposed to technology or people related. For any process there's room for improvement, and if there's a better way to do things, I'm all ears. Also, in our rapidly changing environments, something that works on Monday may no longer be relevant on Friday. We need to be flexible and open to new approaches and brave enough to admit it when things don't work.

What's something that you struggle with as a leader, and how do you overcome that?

As a leader I always get very disappointed when I see good people move on. As an example, I led a team of cybersecurity consultants at a major technology consulting company during the economic downturn in 2008/2009. The business climate was very fluid, and we did not know at that time how long the recession would last. The company decided to

> As a leader I always get very disappointed when I see good people move on.

downsize, and I was required to identify about 15 percent of my team for immediate separation from the company. I fought hard for an exemption to this mandate but ultimately had to see some great people leave the team. I felt a personal loyalty to them—they worked hard to help me be successful, and I worked tirelessly to help them land new positions at other companies. Ironically, later I ended up competing with them for consulting work, but we remained close through the years.

How do you lead your team to execute and get results?
I am a former military officer, and I truly believe in the rule "lead by example." I like to sit deskside with every member of the team to see what they do and the challenges they face. I also don't shun tasks, no matter how small, if I have the time. I never ask a team member to do something I would not do myself. This sends a clear message to my team that I'm in it with them and that I don't see myself above the day-to-day operations. If I have a bad day, I certainly try not to show it, but if I have a good one, I share it with everyone. We share successes across the team and use problems and setbacks as learning experiences for improvement. And we always try to have fun and a few laughs.

> I am a former military officer, and I truly believe in the rule "lead by example."

Do you have a workforce philosophy or unique approach to talent acquisition?
Talent acquisition requires innovative approaches. I started a security associate program many years ago that allowed volunteers in more than 30 countries to be business unit security points of contact. The program provided specialized training and enhanced job titles, and introduced a dotted-line reporting mechanism into the global security team. We quickly learned from these associates about security issues in the field and had someone we could reach out to for valuable information. The associates also assisted with security education and training. We made sure that business unit

leaders were aware of what we learned from the associates to avoid any friction from the dotted-line reporting. We managed to pay small bonuses to these associates, and some ultimately moved into full-time security roles later in their careers.

Retention of top talent can also be challenging. The skills gap has headhunters and recruiters constantly scrambling to identify cyber professionals, and it's not uncommon to see promises of large compensation packages to change jobs. Although it hurts, if someone really wants to leave and it's good for them and their family, you do your best to keep them but ultimately wish them well. I always have a succession plan, and I make it clear what upward mobility opportunities exist. To be clear, though, not everyone can be or should be a chief information security officer.

Have you created a cohesive strategy for your information security program or business unit?

A security program without a credible strategy is like a sailboat without a rudder. You may get where you need to go, but you'll drift and waste a lot of effort getting there. I had the honor as a consultant to help some of the largest companies and security teams on four continents to develop and deploy their security strategies. This was based on my experience and what I learned as a CISO at Global 1000 companies. What I saw is that there is no cookie-cutter approach to security strategy. Every organization is different—particularly international companies—and a security strategy needs to reflect the organization's approach to risk, the opportunities that exist, and the opportunities that may be lost through overly restrictive policies and procedures. Contrary to popular opinion, technology has very little to do with strategy; it's more of an enabler. I believe that an organization's security strategy needs to be communicated widely—internally, to business partners, and to customers—to be effective. It details how the organization wants to be perceived—like Fort Knox or an organization that's easy to do business with, or something in between. There can never be a disconnect between the security strategy and the overall corporate strategy, and this means lots of socialization and coordination with senior leaders. I always include legal in the process, as they are great arbitrators during strategy discussions.

What are your communication tips for interacting with executive leadership?

I believe that successful communication with executive leadership is based on three aspects—planning, research, and flexibility. I proactively plan interactions through their executive assistants, I do research to learn as much as I can about the leader's background and interests, and I remain very flexible in case the executive needs to change the time or place for our discussion. Once these are in place, I communicate in simple, jargon-free terms, and I always relate subjects to the business of the organization. My aim is to use every second of our time together in a meaningful way and to never waste an executive's time. If I need support for an initiative, I state it right up front and don't beat about the bush. My goal is to gain trust, be recognized as an expert in my field, and be someone who applies the right amount of concern directly in relation to the level of perceived risk. And a smile goes a long way in any interaction.

How do you cultivate productive relationships with your boss, peers, direct reports, and other team members?

I develop relationships by being approachable, reasonably interesting, and positive about life. I'm quick to do favors when reasonable, with no expectation of reciprocation, and tend to be the one people want to share their problems with. This is based on trust, and my peers and team members know that what's discussed won't be shared unless I have a legal reason to do so. They know this up front. I teach via storytelling to help junior members of the team put things into perspective, and fortunately I have many stories after so many years of experience and work in more than 100 countries. I try to keep it interesting and tie it back to specific situations. I really enjoy mentoring, and some of my early mentees are now senior security leaders doing great things.

Have you encountered challenges collaborating with technology teams like information technology and software development?

A few years ago, I took a refreshing two-year detour and dove deep into application security. I'd observed that security professionals constantly had difficulties communicating and influencing software developers and engineers. These relationships are generally fraught with mistrust, as developers are always under tight deadlines to deliver functionality and security professionals are single-threaded regarding risk. Before that AppSec detour, I admit that I had had more than a few frustrating encounters with engineers and coders. During my two-year deep dive with a fantastic application security company, I learned how to communicate with developers in their own unique language and established credibility with them that showed I could understand their challenges. By gaining this trust, I was able to help them understand that code riddled with security bugs was like a sleek sports car that could be stolen in 20 seconds by an amateur—great product but relatively worthless in the long run. There were many other similar analogies that seemed to convince developers to think twice about writing better code and testing code prior to release. Engineers and software developers are very clever people, and I find that security professionals don't invest enough time learning about their worlds.

Do you have any favorite books to recommend for people who want to lead cybersecurity teams?

I am an avid reader, but I can't remember the last book I read. I'm sure that there are some great books on leadership and organizational effectiveness, but after 45 years in security, I find these types of books to be too general and theory-based to be applicable to my life.

I tend to follow more timely and topical publications like blogs, opinion pieces, and security research. I really like Krebs on Security, the SANS NewsBytes, SC Magazine, and *Wired*. I also read the *Washington Post*, *The New York Times*, and *Time Magazine*'s digital summary daily to get an appreciation for what's going on in the world and see what our business leaders are reading. I spend several months a year in Israel covering the cyber startup community, and I read everything I can get my hands on regarding this fascinating world.

Every security professional should be on Twitter and follow a representative sampling of their peers. If your company policy allows, actively share your thoughts and tips for success on social media.

"A major problem for many is that most job opportunities are for senior analysts and not entry-level analysts."

Twitter: @RobertMLee • **Website:** www.linkedin.com/in/robmichaellee

Robert M. Lee

31

Robert M. Lee is the CEO and cofounder of the OT/ICS cybersecurity company Dragos, Inc. He is recognized as a pioneer in ICS incident response and threat intelligence and is also an educator as a SANS course author and senior instructor. Robert gained his start in the U.S. Air Force as a cyber warfare operations officer assigned to the National Security Agency, where he built a first-of-its-kind ICS threat discovery mission.

Do you believe there is a massive shortage of career cybersecurity professionals?

There is a shortage of cybersecurity professionals, but the numbers and problem are often exaggerated. Many of the numbers pull from open job listings at companies online where it is common to see job requirements that aren't obtainable (e.g., seven years of experience in technologies that are only four years old), aren't reasonable skills to be found together (e.g., professional engineer with a decade of incident response experience), and more commonly are not offered at market rates (e.g., senior analyst with seven-plus years of experience at $60,000 and a security clearance).

There is no simple answer to bridge the gap, but there are a variety of efforts that are ongoing in different parts of the community ranging from training programs (e.g., SANS has free or discounted classes for veterans, diverse candidates, and high schools) to local conferences and free security challenges and competitions. Cybersecurity training needs to gain more traction in high schools and undergrad programs, but we also need to see companies having more realistic expectations and more intern programs designed similarly to trade schools. A major problem for many is that most job opportunities are for senior analysts and not entry-level analysts. This is also an area in which local and federal government can play a significant role by providing an entry into the community for many, as it has done for decades; with more focus on this, the government could significantly alter the course of the community.

What's the most important decision you've made or action you've taken related to a business risk?

It's always a risk to do things differently, but that's the very nature of creating something new and trying to change the status quo. The most important job at my company is setting the vision and culture. That doesn't mean simply saying good things or writing good blogs; it means making active choices daily that push against the things that distract people from their work. Turning down opportunities that take you too far off-course from your goals, avoiding bureaucracy and processes that pretend to take away risk at the expense of the team's ability to innovate, and not tolerating mediocrity or a**holes no matter what benefits it may bring are daily choices.

How do you make hard decisions? Do you find yourself more often making people, process, or technology decisions?

Hard decisions are almost always best made as a group. You do not want to have death by committee, but when it's truly a hard decision, I find it best to give folks a voice and buy-in. You're not going to make everyone happy, but everyone deserves to be heard, especially when those choices could significantly change your teammates' work experience or the direction of the company. I do not agree with voting on decisions or deliberating too long, but teamwork is there for all times.

What's something that you struggle with as a leader, and how do you overcome that?

As a CEO and cofounder of a venture-backed startup, I've learned that there are a lot of struggles; living up to your mission, living up to expectations, living up to your team, living up to your backers, and living up to yourself are all struggles that grow exponentially with success. Hard is hard, and there's no reason to pretend someone has it harder than anyone else, but for me personally, the weight of my choices impacting one to two investors and five to ten employees is much different than those that now impact nearly a dozen investors, the entire operations technology security market, and nearly 200 employees and their families. I'll turn around twice and it'll be double that. If you stop to think about things in that way, though, it can become destabilizing. Instead, I try to focus on the fact that I've never before had so much support and so many folks pushing in the same direction as me. I try to find the maturity to realize these stresses are strengths. In the same way, I struggle with the realization that I am participating less and less in any given area of my team that I like, and more and more I'm focused on the strategy and enabling my team leads to enable their front-line leaders and team members. Losing control is a scary thing. But it's a good thing. I greatly appreciate this struggle because what's really happening is I'm helping create a scalable and stable team that no longer depends on me but instead is creating something long lasting that can help change the world.

How do you lead your team to execute and get results?

Where I invest my time doesn't fit neatly into a pie chart, nor is it predictable, but if I had to bucket it into categories, I would say that I lead my team by engaging them, engaging their leadership, engaging the community, engaging our customers, and engaging the market.

When engaging them, it is my job to lead the team by being present for them and not dealing with day-to-day conflict resolution (I should instead empower my team leads to handle that) but being available to my team so that they understand how much I care about them and what we're trying to accomplish.

When engaging their leadership, it means being coached and providing coaching to the team leads and my direct reports and ensuring that the choices they are making are constantly empowering their team. A good leadership team is core to a company's success. This is easily stated, but it really takes going through some difficult times to fully appreciate it. If the leadership team doesn't feel empowered or isn't getting the visibility they need across the business, then their folks won't receive that either.

When engaging the community, it's important for me to show my team that it's okay to step away from work to help build the community, and it's important for me to help grow the community. The community to me is the folks who are going to enter this field and participate, not necessarily in conferences or publications but in their day-to-day work and impact. That community is what's going to really change the world; it's our job to engage them and share what knowledge we're gaining without simply trying to sell to them.

When engaging our customers, it's my chief role to ensure the customers' success. You can make the best technology or service in the world, but if you do not have customers who can use it to effect, you aren't going to change anything. The customers place their trust in your company. Most enterprise customers buy into a team, not the technology or service but the team. They are giving you their trust that by partnering with you they are going to be better and more successful on their journey. Thus, it's core for me to get field time with our customers and not hear about them just through others. It is their success that inflicts pain on their adversaries.

When engaging the market, I have to help position the need for what we are creating and explain the nuance at an understandable level about why it matters and is worth investing in. Customers and your team members may get it, but without the market understanding it, you will always have a limited reach. Even companies that aren't venture backed or publicly listed or traded need a viable market if their aspirations are to reach outside their local or national community. There are plenty of companies that are local, though, and there is nothing wrong with that. Not every company needs to be venture backed, publicly listed, or have 500+ employees to find success. But in my own path and in the aspirations we have at Dragos, it is important for me to help build and educate that market if we're to truly safeguard civilization.

Do you have a workforce philosophy or unique approach to talent acquisition?

We have only one company policy: don't be an a**hole. Everything else is a guideline. We have plenty of guidelines to try to provide guidance to folks on things ranging from expenses to training opportunities, but they are guidelines. Guidelines can be broken in favor of common sense, and no one should ever be harassed over that. But everyone knows what an a**hole is, and we don't tolerate them. Our folks are going to work hard. That's not my concern. If someone isn't working hard or efficiently, it's often that there's confusion or misunderstanding of the direction; it needs to be addressed too, though, because burnout doesn't just come from too many hours but often from feeling unproductive. That requires leadership and mentorship. More often, though, folks work too hard and too many hours and burn themselves out. Resourcing the team correctly or asking less things of them is vital. Our philosophy is that everyone gets treated with respect on the way in, during their time, and on the way out. That also guides our talent acquisition. As we are a startup, every hire is added burn on the company's resources, but I ensured we hired HR professionals early in the company's development to be resources to folks around the team. Mental health is important, and it's our job to take care of our people across all fronts.

What are your communication tips for interacting with executive leadership?

I try hard to say the same thing to everyone and in the same way. It's not always possible. As an example, if I write a technical paper, I will have to use technical jargon. But whether I'm speaking to the board of directors or to a new hire, I try hard to engage the audience with my full attention (everyone has cameras on if using online conferencing, especially for the benefit of remote team members) and use as little jargon as possible. I find that the simplest form of communication in the fewest amount of words with the least implied knowledge required works best for all audiences.

How do you cultivate productive relationships with your boss, peers, direct reports, and other team members?

We have a strong remote work culture with more than half the company remote from the main office. We also have offices around the world now. We cultivate good relationships by watching closely how many direct reports any one person has and ensuring that leaders at all levels have the time to be productive themselves while also engaging their staff and having weekly check-ins and 360 feedback sessions. We also have four company on-sites a year; this is an expensive thing with how many employees we have, but it is invaluable to the culture and to ensuring folks get face time with each other and get to sync with each other and the company goals. We also have company tenets that get used regularly and reinforced with each other that focus on candidness and transparency.

Have you encountered challenges collaborating with revenue-generating teams like sales and product development?
No. Everyone wants to do good; if you're hiring people who are just money driven, you're probably hiring the wrong people. I have found passionate and amazing professionals across every business unit, and when the team understands the mission and that they'll be trusted, empowered, and taken care of while being held accountable, people in any team will realize they're part of the larger team and act like it. Understand what motivates people and tie it to the mission.

Have you encountered challenges collaborating with technology teams like information technology and software development?
Everyone needs to be communicated to differently, but it's your responsibility to learn that. I don't expect my teams to adapt to me or my style. I try to meet them where they are since they are the ones doing the mission.

Do you have any favorite books to recommend for people who want to lead cybersecurity teams?
I think there's value in being well read, but I don't really think you can rely solely on books to learn how to be a leader. There are plenty that may give you new ideas and get you motivated, but the most important thing in my experience is to start with personal leadership, then interpersonal leadership, and then put yourself in the position to lead small teams, and work your way up. Experience with a high level of empathy and service-orientated leadership goes a long way.

> "My philosophy is similar to that of many of my industry peers—I believe you can find a great security analyst making pizzas or pushing a broom."

Twitter: @Wh1t3Rabbit • **Website:** www.linkedin.com/in/rmlos

Rafal Los

32 Rafal Los is an industry innovator, strategist, and personality. His career spans 20+ years while working inside companies from a Fortune 10 to a firm of fewer than 10 employees. Rafal's strengths include providing strategic leadership, developing and refining market strategies, optimizing business processes, and bringing people together to solve complex problems.

Rafal is an active member of the Security Advisor Alliance, serving on the advisory board with the intent of creating innovative ways for security leaders to give back to their communities through service and knowledge sharing. Additionally, Rafal is a founder and host of the Down the Security Rabbithole Podcast—an industry podcast delivering a weekly office-friendly format since 2011. The podcast includes thought leadership and industry experts from government advisors to industry founders and everyone in between.

Do you believe there is a massive shortage of career cybersecurity professionals?

While I do believe that there is a shortage of cybersecurity professionals, I tend to be a pragmatist and don't buy into the general hysteria. For years, the "solution" to the problems security professionals try to solve was to throw more bodies at the problem or more tools. The latter has now whipped the industry into a collective panic. The truth of the matter is, no amount of workforce increase will match the current need if we continue to work in a predominantly manual fashion. With new tools and techniques, one person can do many more tasks at an exponentially faster pace—alleviating the need for more people.

> The truth of the matter is, no amount of workforce increase will match the current need if we continue to work in a predominantly manual fashion.

Technology and processes won't entirely solve the talent shortage, mainly because cybersecurity has been a problem neglected for decades that has now gone critical mass.

To truly solve this situation, the collective industry must work with academia and perhaps even establish trade school–style places where people can learn the basics while going through an apprenticeship-type program to hone their skills. The reality is, there is no course, class, or curriculum that will make you a good cybersecurity expert. It is the desire to continuously learn and ask questions and gain new experience. That's something that will have to continue to be built into every aspect of our workforce.

What's the most important decision you've made or action you've taken related to a business risk?

Over and over in my career I've found that the most important business risk decisions I've made have been to see technology (security) problems as a component of business risk. Looking at business risk with the various components—financial, reputational, etc.—and adding technology (security) allows for a balanced analysis. Cybersecurity professionals must always see their role as a component of the overall risk picture—that's the most important thing we can do to be good stewards of our businesses.

Cybersecurity professionals must always see their role as a component of the overall risk picture—that's the most important thing we can do to be good stewards of our businesses.

How do you make hard decisions? Do you find yourself more often making people, process, or technology decisions?
I tend to make difficult decisions by trying to see the collective "big picture." For me, I'm most comfortable analyzing processes, as they impact operational effectiveness and efficiency, so those types of decisions are top of mind. The reason for this, in my mind, is simple: process is the key to bridging between people and technology, and process optimization is the best way to get the most effectiveness and efficiency out of anything or anyone.

What's something that you struggle with as a leader and how do you overcome that?
As a leader I believe the thing I struggle the most with is passion. I'm the type of person who can, sometimes, be led astray by my passion for what I do and how I feel. That said, I believe that decisions can't be made devoid of passion or emotion. Careful analysis should always be supplemented by at least some measure of gut feel.

The most challenging role, repeatedly, in my career has been leading a team at a new organization. Learning and understanding people's individual motivations, strengths, and insecurities and then leveraging that to make good decisions for them, the team, and the company will always be challenging.

How do you lead your team to execute and get results?
As a leader of a team, I tend to lean on my understanding of my team's strengths and weaknesses to put individuals in roles where they can grow, take risks, and have support should they miss. This allows the team to collectively be safer, while giving individuals the ability to take risks at higher levels.

As an individual, I tend to be more risk-averse and conservative without the safety net.

Do you have a workforce philosophy or unique approach to talent acquisition?

My philosophy is similar to that of many of my industry peers—I believe you can find a great security analyst making pizzas or pushing a broom. You don't have to hire someone with "security" in their educational profile to find great talent. I enjoy identifying good cybersecurity talent in the world by simply observing and by finding people with the right blend of curiosity, the ability to cooperate, and the ability to solve problems logically.

Have you created a cohesive strategy for your information security program or business unit?

I've created many security strategies over the years for various companies—as a consultant. The simplest way to align security to the business is to understand what makes the business work. By first learning the core values and key business strategies, security can identify ways to support those in an effective and efficient manner. I've developed an approach that starts with business strategy; digs into individual business drivers, key measurements, and metrics, and then devises a security strategy to support those. What I can say for certain is that without a full understanding of the business and the risk appetite of an organization, security will not succeed in devising a cohesive strategy.

> The simplest way to align security to the business is to understand what makes the business work.

What are your communication tips for interacting with executive leadership?

I believe that experience has taught me that different levels of leadership—executive, board, and on down—have different things they need to hear and a slightly different language they speak. Ultimately, it comes down to knowing the nuances and key points of interest. There's no one bit of guidance that is universal, as I've been in front of a board of directors who had the ability to dive fairly deep into technical jargon and equally witnessed security managers who simply didn't understand the fundamentals of security and business. As in all of life—know your audience.

How do you cultivate productive relationships with your boss, peers, direct reports, and other team members?

There is one universal truth to cultivating relationships no matter who they are with—you must have honesty and respect. Relationships are built on these foundations. Honesty will not always make you liked, but it will make you respected. Giving and working to earn respect is the only way to be trusted and to trust others. If all good relationships are built on trust, then honesty and respect are the way to get there.

> There is one universal truth to cultivating relationships no matter who they are with— you must have honesty and respect.

Have you encountered challenges collaborating with revenue-generating teams like sales and product development?

Of course! The push and pull with these other groups is what makes our jobs fun. No matter whether you're working with a product organization, a sales team, or end users, security's role is to look at their needs and wants and do the best possible job balancing those with the protection and safety of the company and its assets. Companies take risks, and often that means a revenue-generating function will override security guidance. We have to be comfortable with that. Companies make risky decisions every day—some pay off, some don't, but ultimately we are not decision-makers but advisers. That's it.

Have you encountered challenges collaborating with technology teams like information technology and software development?

Yes, and the situations are the same as with revenue-generating teams. We must seek to fulfill wants and needs in a manner that is safe and productive. This is our role.

Do you have any favorite books to recommend for people who want to lead cybersecurity teams?

I highly recommend *The Phoenix Project* by Gene Kim, Kevin Behr, and George Spafford, and *The Four Disciplines of Execution* by Chris McChesney, Sean Covey, and Jim Huling, to all of my colleagues and friends.

"Companies are busy hunting for unicorns when they really just need to stop and look at all the squirrels around them."

Twitter: @InfoSecSherpa

Tracy Z. Maleeff

Tracy Z. Maleeff is an information security analyst for the New York Times Company. She earned a master of library and information science degree from the University of Pittsburgh, as well as undergraduate degrees from Temple University (BA, magna cum laude) and Pennsylvania State University (AA). Tracy holds a SANS GIAC GSEC certification. As an InfoSecSherpa, Tracy is an active member of the InfoSec community and frequently shares her expert knowledge through her OSINT blog and InfoSec newsletter, in addition to Twitter. Tracy is a frequent presenter on a variety of topics and has given talks at DEF CON's Recon Village, DerbyCon, and several BSides events. In her past career as a librarian, Tracy earned the honor of being named a Fellow of the Special Libraries Association and has won the Dow Jones Innovate Award and the Wolters Kluwer Innovations in Law Librarianship Award. A native of the Philadelphia area, she lives and dies with its sports teams.

33

Do you believe there is a massive shortage of career cybersecurity professionals?
No, I don't believe that there is a shortage of cybersecurity professionals. Rather, the shortage is in companies who are willing to train people or develop talent. I personally have been fortunate that my current and most recent past employers very much embraced training and talent development. There are many career changers like myself who came to cybersecurity with a polished skill set from another industry. I was a librarian who made a career change into information security. I had a master of library and information science degree as well as a hard work ethic and transferrable skills. As was said to me during the interview for my first information security job, "We can teach you the tech. We can't teach someone all these other skills you already have that complement the job."

I understand the argument that cybersecurity isn't necessarily an entry-level job. However, every other headline these days screams about how this shortage of professionals is becoming its own security risk and crisis levels. Employers aren't helping themselves by placing unrealistic job requirements on their open cybersecurity positions. A Tier 1 SOC analyst does not need a CISSP to do that job. Yet, it's not uncommon to see cybersecurity job requirements that don't match the actual skill set needed or are appropriate for the job. Companies are busy hunting for unicorns when they really just need to stop and look at all the squirrels around them.

Desperate times call for more creative hiring and training. Whether it's a new graduate or a seasoned professional from another industry, employers need to think creatively about the best person for the job based on their aptitude, their willingness to learn, and their desire to do the job. The HR firewalls that companies put up to filter people are not configured correctly for cybersecurity jobs. Many smart people who are passionate about security are getting stonewalled and frustrated. Many move on to something else eventually. No, there's no shortage of cybersecurity professionals—there's a shortage of good hiring and training practices among employers.

> The HR firewalls that companies put up to filter people are not configured correctly for cybersecurity jobs.

What are your communication tips for interacting with executive leadership?

Be bold. Be brief. Be gone.

- Be bold—Speak or write with confidence. If presenting in person, "mirroring" helps. Meaning, leave the hacker hoodie at your desk. Try to dress like the people to whom you are presenting. Your mileage may vary; base it on what your leadership looks like.

- Be brief—Cut to the chase. Give the bottom line. Don't get mired in storytelling or long backstory explanations. If your discussion involves money, give explanations of why spending x amount now will save x amount later.

- Be gone—After you've given your confident and brief presentation, disappear like a magician in a puff of smoke, if that's an option. It's possible that discussions about what you've just said need to be had and can't take place while you are still in the room. Again, your mileage may vary. Understand before going into your communication if you are to stay or go.

Michael Cooper has great information about communicating with specific brain types. I highly recommend that people check out his Innovators and Influencers site to get more information about communicating with different brain types.

Do you have any favorite books to recommend for people who want to lead cybersecurity teams?

I like to defer to the Cybersecurity Canon for books related to the industry. Those books are vetted by industry professionals and are recommended for information security practitioners, including management books.

- Spencer Johnson's classic *Who Moved My Cheese* is a valuable resource to help understand dealing with change, which is an important skill to have on a cybersecurity team.

- I honestly believe that self-help types of books like *The Four Agreements: A Practical Guide to Personal Freedom* by Don Miguel Ruiz are key to leadership. You must understand yourself, and the feelings and motivations of others, to best lead, guide, and manage.

Choose books that inspire and motivate you and then take those lessons and apply them to leadership.

"Splitting up responsibilities and taking my fair share rather than simply assigning tasks and 'managing' has worked for me more often than not."

Twitter: @MrJeffMan • **Website:** securityweekly.com/hosts

Jeffrey Man

34

Jeff has more than 38 years of experience working in numerous areas and roles of information security within the Department of Defense and later the private sector. He is a certified NSA cryptanalyst and previously held security research, management, and product development roles with the NSA and was part of its first penetration testing "red team." For the past 24 years, he has been a pen tester, security architect, consultant, QSA, and PCI SME, providing consulting and advisory services to many of the nation's best-known companies. Currently he is a senior consultant/advisor for Online Business Systems, a co-host of Paul's Security Weekly, and a host of Security & Compliance Weekly.

Do you believe there is a massive shortage of career cybersecurity professionals?

Well, I wouldn't call it massive, but I do see several problems. First, there is the problem of defining what constitutes a career in this profession. Second, there is the paradox that in most organizations there is an ongoing effort to automate security and the constant quest for "silver bullet" solutions that do all the security work seamlessly and transparently so that nobody has to think about it. Then there's the inequity in terms of being able to hire professionals that exists between industries, between the private versus public sector, and in the large (enterprise) versus small companies. My personal belief is not so much that there is a shortage of people to fill these career roles but that there is a shortage within organizations of people with the appropriate training and understanding of how their current position contributes to an overall goal of cybersecurity. I believe that the gap begins to be closed not by filling "new" roles but by expanding the capabilities and responsibilities of roles that already exist within the organization. There is certainly a need for dedicated cybersecurity professionals, but especially when I think of the limited ability for certain organizations to create and fill these types of positions, I think there is a greater need for internal training to help people understand what they do or can do to contribute to the overall mission.

> My personal belief is not so much that there is a shortage of people to fill these career roles but that there is a shortage within organizations of people with the appropriate training and understanding of how their current position contributes to an overall goal of cybersecurity.

What's the most important decision you've made or action you've taken related to a business risk?
What comes to mind is a time when I was engaged with a client to help them achieve compliance with a certain data security standard after they had suffered a major breach. The CEO of the company went on record that they would achieve compliance by a certain date (it was about 45 days as I recall). This required a no-holds-barred approach, which resulted in my challenging the customer on the need to conduct an on-site assessment of a particular business unit (their call center) even though they believed it was not necessary to focus there. I was insistent that it did need to be evaluated and did so in a rather

abrupt manner. When the CISO stated that we didn't need to
focus on or visit that particular business unit, my response was,
"Your posture right now should be bent over, firmly grasping
your ankles." The reason I chose this path was my belief that
as a breached entity the company should have everything
scrutinized—even if it was to validate the assertion that the area
was of little to no concern. We visited the business unit, and
it was a good thing; it turned out they were mistaken, and the
business unit required the bulk of the remediation efforts to get
them to a secure and compliant state.

How do you make hard decisions? Do you find yourself more often making people, process, or technology decisions?

I try to make decisions based on the most practical approach
possible. To accomplish this, I often chart out the possible
decisions based on a spectrum from "do nothing" to what is
perceived to be the most expensive/complex/ideal solution. The
choices also tend to correlate to a level of risk or risk reduction.
Once the decisions are listed, I try to document as many pros
and cons that I can for each one. This process often leads to the
best decision becoming fairly clear, depending on the desired
risk posture or risk appetite of the affected parties. I would
say that these decisions most often involve a mix of processes
and technology, but in terms of people, I try to identify who is
impacted by the decisions and what level of capability, training,
and workload is involved in the decision—particularly when it
comes to the perception that a technology-leaning decision
would reduce or eliminate the need for people being involved (which is rarely the reality).

> The biggest struggle I have as a leader, and this is most often when I am in the role of a trusted adviser, is getting my client to understand that I really do know what I am talking about and that I am recommending or doing what is best for them.

What's something that you struggle with as a leader and how do you overcome that?

The biggest struggle I have as a leader, and this is most often when I am in the role of a trusted adviser, is getting my client to understand that I really do know what I am talking about and that I am recommending or doing what is best for them. The most challenging role I've had is as a trusted adviser, particularly when I am viewed as the annoying "auditor."

The challenge takes many forms, depending on who I am dealing with at the client. The security teams don't want to deal with me because they don't want to be judged as deficient, they think I am taking them away from their real jobs, or they don't believe I actually understand what they do or at least not as well as they do. IT teams are similar but probably lean more toward they don't want me to tell them they are doing something wrong (or not doing the right or necessary things) or that I don't understand what they do well enough to give them any guidance. The compliance/internal audit managers (who are often the direct customer) do not expect more than just a "checkbox" response from me and are surprised that I provide them with guidance and explanations of why things are deficient and how they need to change. I have had reasonable success in this challenging role by demonstrating competency, helping them understand the problems and deficiencies, and fostering a partnership based on the trust that I am able to build with them.

How do you lead your team to execute and get results?
I most often lead by being a participant as much as possible in the project or task at hand. My contributions as an individual are the key ways that I help the team to complete the project. Splitting up responsibilities and taking my fair share rather than simply assigning tasks and "managing" has worked for me more often than not. I also find it helpful to split up duties based on interest, experience, and capabilities so that people get to do what they want to and like to do as much as possible.

Do you have a workforce philosophy or unique approach to talent acquisition?
I have not often had direct responsibility for talent acquisition; more often I participate in the technical interviews or simply meet the prospects to provide feedback on whether they "fit" in the culture of the organization. In terms of a workforce philosophy, I find that what makes a good team is finding people who not only bring the right experience and skills to the team but also are able to share their knowledge with

In terms of a workforce philosophy, I find that what makes a good team is finding people who not only bring the right experience and skills to the team but also are able to share their knowledge with others, are willing to pitch in and help to get the job done, but do so with a certain "team spirit" and camaraderie.

others, are willing to pitch in and help to get the job done, but do so with a certain "team spirit" and camaraderie. We all try to teach when possible but are also willing to learn from each other as well.

Have you created a cohesive strategy for your information security program or business unit?
Not in so many words, but we do try to create an atmosphere in our team of having a work hard/play hard attitude. I work for a consulting practice, so the overall corporate strategy is that we find and retain our customers by working hard, being capable, being fair, and creating a partnership with our customers so that they understand that we are putting them first—even if what we are recommending/requiring of them is difficult and sometimes expensive. Our company succeeds when we succeed, and that is often reflected by testimonials that our customers send to our management team, usually without prompting, that express appreciation for our hard work and the overall effectiveness of the engagement. The best compliment I ever received was a testimonial from a client who said, "That was the toughest assessment we've ever been through, but we learned a lot. Thank you."

My communication tips in general revolve around knowing your audience—whether the audience is one or a thousand—and that includes understanding who they are, be they executives, managers, bosses, peers, or whatever.

What are your communication tips for interacting with executive leadership?
My communication tips in general revolve around knowing your audience—whether the audience is one or a thousand—and that

includes understanding who they are, be they executives, managers, bosses, peers, or whatever. Having conversations with executive leadership in our line of work usually involves decision-making, so my communication is a form of persuasive speech, or more simply I am selling them something (or trying to get them to purchase or invest in something). Knowing your audience has main elements including learning to speak their language, understanding their interests so I can make comparisons or analogies they can relate to, and—hands-down the most important communication skill—listening. Listening involves not only hearing what they are saying—I often ask, "What did you hear me say?"—but also paying attention to nonverbal communication such as facial expressions and body posture. I believe effective communication is probably the most important skill to achieve in this industry but often the most neglected. To that end, I have given numerous talks and training workshops that I call "The Art of the Jedi Mind Trick: Learning Effective Communication Skills."

How do you cultivate productive relationships with your boss, peers, direct reports, and other team members?
First, I make sure I am doing my part by fulfilling my own responsibilities. Beyond this, I spend a good deal of time listening, asking questions, providing feedback, and sometimes critiquing, teaching, explaining, and telling stories from previous experiences. I would be remiss if I didn't say that I overlay this with a certain amount of humor to try to set people at ease.

Have you encountered challenges collaborating with revenue-generating teams like sales and product development?
I try to emphasize that I understand that they are the most important part of the organization, because they produce income—which is why most companies exist in the first place. But I temper that with easing them into the reality that while what they do is of primary importance to the success of the organization, they also need to follow certain rules and do things a certain way, and that is equally important. The goal is always to get them to buy in to the necessity of secure practices and processes and following certain rules, and to work together to find a path forward that works for them within the boundaries that are put in place around them.

Have you encountered challenges collaborating with technology teams like information technology and software development?

I take a similar approach to these types of teams, but where they typically differ from the aforementioned teams is that they more likely have an attitude of "We know what we're doing" or "We're smarter than you" or "We know what's best and what works." The success I have in getting them to buy in to a collaborative approach that placates their egos while nudging them toward changing their behaviors and processes varies greatly.

I use the "Art of the Jedi Mind Tricks" techniques here as well, but I also have had to prove technical competency more often than not to get them to listen. That translates into having to demonstrate that I understand what they do, not that I've done the work necessarily, but that I understand their point of view. I have had many conversations that have started with, "Let me guess what you're dealing with, or how things work here." Once they see that I "get them," they tend to at least participate, if not actively engage and start volunteering what they see as the real issues, the roadblocks that they encounter, and so forth.

Many times, I have helped them to get what they need simply by crafting their problems as part of the problem I am there to help with (compliance with a certain data security standard). I simply tell them, "Let me paint your problem within the context of compliance, and you'll get what you want and need. Just try me." Works like a charm.

Do you have any favorite books to recommend for people who want to lead cybersecurity teams?

I'm more of a movie person than a book person. For example, to help gauge corporate culture, I often ask people if they've seen *Office Space* and ask them what their favorite scene is. If a movie was in any way based on a book, I'd recommend reading that. Years ago I was given a book called *Who Moved My Cheese?* by Spencer Johnson. I never read it, to be honest, but I know a lot of people who did and said it helped them.

The other book I would recommend for looking to the future of our industry is *Analogue Network Security* by Winn Schwartau. Honorable mention goes to *The Cuckoo's Egg: Tracking a Spy Through the Maze of Computer Espionage* by Cliff Stoll, because this book is required reading for whatever you do or want to do in this industry.

"Learning from others' mistakes is useful, and I try to share my mistakes with others as well when I am the one giving advice."

Website: linkedin.com/in/angela-marafino

Angela Marafino

Angela Marafino is an Evolve Security Academy alumna and is currently an associate consultant engineer on CDW's InfoSec team. With no background in IT or computer science, Angela did not take the traditional route to obtain a career in cybersecurity. However, the desire for a more challenging career led her to enroll in a cybersecurity bootcamp, which gave her the skills and mindset necessary to become a cybersecurity professional. She is CompTIA Security+ and Network+ certified and holds two bachelor's degrees, one in fine arts and another in pre-law. Angela is also the organizer of her local Women of Security (WoSec) chapter.

35

Do you believe there is a massive shortage of career cybersecurity professionals?

I absolutely believe there is a massive shortage of cybersecurity professionals. I base this response on the research others have done to determine the shortage percentages and, specifically, the number of women in the field compared to the number of men. I think companies should give junior employees a chance to train and learn on the job in order to fill more senior-level positions. Waiting to find candidates who meet the requirements for roles that need "years and years of experience" is not going to get the positions filled. There are high-quality cybersecurity professionals just starting out who have put in a lot of time and effort to become educated in cybersecurity and could help fill these gaps.

How do you make hard decisions? Do you find yourself more often making people, process, or technology decisions?

I have a really amazing mentor and a large network of cybersecurity individuals that I feel comfortable asking for advice if they have been in a similar situation to see how they might have handled it and why they made the decision they made. Learning from others' mistakes is useful, and I try to share my mistakes with others as well when I am the one giving advice.

I tend to make process decisions more frequently, and I believe this is because I have a knack for spotting errors and paying attention to details that others may overlook.

What's something that you struggle with as a leader, and how do you overcome that?

As a leader, I feel as though I struggle the most with remembering that if I have accomplished something one way that it may not be the best way for someone else to accomplish that goal or task, even if it was a successful path. Trying to foresee the possible outcomes of many different routes, and being open to creativity, helps overcome the urge to push for one way of doing things. Trial and error are also a big part of the learning process.

What are your communication tips for interacting with executive leadership?

When interacting with executive leadership, I always try to focus the conversation on the exact point or points that I want to get across and nothing more. Having more frequent interactions with my boss, co-workers, and team members leads to more relaxed relationships where conversations can get off-topic solely based on our involvement in working so closely together and being more involved in each other's day-to-day business.

How do you cultivate productive relationships with your boss, peers, direct reports, and other team members?

Communication! Responding in a timely manner and following up on things you need responses to are great ways to stay productive. Picking up the phone never hurts either; sometimes we can all get overwhelmed with email messages, and a quick phone call may be an easier way to respond or obtain a quick reply. It also helps build relationships.

Have you encountered challenges collaborating with revenue-generating teams like sales and product development?

Yes, collaborating with revenue-generating teams has not always been the easiest. The best approach to making these collaborations better is one of clear communication and education if necessary. Many times, it has been brought to my attention that those on other teams, such as sales, are left in the dark on what it is exactly that my team is doing. A high-level overview and explanation in the beginning of the collaboration phase can go a long way to making sure we are on the same page and trying to accomplish the same goal, specifically in the eyes of what "done" will look like, in order to offer our clients the best outcome.

Have you encountered challenges collaborating with technology teams like information technology and software development?

Personally, no. I have had discussions with others in those roles, however, who clearly did not understand the goals of information security and why it is important that we all work together.

Do you have any favorite books to recommend for people who want to lead cybersecurity teams?

Two books that I recommend that were recommended to me are:

- Carol Dweck's *Mindset: The New Psychology of Success*
- Shane Anastasi's *The Seven Principles of Professional Services: A field guide for successfully walking the consulting tightrope*

I am a part of many online communities that provide a wealth of recommendations for reading material. These two were recommended by my mentor and by my manager, both of whom have led teams and are very good at their roles.

"You can learn from both good and bad leaders, learn what not to do from the poor leaders you encounter, and adopt the good leaders' attributes as your own."

Twitter: @SATCOM_Jim

James Medlock

36 James Medlock is a 25-year Army veteran with multiple job skills, a cyber operations specialist, a satellite network engineer, and an SME. He also has worked on designing and supporting communications systems for the military as a senior satellite engineer and staff engineer for General Dynamics, has written his name on a Milstar communications satellite before it was launched into space, has a bachelor's and a master's degree in management of information systems, has eight years working with IT and OT in the oil and gas industry, has a bunch of certificates in a box in his closet, serves as a high school cyber patriot mentor, was the technical editor for three books, has written multiple technical manuals for Army communication equipment, is a board member for a couple of conferences, is a DEF CON walker of 15,000 steps a day, was an illuminati party-goer, and is a friend to many, father of five, and spouse to one.

What's the most important decision you've made or action you've taken to enable a business risk?

Having 24 years in the Army including combat operations, I have been a part of decisions where people got hurt. I'll exclude those decisions from this topic, but of note, those decisions help guide my understanding of risk. I started in the satellite communication field in the military and then added IT and networking, while sprinkling on some information assurance long the way. The hardest decision I had was going from being a recognized SME in my previous field to being the n00b in the radically different and ever-changing field of information security.

Over the last decade, InfoSec has become my hobby. Most of the people and groups I hung around with were in InfoSec, and the work I enjoyed doing the most revolved around InfoSec. When I finally made the jump, I was able to turn my hobby into how I made money to put food on the table for my family. This was both the hardest and most rewarding decision at the same time. I was helped and encouraged in making the decision by many people along the way, especially my DEF CON friends, my Texas InfoSec peers, and my friends from the military. I have many people to thank for their counsel and support in making this decision.

Do you find yourself more often making people, process, or technology decisions?

Determining what drives business success for the company you are in helps define the way to answer this question. The answer is further complicated by business size, segment, personnel, and leadership personalities. Examples of external forces that drive decisions are compliance, governance, legalities, safety, personnel turnover, risk appetite, automation, and the business segment. Automation is one of the few ways we have to harness the tribal knowledge and wisdom of our elders in any industry.

Personally, I try to invest in people. It takes effort and money to find, train, and retain quality talent. When you can find the right people who have the inquisitive mindset and their work and passions are in alignment, there is no limit to their capability.

I've worked in larger organizations where implementing process was the first step in establishing a level of constancy in business operations, while you build or find the talent. Developing processes that increase efficiency and are in line with meeting compliance standards can provide significant business value to your business.

Technology is similar to this in that you might not be able to use open-source tools due to compliance. With the right technology, you can address a lot of ankle biters to free up your employees, increasing their efficiency and allowing them to focus on stopping the fires from happening versus just putting out fires all day. Just always remember to be requirements-centric and vendor-agnostic.

What's the most difficult part of your current role?

I recently changed jobs from oil and gas to the government sector. My current role has me drinking from a fire hose while working as a cybersecurity program manager. I provide support for a large government program that has been ongoing for several years and am playing catchup and learning all of the ins and outs of technology and people, as well as the history of the program and the politics of business relationships, projects, and people.

I will use the oil and gas industry for this question, as I recently left after eight years. The most difficult part was understanding the business realities or pressures of my senior leadership, compared to my realities as seen from the point of view of my "foxhole." An example is when I thought that they made a very poor and nearsighted business decision. Though I expressed that I adamantly disagreed with the reasoning and justification, they moved ahead with it. Less than 18 months later, it bit us in the backside pretty badly. My learning opportunity from that scenario was to find the driving force of the external pressures on my senior leadership. It could be revenue, pending layoffs, governance, compliance, legal issues, or in my case them being technology adverse. I needed to change the way I communicated to them to ease them into technology decisions. I consulted several friends and tried changing the way I put my business justification presentations together and really tried to cater to solving problems for my boss and my boss's boss. This paid dividends nearly immediately as my team was providing solutions to directly address their pain points.

How do you lead your team to execute and get results?

The definition of leadership I learned while at Skyline High School JROTC was "the ability to motivate others to perform a mission or task by providing direction, guidance and end result expectations." I was blessed to have a couple of Vietnam veterans who were program mentors, and they always said to fulfill your role in the leadership process and let your subordinates surprise you with their outstanding results. I still try to apply that leadership mentality, minimizing micromanagement and providing an environment for my employees to buy into the project, culminating in personal excellence and creating both individual and team successes.

As an individual contributor, I try to provide the best effort I can to whatever the job is at hand. I tend to express my opinion as an advisor, and I have had leadership reactions across the range, from excellent responses to being told to go back to my desk and color. I don't let the dismissal of my ideas be a reason to not do my best work. That comes off a bit stoic but, in reality, was a hard lesson. Many years ago, I had multiple experiences with poor leadership. I talked trash about it to my peers and only created more drama for myself. To prove a point, I lowered my own standards of performance under the self-justification that my job performance was making my supervisor look better. I was nearly kicked out of the military. I learned from that experience, realizing that I was actively choosing to lower my own personal standards of performance to spite someone I didn't even care for. My point of view and advice on the topic of leadership is different now. You can learn from both good and bad leaders, learn what not to do from the poor leaders you encounter, and adopt the good leaders' attributes as your own.

Do you have a workforce philosophy or unique approach to talent acquisition?

The million-dollar question: how do you identify, train, and retain quality talent in such a growing technical field? My opinion: it is about culture. I want to be the person who people want to work with. Get involved with the InfoSec community and establish relationships over a common desire to teach each other and have the open mindedness to learn new things. I have found talent in many areas, some who were not even in the security field, but with some exposure they are thriving and, in some cases, they have surpassed me technically. In my mind, ultimately, that is the goal of a mentor.

One of the hardest problems in this field is talent management, which doesn't mean just paying more but providing a culture people want to be a part of. Try to establish a culture of excellence while empowering people, supporting continual growth, and rewarding both individual and team successes. It is about being happy with what you are doing, your work having meaning, and getting to express yourself in your work. Cross-training your people in critical areas is a must. As a leader, I understand that I am both a mentor and a stepping stone, and you need to have a level of understanding in your role. As with most emotional relationships, try not to burn bridges with employees who choose to leave your employ. It hurts when folks leave your organization, but in the majority of cases I am extremely happy for them and their new opportunity. It is not just about money for many folks in this field. However, for the right price, just about any talent can be bought, and I don't hate on them for getting an amazing opportunity. When (if) the grass ends up not being greener, I welcome them back with open arms. Some will warn that if an employee leaves once, you don't want them back, because they will just look for the next opportunity to leave again. I disagree for a couple reasons.

- One, I got a talent back who can fill an important gap.
- Two, when they return, it will solidify to the others that they have a good work culture.
- Third, the person who left can become an advisor to anyone else who might be looking at other opportunities, which might reduce the "grass is greener" illusion.
- Lastly, accepting someone back who left shows that they weren't just a number, but a valuable asset, and usually it will increase the psychological connection with the leader and team.

Have you created a cohesive strategy for your information security program or business unit?
Short answer, it is in progress. In the previous eight years in the oil and gas industry I worked on formulating a business strategy focused on providing effective communication, defining clear requirements, soliciting feedback, and then executing the plan. This was developed utilizing experience gained in my time in the military and focused on the people around me, my direct influencers. From my position, they were to my Up, Down, Left, and Right.

Up—from my position to senior leadership
Down—my position to subordinates

Left—my group other business units

Right—my group to customers

Reviewing and updating this strategy is a defined task on my weekly agenda.

As a leader, you have to have your finger on the pulse of your senior leadership and understand the internal and external influences that drive their "lines of questioning" during meetings. In a past life, I figured out before our security meetings that some of the senior vice presidents would scan the latest Gartner Magic Quadrant or technology-focused report and ask things like, "How are we integrating next-, next-, nex-gen artificial intelligence/ blockchain/zero trust/machine learning into our solutions..." *ad nauseum*. We could literally play InfoSec Bingo during the meeting, and it was not productive. All joking aside, ask yourself if you can clearly articulate the vision of your senior leadership and business unit. Reverse engineer that vision into the key lines of effort for your group. Define and write out these lines of effort to your boss and solicit feedback to make sure you are in line with or leading the effort to define the lines of effort and expectation, effectively making a rubric. At that point, you have to clearly define the expected results and then look to gap analysis.

I use derivatives of the Project Management Institute (PMI) or PM Body of Knowledge (PMBoK) to help quantify measurables and milestones based on the size and scope of the task or project. I'm a firm believer that not everything should be a "project," but that doesn't mean we should not utilize project management principles in tasks that would benefit from abridged versions of process.

What are your communication tips for interacting with executive leadership?

Develop processes for quick ingestion of relevant information in order to minimize time required in meetings. I work to find out what format my senior leadership uses for briefs, and make my reports where they are relevant to their pressures and can be copied/pasted into higher briefs. I train and ask my team to do the same thing. This minimizes our need to have excessively long meetings. I believe an executive update meeting should not exceed 15 minutes. It took some intentional practice to try to put myself in the shoes of the person I was trying to communicate with. It takes practice to learn when to take the engineer hat off and put the business manager or project manager hat on, with each having different agendas, priorities, and expectations of results.

How do you cultivate productive relationships with your boss, peers, direct reports, and other team members?

Honesty, openness to ideas, actively trying to bring people into the conversation (as applicable), respecting opinions, minimizing distractions during meetings, and making a point to be respectful of people's time during meetings.

For my boss: I try to be a trusted advisor, including providing recommendations about decisions at his or her level, not just about our direct scope of work.

For my peers: I try to be a sounding board, regardless of topic, providing a listening ear and asking detailed questions. In most cases, they have the right answers, but they need a trusted person to talk through it with them who will be brutally honest.

My direct reports: I try to be a mentor, checking in on them routinely, not just about work but asking about family or plans for the weekend. I'm not trying to be a best friend but taking an interest in what they enjoy. With various personalities, this helps me understand what makes each employee tick in regard to their psychological personality and what they value in work and reward systems. With direct reports and other team members, I strive to make myself approachable and available.

Short story, when I was a young pup of 25 years old in the Army, working for National Command Authorities (NCA) in the DC area, I was the SME on a highly technical communication system. I would make jokes about others' lack of competence when they didn't comprehend technical issues. I had a civilian supervisor who gave me a less than stellar annual review (I was livid), and he clearly identified my actions and attitude as a weakness in leadership. I had not realized what I was doing to others. I was part of the problem—I was making myself unapproachable to my peers and subordinates and even some leaders. I learned a lot, and it made me a better person and a better leader. After that, I changed my motto to "always training my replacement."

Have you encountered challenges collaborating with revenue-generating teams like sales and product development?

After a couple of years learning how the various business units worked and understanding where the priorities of different groups were focused, I started introducing my department during some leadership meetings, just to clearly lay out a foundation of understanding and perspective.

"Howdy, my name is James Medlock. I am the international product line manager for communications; I manage one of the most important non–revenue-generating entities in our entire company. Though we have a shoestring budget, several hundred million dollars in revenue is riding on communications links."

As I was learning how to better understand and communicate with my leadership, I received some great advice from our engineering director about understanding senior leadership pressures, which I have already shared. The best advice I received was how to communicate your position as a non–revenue-generating entity. I adjusted my group's mission from satellite network communications to "content and data delivery platform." I related our role in the business to terms that were easily understood. This simple change in ideology caused a major change in perspective for the higher-level business unit, and it flowed down to my leadership along with funding for additional equipment and personnel.

Have you encountered challenges collaborating with technology teams like information technology and software development?

The company I previously worked for had a huge period of growth through acquisition under an amazing strategic leader (PM). In a period of 10 years, they acquired 200+ companies. This was an amazing feat in itself, but it created a lot of functional silos in development and operations. My groups provided communications on and off the drilling rigs, crossing between IT and OT services. I made it a point to reach out and become acquaintances and friends with the IT communications and security teams at the highest levels of the company. It took about two years before we became colleagues and friends, as I would actively make a point to coordinate a visit anytime I was in town. My group was brought in on some R&D projects. When communications projects were being briefed to the higher business units, they would refer the project leads to my group for integrations of IT and OT services. This relationship resulted in driving intercompany revenue into my business unit, which helped provide business value. Actively reaching out to peered and higher-level groups was a goal to get my group a seat at the table, becoming relevant and involved in the strategic direction of the company at the corporate level.

Do you have any favorite books to recommend?

I'll tend to listen to audiobooks on flights, while commuting to work, or before bed. I like to take recommendations from friends in the industry; they have usually gone through similar issues. In most of the larger companies I've worked for, there has been a decent reading list, usually over management or leadership. Books on shelves look pretty and can be useful for reference, but most are meant to be shared. It is a good investment to have a small book library at work.

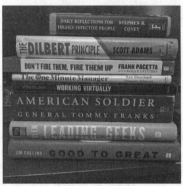

Image courtesy of James Medlock

I definitely recommend *Phoenix Project* by Gene Kim, Kevin Behr, and George Spafford and the *DevOps Handbook* by Gene Kim, Patrick Debois, and John Willis for entry to mid-level IT managers to help break down and analyze IT tasks, processes, and constraints on workflow. Here are some others:

- *Daily Reflections for Highly Effective People* by Stephen R. Covey
- *The Dilbert Principle* by Scott Adams (yes, the comic strip)
- *Don't Fire Them, Fire Them Up* by Frank Pacetta
- *The One Minute Manager* by Kenneth Blanchard and Spencer Johnson
- *Working Virtually* by Trina Hoefling
- *American Soldier* by General Tommy Franks
- *Leading Geeks* by Paul Glen
- *Good to Great* by Jim Collins

"If you have a strong team, then leading is often about clearing the area and providing tools for people to work."

Kent Nabors

Kent Nabors has worked in bank examinations for the FDIC and the Federal Reserve. After leading the networking infrastructure team for a national midmarket bank, he went on to build their cybersecurity practice and then served as the institution's first CISO. After more than 20 years in the banking industry, he recently took over as the cybersecurity leader for a national retail chain with more than 800 locations and a significant e-commerce presence. Kent is also the co-author of *Dissecting the Hack: The F0rb1dd3n Network*. When not practicing cybersecurity, Kent is an occasional speaker on the topic for industry, university, and civic organizations. He also does volunteer work for community cybersecurity activities. In what spare time remains, Kent owns a small business with his wife. He received his MBA from the University of Oklahoma.

37

Do you believe there is a massive shortage of career cybersecurity professionals?
We haven't suddenly run out of intelligent humans. In fact, I think we have more educated people today than at any point

in history. We do have a lot of demand for particular skills right now, but that can be filled with bright people...but are we making cybersecurity an interesting and engaging option for them? If your organization can't find someone to fill a particular opening, are you being creative in solving your problem or just waiting for a unicorn to walk down your street?

You can succeed in gathering a bunch of people together if you throw money at the problem. But that won't get you an effective team. Building a team of cybersecurity professionals takes time. You shouldn't just be looking for someone to fill a slot today. You should be hiring someone for who they will be in two, three, and five years from now. Look outside of normal career paths.

What's the most important decision you've made or action you've taken related to a business risk?

I was a year into a job as a network admin. I had been tapped to lead part of the effort for a major system conversion at a regional bank. It was late at night after an initial system test had gone poorly. All of the tech team was in our "war room" trying to figure out what had happened. The executives had come to watch and then huddled in a nearby conference room after things broke. My boss pulled me out of the room and started quizzing me on the problems. He quickly came to the bottom-line question, "Can you make this work?" He had to walk back in the conference room with a go/no-go recommendation, and I suspected I was betting my job with my answer—"We can do it."

Why did I choose that path? They hired me to make things work. I didn't know how to fix all the problems yet, but I knew the people I was working with. Sometimes you bet on the how and sometimes you bet on the who. I had worked with the team long enough to believe it was a good bet.

A week later we went through with the systems conversion, and it worked. I ended up staying with that company for 18 years.

How do you make hard decisions? Do you find yourself more often making people, process, or technology decisions?

Some decision-making is shorthand for data processing that builds over time. It's possible to lose awareness of the variables you process as you become more familiar with the industry, your organization, and your team. When you move to a new company, your business changes strategy, or a regulation changes, and you have to be more deliberate in collecting the data you evaluate.

I tend to make people and process decisions. Those are the decisions where action happens. Technology is a tool. People and process are what turns that tool into action. Even if you have the technology right, if the people (first) and processes (second) are not ready, the technology won't do you any good. There are a few principles that help when it's time to make a decision.

- *Simpler answers tend to be better answers.* They are more likely to be implemented successfully, and they are more likely to be understood by those who have to carry them out. If your answer is overly complex, you probably don't yet understand the problem.

- *Know who will be impacted by your decision.* Have you talked with the right people to get their perspective? Do you understand organizational objectives? Do you know what your leadership wants/needs (not the same thing)?

- *Don't overvalue the most expensive opinion.* Just because the person with the biggest title gives an answer, you need to keep exploring. There may be a very quiet engineer/admin/developer who knows the one reason that answer won't ever work.

- *Someone has to make a call.* There will be a point in the process when a decision has to be made. You have to develop an understanding of how much data you can collect. Some situations require an answer with the best data in the moment. Others require a collaborative and/or deliberative process.

What's something that you struggle with as a leader, and how do you overcome that?

I had worked for the Federal Reserve as a network admin. Then I was recruited to be a manager over a tech team for a call center owned by an airline. It was my first manager job, and I jumped at the chance. Less than a year later I was laid off when the company shut down all their operations in the state. At that point in my career, I was impatient. If there was an opportunity, I took it and ran. But I didn't do my homework, so I didn't understand the business risks I was walking into. I spent 11 months with nothing but problems—not enough resources, internal staff problems, inconsistent leadership, a losing business model, and more.

It took me a while and a few more hard lessons along the way, but I got better at reading the room and doing background research. I learned job interviews are two-way evaluations. Leadership starts with how you are set up in a position. If you walk into a mess, you better know you have the resources to fix it. If you don't, then turn around. There will be places where you can succeed, but they have to be the right fit for the skills you bring.

How do you lead your team to execute and get results?
You behave differently as a leader depending on the people you lead. If you have a strong team, then leading is often about clearing the area and providing tools for people to work. If you don't have a strong team, then you have to find ways to fix that—either through building talent or finding talent (or both).

But some things are consistent. Ask good questions. Be honest. Be fair. Don't ask something of someone you wouldn't do yourself. Do your homework and expect the same of everyone you lead. Listen more than you talk. Know what is important to your organization and remind your team of that purpose through words and actions. Treat people as people and not assets. Live a balanced life and expect the same of your team.

Do you have a workforce philosophy or unique approach to talent acquisition?
- *Value aptitude over knowledge.* People can get more knowledge if they have the ability and motivation (must have both).
- *Be patient.* If you haven't found the right fit, don't settle. Putting the wrong person on a team can wreck a team.
- *Respect your people.* If you hire right, you will end up with people who have the potential to do good work. Don't give them reasons to walk away.
- *Have fun.* If you don't like what you are doing, then the people around you probably won't either. If this business isn't fun for you, go do something else!

Have you created a cohesive strategy for your information security program or business unit?
Yes, in my career I've had the opportunity to create a strategy and implement it. But often what happens is you are presented with a "current state" that isn't where you think the organization should be. You could spend time creating a coherent plan and find that no one wants to go in that direction. That isn't

leadership. Leadership is about execution, and that can't happen just through your work. It's the product of many people.

First, don't try to be the author of the strategy. If it's your vision, it probably won't be implemented. It also needs to be something that can be communicated simply and connects with the organizational mission. Make sure you know why your organization exists. What is its purpose? Now, what does the information you protect have to do with that purpose? Make the connection simple and clear. Bonus points if you can say it with fewer than five words.

What are your communication tips for interacting with executive leadership?

- *Listen first.* You need to know what is important to them and to the organization. How do they communicate? Some companies want lots of numbers and analysis. Some want a story.
- *Listen with your eyes.* Do you see signs of engagement or boredom? Watch for visual cues. Did the executive just flip your report over and look at their phone? Better luck next time.
- *Respect their time.* Executive life is about time-slicing. The topics are wildly diverse, and only the hard questions get to the executive office. Give good data (check your work) and make a clear recommendation.
- *Be deliberate with your language.* Tech-speak used to be a problem for these conversations. That's less true today, but you still need to be careful. The technology dialect is constantly adding new words, and you have to be cognizant of what language is right for your organization.
- *Don't fake it.* If you don't know the answer to a question, say so, and then go find the answer.

How do you cultivate productive relationships with your boss, peers, direct reports, and other team members?

The basics are true for everyone. Be honest, be diligent, and produce a good product. That will probably make you better than the average. The next step, however, is to actually care about people. You can't fake it. I once had a colleague who ended up in the hospital for an emergency surgery. He had been a challenge to get along with. So, I showed up the next day at his recovery room with a stack of magazines that included some info on his hobbies. I later learned it surprised him that someone from work actually cared to stop by and check on him. I could only do that because I had paid attention to his interests.

But you can't do things like that because they work for an outcome you expect. You do them because they are the right thing to do. Cybersecurity is similar. You do the right things, and sometimes people notice. Sometimes they don't. Recognition should not be determinative for your actions.

Have you encountered challenges collaborating with revenue-generating teams like sales and product development?

Oh, yes. Especially in the 2000s—cybersecurity was important, but many organizations hadn't made the direct link between protection and their organizational success. For those who were business leaders then, they didn't have experience to draw from about the cyber risks they were accepting. That made it easier for revenue teams to have greater impact on decisions.

I think that pendulum has swung, but how far depends on the industry. Banking has a lot of regulatory pressure that pushed them farther and faster than others. Retail is a bit of a mixed story, with some players learning lessons (including some learning through direct painful experience). There is still plenty of opportunity across all industries for cybersecurity leaders to shape strategies and provide real value to their companies. Attitudes will also continue to change as leaders change with time. If you are early- or mid-career right now, do your homework to be ready to step into leadership.

One of the keys to partnering across teams is establishing mission credibility. Companies don't exist to do cybersecurity. They do cybersecurity (and other things) to service their customers. Cybersecurity leaders have to understand how their work fits into the corporate mission and speak up with ways to protect and fulfill that mission's success. Know what is critical and work out from that knowledge. Grow and keep your credibility by speaking from facts and not fear.

Have you encountered challenges collaborating with technology teams like information technology and software development?

Oh, yes. I moved into cybersecurity from network infrastructure many years ago. I think it took about a week before I had issues collaborating across the IT teams, including the one I came from. There is a natural tension just because teams are measured differently. As long as goals are different among teams, then collaboration will be difficult. I've even had bosses who have cultivated that tension.

I've seen this naturally improve over time because cybersecurity is more of an acknowledged and understood requirement now. More people have been personally impacted by breaches and understand they need to prevent them where they have the power to do so.

Partnering takes time. You have to stay professional and not break relationships. Build trust, be accountable, and tell the truth. Sometimes that will require you to make a difficult stand. When that happens, be tough on the issue but not the person. It won't always work. But it works more often than not, and a career is a game of averages over time.

Do you have any favorite books to recommend for people who want to lead cybersecurity teams?

I've recommended *Team of Teams* by General Stanley McChrystal several times—he has a good story to tell about overcoming units that were cohesive at a small scale but failed at the overall mission. That's a similar challenge to technology teams today. They may be individually capable, but if they lose sight of the business mission, the organization doesn't get the full benefit of their abilities.

The book *Unthinkable* by Amanda Ripley is a darker suggestion. It's about how people react to disasters and what types of decisions are necessary to survive. If you work in cybersecurity long enough, you are going to see people under significant pressure (yourself included). It wouldn't hurt to think about what it takes to survive the worst of times before you find yourself in the middle of such a situation.

The older I get, the more I am drawn to reading older books. We work in a perpetually new business that requires constant study and monitoring for changes and innovations. We may be the first few generations to deal with this current pace of change, but we are not the first to deal with changes like new threats, innovations, and technologies. I've been reading more history and biographies and found that they help me think about the human condition. No matter how innovative we think the latest tool is, it's still a tool made by humans with human flaws. So, my last book recommendation is for every new book you read, go read at least one old one that has been tested by time and proven true.

"I believe that being transparent about my shortcomings and being vulnerable and creating that environment will allow individuals to grow into their best selves."

Twitter: @charles_nwatu • **Website:** www.linkedin.com/in/cnwatu

Charles Nwatu

38

Charles holds a B.S in Information Sciences and Technology from Pennsylvania State University, where he specialized in Information Assurance and Security. He has over 13 years of experience and is currently the Engineering Manager, Corporate Security for Netflix. Charles is known for creating dynamic teams that develop and engineer robust security capabilities with a constant awareness of the threat landscape balanced with an understanding of business risks. Mr. Nwatu believes that diverse talent working in a diverse environment allows for great opportunities and discoveries to take place, so he is very active in the community as a member of /dev/color and is a current ally of Women's Society of Cyberjutsu.

Do you believe there is a massive shortage of career cybersecurity professionals?

I actually do not believe there is a massive shortage of career cybersecurity professionals. I do believe there is a massive shortage of entry to mid-level cybersecurity opportunities for individuals to learn and develop their cybersecurity principles and best practices.

To bridge this gap, I believe that as an industry we must be open to providing entry-level to mid-level career opportunities. Within our companies we have the opportunity to offer a nurturing environment for our employees to grow and learn from obstacles and victories.

What's the most important decision you've made or action you've taken related to a business risk?
Taking a step back to talk about risk differently. At the end of the day, words matter, and understanding what risk means and how to articulate it as part of my day-to-day activities is important. Over the last several years I have been going through a risk journey, thanks to folks like Ryan McGeehan (@magoo) and Travis McPeak (@travismcpeak), in pushing the envelope around how we talk about risk within cybersecurity. I have expanded into using Factor Analysis of Information Risk (FAIR) and continue to find ways to normalize how cybersecurity and business risk are discussed within the industry.

> Within our companies we have the opportunity to offer a nurturing environment for our employees to grow and learn from obstacles and victories.

How do you make hard decisions? Do you find yourself more often making people, process, or technology decisions?
I love people. Making hard personnel decisions is a balance of understanding what is right for the individual and the company. I recently read *The Advantage: Why Organizational Health Trumps Everything Else In Business* by Patrick Lencioni and the following quote really resonated with me: "Accountability is about having the courage to confront someone about their deficiencies and then to stand in the moment and deal with their reaction, which may not be pleasant. To hold someone accountable is to care about them enough to risk having them blame you for pointing out their deficiencies." When it comes to making hard decisions, I am accountable, caring, and thoughtful about the decision I make and its impact.

What's something that you struggle with as a leader, and how do you overcome that?

Time. What do you spend it on and why did you spend your time on that? As a leader I am asked often how I spend my time. I continue to ask myself, "Am I spending my time on the right thing, or is this the right thing that I am working on?" My current role at Netflix is challenging me in a healthy way to develop my own philosophy around my time and how it reflects on impact.

How do you lead your team to execute and get results?

Communicate and recalibrate. I am a firm believer in communicating and finding the right medium to communicate through. Communicating the desired outcome and nurturing the team and its contributors to set the path for resolution is how I like to approach team execution. In addition, part of executing and getting results is also having a healthy understanding of the work that you consciously decide not to execute because of various factors.

Do you have a workforce philosophy or unique approach to talent acquisition?

My workforce philosophy centers around meeting people with grace and humility and hiring people who want to work together to better themselves, the people around them, and the company. I recognize that as a security professional and as a human, I am not perfect, but I believe that being transparent about my shortcomings and being vulnerable and creating that environment will allow individuals to grow into their best selves and execute with consistency and rigor.

Have you created a cohesive strategy for your information security program or business unit?

I had the opportunity to develop a security program from scratch for a startup. It was not easy; it was challenging to find my style and ensure that my content was being understood by the executive team and ultimately the business. To ensure proper strategic alignment with the business, I focused on growing relationships with key business partners and communicating the narrative in order to bring them along on the journey.

What are your communication tips for interacting with executive leadership?

There is this term that gets thrown around: *executive presence*. I keep searching for its definition and come up short. With that in mind, I focus on ensuring that my narrative focuses on what information my executives need to walk away with. I focus on understanding what the purpose of my communication is. Is it to inform, seek alignment, or establish a direction? With each of these approaches, I tailor the appropriate narrative, keeping in mind my overall communication goal.

How do you cultivate productive relationships with your boss, peers, direct reports, and other team members?

Meet people with grace and humility. Be true to yourself and develop your personal narrative. I believe that people want to be respected, valued, and recognized for the work they do. I focus on accountability: are my relationships holding me accountable, and am I doing the same in return?

Have you encountered challenges collaborating with revenue-generating teams like sales and product development?

I personally have not had challenging relationships with revenue-generating teams. I do ensure that the cybersecurity narrative is not just technically driven but aligned to key business risks that may impact the company.

Have you encountered challenges collaborating with technology teams like information technology and software development?

Friction. At the end of the day I look to partner with technology teams and focus on how we can decrease friction by working to establish the proper end-user incentive and end-user experience.

Do you have any favorite books to recommend for people who want to lead cybersecurity teams?

The following quote from *Black Box Thinking* by Matthew Syed wraps up how I look at failing and being self-aware that it is okay to fail. I have to thank Bob Lord for the recommendation. "Failure reveals a feature of our world we hadn't grasped fully and offers vital clues about how to update our models, strategies, and behaviors."

"I've learned to start balancing my technical focus and expertise with empowering my team members to develop their skills and to take the lead on certain day-to-day work."

Twitter: @gose1

Greg Ose

39

As a senior manager of security engineering at GitHub, Greg leads a team dedicated to finding and fixing vulnerabilities within GitHub's products and applications. He has a strong passion for keeping applications secure, whether through security assessment, automation and static analysis, or developer training and awareness. For more than a decade he has focused on application security, previously securing applications at CME Group, as a senior security consultant at Neohapsis, and as an adjunct professor at DePaul University teaching a graduate course on software security assessment and exploitation.

Do you believe there is a massive shortage of career cybersecurity professionals?

I do not believe that there is a massive shortage of cybersecurity professionals. However, meeting the growing needs of this industry will require us to change our pre-existing ideas about the required background and experience of individuals on a security team. Not all experienced security engineers will come with a decade of heads-down security work. The key to expanding hiring reach is to look for great engineers with a passion for security. For example, my team members spend a large part of their day performing code and architecture review, the same responsibilities one would expect of an experienced software engineer. The main difference is that our review provides a focus on security. Bridging an individual's gap of security expertise is sometimes easier than a gap in engineering experience.

The same line of thinking applies when hiring for roles requiring less experience. Many software engineering graduates are not sure what area of development will be the focus of their career. The security community needs to ensure that we make security an attractive specialty for these less experienced engineers.

What's the most important decision you've made or action you've taken related to a business risk?
Some of my most important business risk decisions were made as my company went through the rapid growth of its service offerings and technologies. Initially, when a product or engineering team comes to security with complex initiatives, it is tempting, as a security advocate, to push back and hope the rest of the company shifts in a different direction.

However, by taking a step back and looking at the overall business opportunities these new initiatives presented, I was able to help enable product goals while keeping security's concerns and recommendations intact. My team and I worked closely with engineering and product teams to identify security requirements, ensure that the decisions being made were architecturally sound from a security perspective, and see that the features were implemented in a way that kept our infrastructure and customers secure.

Looking back, I know it was imperative that I shifted my focus from being a blocker, trying to shut these initiatives down, to instead accepting the fact that our threat model and risk profile would change. I could then dedicate my team and my efforts to enabling this growth while minimizing its security impact and building security resilience into these new features.

How do you make hard decisions? Do you find yourself more often making people, process, or technology decisions?
I lead an application security team, so the difficult decisions I typically encounter involve weighing a technical security risk

against the impact of changing the direction of a product feature or its timeframes. These difficult decisions typically come up when an architectural flaw leading to some security risk is identified late in the development cycle. For these situations, the risk and correct remediation are not as clear-cut as a specific vulnerability in the implementation of a service. Often, these architectural vulnerabilities can be fixed only by re-architecting or redesigning a specific feature that the engineering and product teams already have a set vision for.

In these cases, it is important to clearly and realistically state the security risk identified. It is equally important to understand the perspectives of all the teams involved and how your own view of risk differs from those of other teams. For example, a fix to a specific security issue might satisfy the need of security but at the same time may introduce a workflow that could cause user adoption to plummet or introduce significant technical debt to engineering teams. The right decision in these cases is almost never the decision that I want from a strictly security-focused point of view, but one that takes into consideration all of the viewpoints at play to ensure an outcome that strikes an acceptable balance with all of those involved. This collaboration is what has allowed me to confidently make decisions in difficult situations.

What's something that you struggle with as a leader, and how do you overcome that?
As a leader of a team of application security engineers, I constantly struggle with how I can best contribute my time to the team. I'm often tempted to spend my time digging into code or architecture reviews, contributing my technical skills toward the immediate goals of the team. I've learned to start balancing my technical focus and expertise with empowering my team members to develop their skills and to take the lead on certain day-to-day work. As the team and company have continued to grow, my shift to a strategic focus has continued, and I can rely on my team and trust them to perform solid technical work that doesn't require my oversight.

How do you lead your team to execute and get results?
Like most security teams, my team of application security engineers is greatly outnumbered by our peers in engineering. We need to continually improve the efficiency of our work to keep up with the pace of development. I push my team

to identify areas where our work is redundant, is repetitive, or doesn't require our core skill set of finding and fixing vulnerabilities in our applications. In these cases, I work with the team to lay out initiatives where we can automate this work to reduce this overhead.

For example, we've invested a significant amount of development effort into automating the initial triage of submissions for our bug bounty program. With this tooling, we've been able to shift away from issuing repetitive responses to the same invalid or known low-risk reports, leaving more time to focus instead on working with the appropriate engineering teams toward a fix for valid and impactful vulnerabilities identified by the program.

This mirrors my own individual work style, looking to focus my attention and time on the most impactful work I can and limiting the time I spend on repetitive or redundant tasks.

Do you have a workforce philosophy or unique approach to talent acquisition?

When hiring members of my team, I look for experience in software engineering and a passion for security. A passion for security may be demonstrated by experience in bug bounty programs, vulnerability research, and disclosure, or by taking on a security focus within an engineering team. A successful application security engineer must be able to confidently enter technical conversations with developers and understand their goals, daily work, and requirements. A strong background in development allows members on my team to accurately assess, identify, and communicate security vulnerabilities in terms that align with engineers' daily work.

Have you created a cohesive strategy for your information security program or business unit?

To guide strategy for initiatives and priorities, I am always looking for ways that my team can most efficiently push forward our goal of reducing the risk in our applications and services. I look for new processes or tweaks to existing processes and tools we can make to increase productivity and improve collaboration with other teams.

It is important to be nimble and quickly react to changes within the company. If the usefulness of a process that worked a year ago starts declining, it is time to re-evaluate that work and see if it can be restructured to be useful in today's environment or if it should just be scrapped. This ensures that security's work naturally flows with the work of the teams that we collaborate with and that we can most efficiently make progress toward our goals.

The best way to ensure that our goals are aligned with the overall corporate strategy is to work with leadership to push the importance of security from the top down. Make sure the work your team does is known and it is known why it is important. When security awareness is instilled as part of the company culture, making progress toward reducing security risk becomes a natural and expected requirement of all initiatives.

What are your communication tips for interacting with executive leadership?
When communicating with executive leadership, it is important to be confident and decisive in your guidance. In my experience, executive leadership is looking to me as a subject-matter expert. Sometimes I'm tempted to say, "Here are all the facts, but it's not my decision to make," but as the subject-matter expert, my guidance *is* my decision to make.

In security it's often hard to make decisions that don't solely reflect our adversity to technical risk. To confidently make decisions for leadership, you need to consider all of the risks a decision may introduce. Make sure you have the complete picture and details from other experts, especially from those from areas outside of security that would be impacted. If there is not enough information available to you to make a decision, dig into how to get that data. In the end, with all of the information in hand and by utilizing your own experience and expertise, you can communicate and present the best possible guidance to leadership.

How do you cultivate productive relationships with your boss, peers, direct reports, and other team members?
To cultivate productive relationships, I find it's imperative to enter all conversations and situations with empathy, leaving aside your assumptions, stress, and frustrations. I frequently am involved in potentially tense situations, either during a security incident, while discovering a vulnerability, or when trying to determine the root cause of issues. These situations are when either strong relationships can be formed or bad impressions of the security

team can be made. It is important in these conversations to realize that incidents are part of the nature of security work, and it is our job to collaborate and find the best path forward.

In these situations, strive to understand why things happened from multiple perspectives. It may be the case that the product team rushed engineering timelines and efforts, maybe engineers didn't have enough training to write their code securely, or maybe it was just a fringe scenario that no amount of foresight could have prevented. By working and understanding from the viewpoint of engineers, you are able to become a strong supporting member of their team, giving them confidence to make their own security decisions and being a reliable resource when they need guidance.

This approach is equally effective when performing retrospectives with my own team members, trying to answer the question of why a security vulnerability was introduced and why we did not identify it during the development life cycle. I've learned that no security program will mitigate all the vulnerabilities, and setting this understanding with the team empowers them to do their best work. Any time we're able to dig into where things went wrong, we can use the experience not to place blame but as an opportunity to identify where we have gaps in our knowledge or processes and work toward filling them.

Have you encountered challenges collaborating with revenue-generating teams like sales and product development?

The most difficult challenge when collaborating with product and sales teams is aligning their goals of creating and selling products with security's goals of reducing risk to our customers and infrastructure. When partnering with these teams, I try to clearly communicate to them why security is important, not just to the security team but also to our customers. Customers are becoming increasingly security conscious, and strong security practices have become an attractive product feature and one way our service can stand out from the competition.

In these conversations, it is also important not to be a security absolutist. You have to realistically scope security concerns and clearly communicate their actual risk. Realize that accepting a product direction that introduces security risk might end up being the best path forward for the company and enable a product to grow and evolve. It is important in these situations to ensure that you find the middle ground that helps the product grow but also helps minimize the security concerns. This is where collaboration and creativity across multiple teams can help come up with non-obvious solutions on which product, sales, and security can confidently agree.

Have you encountered challenges collaborating with technology teams like information technology and software development?

My team collaborates most closely with software engineering teams, and we view these engineers as our customers, continually looking at how we can provide the best services that support their work. Our engineers' time and attention are our most valuable resources in securing our applications and infrastructure. So, it's critically important to make sure that our interaction with these teams is efficient and provides the best possible value. We continually look to build trust and rapport with these teams, ensuring that when they have security concerns or questions, we are their first resource.

Challenges arise in our work with engineering when we communicate without empathy, come to these conversations unprepared, or set unrealistic expectations. We must ensure we do not waste our engineering teams' time or they will not seek out our help in the future. To avoid this, it's important to understand the viewpoint, goals, previous security discussions with the team, and existing architecture decisions. We asynchronously collect all the information possible to get up to speed on their work and can enter these conversations the same way a peer on their team would.

In these conversations, it is important to establish that the security of their work is a collaborative effort and we are available as experts whenever they have concerns. My team's goal is to allow engineers to ship their applications and services with confidence in their security posture. When issues do occur, we will be working with the same team during an incident, and establishing this collaborative relationship helps us to efficiently handle and mitigate security issues as they arise.

In the end, to be successful, we must be viewed as a useful and important partner of engineering teams. If we are viewed as an adversary, a hindrance to their progress, or just a checkbox that provides no value, we cannot effectively collaborate to meet our security goals.

"It's helpful to see risk appetite cleanly aligned to decisions and strategy; that enables me to make smart calculated risks."

Twitter: @edwardprevost

Edward Prevost

Edward Prevost is currently a staff security engineer II at Squarespace, the all-in-one platform for websites, domains, online stores, and marketing tools. Edward got started with computing at a young age when his uncle gifted him C and BASIC textbooks. The son of a master stonemason (who happened to work at Rensselaer Polytechnic Institute [RPI]), he was raised with no computers at home but had access to the converted-cathedral computer lab at RPI and eventually an IBM Aptiva, on which he grew his expertise leveraging dial-in access to the RPI network.

40

Many late nights on IRC and BBCs later, Edward began his formal career at Albany Medical Center as an application specialist, tackling complex technical problems found in academia and healthcare. Over the course of his career, he helped to build the Information Security Technology Center of GE in Glenn Allen, Virginia; design, review, and deploy core security architectures for Adobe—most notably adobe.io; lead an ICS research team at Tenable; and build and direct the Fraud Engineering, CIAM, and IVR teams at Zions Bancorporation.

Most recently, Edward joined Squarespace to help drive and promote growth and maturity of the organization's security engineering and security architecture practices.

With roughly 20 years of information security experience, Edward is very active in the community. He can be found volunteering each year on the CFP board for BSidesLV, teaching Hour of Code in his local rural community, and responding to questions on Twitter.

When not hacking on systems or software, he can be found wrestling, farming, powerlifting, soccering, tabletop gaming, reading theology, forging friendships, and making people laugh.

Do you believe there is a massive shortage of career cybersecurity professionals?
Yes, and no.

Yes, there are many open positions currently, some in critical roles, and this can lead to some of the hysterics around hiring in this space. No, because in the past 17+ years of working within InfoSec I've met hundreds of technical and nontechnical people who would suitably, and in some cases incredibly, fill those current vacancies. The issue is they aren't currently within InfoSec.

Bridging the gap requires companies to embrace creative learning and education practices. Grow-your-own programs are incredibly successful, as demonstrated by the efforts at Whitehat Security in years gone by. Any opportunity that an organization offers for interested personnel to research and investigate a cybersecurity career is going to be a boon for the industry.

What's the most important decision you've made or action you've taken related to a business risk?
I once made a concerted effort to establish a dedicated group of data scientists focused on machine learning applied to various InfoSec issues, instead of purchasing an expensive but proven platform of premade models. Underneath this decision were two main factors: I prefer people over machines, and I prefer people over machines.

On the one hand, having staff empowers an organization to pivot quickly; it means not relying on a vendor or technology to dictate your speed. On the other hand, investing in vendors means being able to have recourse; however, that recourse is typically litigation. In the end, it was a good decision, and the team proved its worth within six months, significantly cutting loss by tens of thousands per month. Moral of the story, always pick people over machines and code.

How do you make hard decisions? Do you find yourself more often making people, process, or technology decisions?

There is a spreadsheet I created many years ago at GE that allows me to assign weighted values to various aspects of benefit, risk, etc., to any given decision. Once completed, the sheet helped me make a weighted calculation as to the challenge I'm evaluating. It's helpful to see risk appetite cleanly aligned to decisions and strategy; that enables me to make smart calculated risks. Of these decisions, I find they are almost always people or process in nature. Technology changes rapidly, not only within the industry but also within any given organization. So long as engineering is transparent and contains a high level of trust, there is little adjustment needed in that space that they won't make themselves. People and process, however, are a far different breed. Sometimes people don't see their gifts or the place they are needed most. Sometimes processes are perpetuated blindly.

What's something that you struggle with as a leader, and how do you overcome that?

Delegation. It's easy to try to execute on technical efforts rather than allowing team members, in their appropriate roles, to execute. I feel this is a common issue for leaders who have come into leadership from development backgrounds.

One of the most challenging leadership roles I was in was an early position with a startup in upstate New York. I had been promoted into management because of the technological facelift I gave the organization within a short time after being hired. It had led to our gainful acquisition. The promotion, however, was not happy for all parties. I learned that office politics can be brutal. Having a philosophy of "charity always wins," I found myself in some desperate situations and then eventually exiting the organization. At the time, I was devastated; I thought I could never lead again. That leadership was rife with lies and deception (have you ever *really* read Sun Tzu?). But, I was wrong. Soon after I was given an opportunity to lead a new team, and it was a smashing success, no deception required.

How do you lead your team to execute and get results?

As a leader, my focus is on charity. Everyone has bad days. And you never know when it's someone's bad day. Patience and communication, charitably applied, are the most effective means to productive ends. Having honest and open conversations, seasoned with understanding and charity, helps identify and deal with issues as rapidly as it helps identify improvements. It also tends to have a familial effect of drawing the team together as friends and, in the best cases, as family.

I find little difference in my philosophy between leading and following. Charity always wins.

Do you have a workforce philosophy or unique approach to talent acquisition?

Having a vast personal network built up from years in the industry, I do tend to reach out to those I've worked with before. The net benefit is I've seen them perform on my or another team and know they can deliver on X and Y.

During hiring, I look for candidates who are passionate in a humble way. Those who dig into problems head-on, Googling like crazy and asking flurries of questions, but who aren't afraid to ask for advice. Once hired, most folks who have worked for me have attested to my "charity always wins" approach as being the cornerstone of why they enjoyed working at the organization.

What are your communication tips for interacting with executive leadership?

Perhaps the main theme of my leadership style (that charity always wins) has now been repeated ad nauseum. If so, I'd say "be kind." Regardless of who you're interacting with, remember they all have a limited resource, time. Listen actively. Consider the information they are sharing or the question they are asking. Ask clarifying questions if you're uncertain exactly what is being communicated. Be able to reply in a succinct way that leaves them with few questions but several points to ponder and valid directions to consider.

Have you encountered challenges collaborating with revenue-generating teams like sales and product development?

Ah, the old business versus technology battle. In my opinion, this is a falsely premised and perpetuated issue. Historically, the InfoSec division, in its infancy, tended to be a group of technologists who showed up to meetings, listened to the issues, and then sternly said "no." They were a secret group of unknown origin who had the power to halt projects, well, because. As the industry matured, we've moved into realizing that InfoSec is an enabling division of any healthy, functioning organization. If challenges exist between your team and sales/product/business, then I would suggest you're still leading the team as a "no" team. Pivoting into partnership with these groups is going to require an approach based on clearly defining risk appetite and then clearly articulating the spectrum of options to move forward with any given effort, in light of a range of risk ratings/saturation. Think of it this way: someone approaches you and asks if you'll "teach them computers." You have a few options, other than "Nope, see ya kid." You could start by offering them instruction on electronics, you could start by offering them some simple C instruction, you could start by offering them some Scratch tutorials. But you would make your decision based on where the person was at. You'd be unlikely to offer deep electrical engineering instruction to a four-year-old. This same principle, as gut level as it is, needs to permeate through all your InfoSec leadership interactions with sales/product/business. Meet them where they are. Truly partner with them, looking to enable them in what their end goal is, in the most effective way, currently. You can always work together on incremental improvements, but if you haven't worked to enable them where they currently are, that incremental improvement isn't going to follow.

Do you have any favorite books to recommend for people who want to lead cybersecurity teams?
It may be strange to anyone other than Donald Knuth, but I read a lot of theology. I find that spending time reading about deep, meaningful topics that pose complex philosophical challenges has a tendency to produce greater appreciation for those around you and a deeper contemplation of issues that arise at work.
Here are some books I recommend:

- *The Scriptures* (66 books of the Textus Receptus)—God
- *Things a Computer Scientist Rarely Talks About* by Donald E. Knuth
- *Theistic Evolution* by J.P. Moreland, Stephen C. Meyer, Christopher Shaw, Ann K. Guager, and Wayne Grudem
- *This Is Water* by David Foster Wallace
- *What Color Is Your Parachute?* by Richard Nelson Bolles

"I believe strongly in leading by example. In many cases, this is the difference between being a manager and being a leader."

Website: RayRedacted.com

Ray [REDACTED]

41

Ray [REDACTED] is the vice president of technology at a global solutions provider focusing on cybersecurity solutions for multinational corporations. In addition to a degree from Purdue University and numerous industry certifications, he has 22 years of frontline experience in the prevention and mitigation of attacks from cybercriminals, hacktivist groups, and nation-state actors. Ray frequently teaches advanced security for global corporations, as well as federal and international law enforcement agencies. Ray has spoken at InfoSec conferences such as Black Hat and Shmoocon, as well as teaching classes on operational security (OPSEC) at cryptocurrency conferences globally.

Do you believe there is a massive shortage of career cybersecurity professionals?
There is no question that we are facing a massive shortage of cybersecurity professionals. Analysts and statisticians say this gap may soon be as large as three million unfilled jobs

worldwide. To bridge the gap, we need to both increase the supply of workers and decrease their workloads.

First, this means making serious and concerted efforts at diversity and inclusion initiatives, including providing more opportunity for members of under-represented communities. Increasing diversity in the InfoSec workforce has the additional benefit of making our security teams not only bigger but also stronger, because having different backgrounds and experience provides better views of events and more thorough problem solving.

Beyond increasing the pool of workers, we should strive to reduce the workloads for cybersecurity professionals by reaching out to "deputize" other departments to become part of the cybersecurity workforce, even within their current roles. Security should not be considered the sole responsibility of a "department," just like fire prevention should not fall on one department. The entire corporation should be aware of how to prevent fires, where the fire extinguishers are, and how to respond when they smell smoke.

> Security should not be considered the sole responsibility of a "department," just like fire prevention should not fall on one department.

Additionally, I believe that we have technologies and tools that can significantly reduce workloads by acting as so-called force multipliers. Machine learning and artificial intelligence show incredible promise here, and their impacts will continue to grow.

What's the most important decision you've made or action you've taken related to a business risk?
The hardest decision I have made was leaving a job I was extremely comfortable in so that I could start a new career that stretched both my abilities and my comfort zone. I chose this path because I saw an opportunity to grow both in technical ability and business acumen. In hindsight, this decision now seems obvious, but at the time it was rather scary.

How do you make hard decisions? Do you find yourself more often making people, process, or technology decisions?
I find that the three are inextricably linked, especially on the most difficult decisions. When faced with making the most

difficult decisions, I try to never do it in a vacuum. This usually means discussing challenges and ideas with my support networks, including the informal ones.

> ## It is extremely important to both be a mentor to others and to have a mentor yourself.

Mentors are important in difficult decisions. It is extremely important to both be a mentor to others and to have a mentor yourself. As supported by countless studies from multiple social science fields, mentorship is directly associated with professional success for all parties.

What's something that you struggle with as a leader, and how do you overcome that?

I frequently speak to large groups, giving prospective customer presentations, training, and even keynotes at conferences. In this role, especially the last one, I often struggle with what psychologists call *imposter syndrome*. For me, these feelings of self-doubt or inadequacy often result in procrastination. The connection between procrastination and imposter syndrome is that by waiting until the very last minute to work on a speech or keynote, even if the job isn't done well, you can rationalize the outcome. "Well, that wasn't so bad, considering I didn't even start it until the last minute." I have been struggling to overcome this as a leader. While I don't have a solid solution for it, I try to stay cognizant of it. Awareness is step number one.

How do you lead your team to execute and get results?

I believe strongly in leading by example. In many cases, this is the difference between being a manager and being a leader. As is often cited, "Managers have people who *work for them*, but leaders have people who *follow them*." It is important to know the difference and to strive to do both.

Do you have a workforce philosophy or unique approach to talent acquisition?

At the company I work for, we strive to promote from within to "grow our own" talent. This is particularly true in the SOC environment, where alert fatigue and burnout can cause morale issues.

Have you created a cohesive strategy for your information security program or business unit?

While it is extremely important to create strategies and plans, in my experience it's the execution that often presents more challenges than the creation of strategy. The path to ensuring that these goals are aligned with corporate strategy is simple: communicate, communicate, communicate.

What are your communication tips for interacting with executive leadership?

One of my mentors has a somewhat tongue-in-cheek expression: "Ray, there has never been a single important piece of information that was delivered after the 30th minute (of a conference call) or after the third slide." I always try to remember this when presenting information to executives. Keep it short, concise, and clear.

Another often cited (but often forgotten) tip is to never present a problem without presenting at least one proposed solution. This is often easier said than done but is absolutely vital when communicating with executive leadership.

On the other hand, when communicating with your peers and direct reports, brevity is not nearly as important as it is with executive leadership. In this case, it is much more important to be thorough in your communication and especially thorough in listening and absorbing their viewpoints.

> Never present a problem without presenting at least one proposed solution.

How do you cultivate productive relationships with your boss, peers, direct reports, and other team members?

One of the most important things to realize is that almost everyone has a preferred mode of communication: some people naturally prefer face to face or phone calls, some prefer emails, and many prefer instant messages. You should not necessarily use that method exclusively, but most people are more receptive when you communicate with them via their natural channels. Beyond this, it is important to emphasize that you have a shared mission. In the InfoSec arena, this is about identifying and reducing risk.

Have you encountered challenges collaborating with technology teams like information technology and software development?

I would say the biggest challenge when collaborating with software development and other IT teams is that their priorities are not necessarily aligned with yours. Additionally, security is often (erroneously) viewed as an impediment to software or product development. However, this should not be the case, and here is why...

One of my favorite analogies about InfoSec has to do with the Shinkansen trains in Japan. These are the so-called bullet trains that regularly travel at 200 mph. The reason these trains travel so fast is not because of the technology involved in the acceleration; it is actually because of the innovations in *braking*. The brakes aren't there to make the train constantly go slower; they are there to enable the train to travel faster! Similarly, properly implemented information security controls can be a business enabler rather than a hindrance. Good brakes empower faster trains.

Do you have any favorite books to recommend for people who want to lead cybersecurity teams?

The Woman Who Smashed Codes by Jason Fagone. This is the incredible story of Elizebeth Smith Friedman, who helped start what we now call the NSA and was an absolute badass.

Cult of the Dead Cow: How the Original Hacking Supergroup Might Just Save the World by Joseph Menn. This is an absolutely compelling tale about one of the most influential hacking groups ever.

Sandworm: A New Era of Cyberwar and the Hunt for the Kremlin's Most Dangerous Hackers by Andy Greenberg. This has incredible in-depth reporting on nation-state activity.

Dark Territory: The Secret History of Cyber War by Fred Kaplan. Basically this is a textbook on the newest realm of warfare.

The Hitchhiker's Guide to the Galaxy by Douglas Adams. It's still one of the funniest sci-fi books ever written.

I tend to choose my reading materials based on what I see on InfoSec Twitter. This probably explains why all my recommendations are InfoSec-related!

"I've only learned recently that it has become really valuable for me to give myself time to allow the creative process to happen."

Twitter: @s7ephen • **Website:** about.me/s7ephen

Stephen A. Ridley

42

Stephen A. Ridley is a security researcher with more than 15 years of experience in software development, software security, and reverse engineering. Within the last few years, he has presented his research and spoken about reverse engineering and software security research on every continent except Antarctica. Stephen and his work have been featured on NPR and NBC and in *The Wall Street Journal*, *The New York Times*, *Wired*, *The Washington Post*, *Fast Company*, *VentureBeat*, *Slashdot*, *The Register*, and other publications.

Stephen has authored a number of information security articles and cowritten several texts, the most recent of which is *Android Hacker's Handbook*, published by John Wiley & Sons. Stephen has guest lectured at NYU, Rensselaer Polytechnic Institute (RPI), Dartmouth, and other universities on the subjects of software exploitation and reverse engineering.

In late 2019 Stephen became adjunct professor of Hardware & Software Exploitation at the NYU Tandon School of Engineering in New York, an NSA Center of Academic Excellence in Cyber Operations. Stephen has served on the programming/

review committees of USENIX WOOT, Securing Smart Cities, BuildItSecure.ly, and others Stephen also serves on the board of IndySci.org, a California nonprofit devoted to making "open source" pharmaceuticals a reality.

Do you believe there is a massive shortage of career cybersecurity professionals?

This is really a tough one. I go back and forth on this. Companies and governments definitely need higher-quality cybersecurity professionals, but I sometimes wonder where that demand is coming from. I am sure there was a healthy demand for talented farriers (the people who make horseshoes) right up to a time when the first automobiles were being delivered to early adopters.

In a lot of organizations, the status quo is to just throw money and bodies at a problem, but this doesn't necessarily mean that the problem demands either of those...the problem may just need clever solutions. Clever solutions come from really passionate (and/or smart) people creating things. I'm not really sure if we need more cybersecurity professionals or just more of the existing professionals focusing on creating solutions.

Social media certainly isn't helping. It rewards people who haven't actually done "the things." It rewards people who say they have done "the things." This is an epidemic for a number of industries, InfoSec included. It is unfortunate because if the skills gap and the shortage is in fact real, then it comes at a time when the supply of competent people is *also* actually a bit diluted with noise.

What's the most important decision you've made or action you've taken related to a business risk?

I am technical, and I like creating things. So most of the recent business risks I have had to take in the last few years (as a founder) have mostly involved trying to balance two things: running the business and finding time to be creative and focus on the very projects (and "art") that created the business to begin with. The hardest part for me about this balancing process is that oftentimes the creative process actually includes things like procrastination and boredom, but I'm conditioned to believe that "downtime" like that is actually counterproductive. I've only learned recently that it has become really valuable for me to give myself time to allow the creative process to happen. This includes allowing myself to "play" around on the computer by doing small technical things that may not have a direct line to the task. It is often during these moments that the epiphany comes about how to leapfrog to your mission objective.

How do you make hard decisions? Do you find yourself more often making people, process, or technology decisions?

Hard decisions are hard. Perhaps the hardest thing about hard decisions is that you can't hide from them. You can't delegate them away. You can't procrastinate them. Jeff Bezos has a great quote about this: "Stress primarily comes from not taking action over something you can have some control over." This (I think) is also why hard decisions are so stressful. While you are deliberating, the clock is ticking, and you still haven't taken action. Finally, I think the worst thing about hard decisions is that they isolate you. And this is where things can get negative. It is very easy to begin spiraling once you are stressed and struggling with something that keeps you isolated. So, the best thing I have learned to do is to have great advisers, friends, and colleagues I can safely share things with to help me work through.

What's something that you struggle with as a leader and how do you overcome that?

Acting as CEO of a venture-backed technology startup was the biggest challenge of my career (and my life of recent memory). I struggled a lot with Intentionally taking the time to do the kinds of things that rejuvenate me professionally (research, development, tinkering, etc.). These things seemed less relevant to the immediate needs of the startup, so I triaged them away, but what I didn't take into consideration was how those very things stoked my optimism. They kept me engaged in the subject matter. Without that time to "play," I was grinding metal-on-metal without any lubrication.

How do you lead your team to execute and get results?

I was fortunate that my most recent team and those of the past were technical. Furthermore, I was fortunate that all my colleagues somewhat respected my abilities. This made my job easier. What I really struggled with was working with team members who weren't "my people." It is easy to get along with people who come from the same "tribe" (similar humor, understanding, worldview), but I had to learn a bit about how to work with people outside my tribe. That was difficult, and I am still learning.

Do you have a workforce philosophy or unique approach to talent acquisition?

I believe that if you treat people like adults, you'll have the best results. I tend to not micromanage, or "hover." I prefer to treat team members like equals. I think this is because most of my career I have worked in "think tank," "skunkworks" teams that are small but highly skilled and specialized. So, I prefer to just review the objective with everyone, make sure they have what they need, and then let them get to work. But, that said, the hardest part of doing things this way is that you have to get very good at firing at the first sign that your style is being taken advantage of. I have historically not been good at this and had people take severe advantage of this. It is always extremely disappointing when you realize that people are taking advantage of the freedom you yourself would want to be given in the workplace.

Have you created a cohesive strategy for your information security program or business unit?

I hail from the R&D side of InfoSec, so the hammer doesn't fall on me for these kinds of things.

That said, as a consultant, I often helped companies fix or architect away these things. The three most important things in that capacity seem to be competence, situational awareness, and boldness. You need at least one person in a position of prominence who is deeply competent but also situationally aware enough to see when things are off course. They also need to be bold enough to say something about it and use their competence to suggest a solution. Every organization is different, but as a consultant, where I saw the healthiest programs was where there was a person of prominence with those three characteristics...and also where this role was mostly "left alone" and not so mired with day-to-day operations that their heads-up situational awareness subsequently suffered.

What are your communication tips for interacting with executive leadership?

This is an interesting one. I don't know how to articulate the nugget at the root of my answer to this question, so I will beat around the bush...Miyamoto Musashi is the author of a book called *The Book of the Five Rings*. Musashi was the self-taught swordsman who eschewed formal swordsmanship and pioneered his own style. He traveled around Japan defeating the masters of each prestigious school of swordsmanship in duels to the death. To add insult to injury, he won all those duels using wooden practice swords against his opponents' priceless razorsharp steel.

I can't articulate what I mean, so I offer this: communicating with competent and high-quality executive leadership is what I imagine swordsman duels to be like. No frills. Concise, sharp, and straight to the point. But you also don't need fancy sword lessons or expensive swords to be a great swordsman.

How do you cultivate productive relationships with your boss, peers, direct reports, and other team members?
I actually learned this by observing one of my advisers. Whenever interacting with him, I noticed I always felt like he was "sneaking away" to give me more time than he gave everyone else. He always made time for me. Then I realized that it was virtually impossible that he was giving just me so much time; he just had a magic way of making people feel as though he was giving them this time. Ever since I started trying to model my interactions with people based on his ways, my work and personal relationships improved quite a bit.

Have you encountered challenges collaborating with revenue-generating teams like sales and product development?
This actually harkens back to my earlier point about "different tribes." It can be easy to interact with people from the same "tribe," but for an organization to succeed, it (much like a biological organism) needs to have different parts that specialize in different things. The mistake I made as a founder was assuming that "sales guys" had to be from a different "tribe." In reality, this is not true. You can find "your people" in a whole series of disciplines. The challenging part (especially for a startup and a founder) is finding those people in a timely fashion. This latter point I can't recommend anything for...I still struggle with this.

Have you encountered challenges collaborating with technology teams like information technology and software development?
Many years ago as a mid-20-something researcher at McAfee, I sat in the office of the CTO.

When not auditing the code of all the McAfee products with my research partners, Mark Dowd and Brandon Edwards, I had to advise the CTO on technical due diligence for acquisitions. So I had to interface with *a lot* of different parts of the organization within McAfee and without. Even at an InfoSec company like McAfee, security can be high friction to the needs of the organization. For example, at best, code auditors can only slow things down and deliver bad news.

So I think I learned the most about how to handle this when I was building a team at my startup. Information security is actually quite a bit more multidisciplinary than many may give it credit for.

There are so many great specialties within InfoSec that can be leveraged to interface (as an InfoSec company) with the real world. For example, the social engineering InfoSec types may make great salespeople. The extraverted "con scene" kind of people make really good sales engineers, consultants, and customer-facing subject-matter experts. Researchers can do everything from being content marketing engineers (blogposts, videos, published research) to VP of engineering, VP of research, or VP of product. Within InfoSec alone, we actually have a wealth of diverse personalities and disciplines to pull from.

Also, at the end of the day, smart people can do whatever they set their minds to, so never underestimate what smart members of your team can do.

Do you have any favorite books to recommend for people who want to lead cybersecurity teams?
I am actually a reluctant leader, so I may not be the best person to ask this question. I didn't ever want to start companies or lead anyone. I just wanted to do "the thing," and starting a company or rallying a group of people to help out was the only way to do it at any appreciable scale. So, I cannot recommend any great books about leadership, since I never really sought it or studied up on it. I think if I had to summarize the single most influential advice I have ever read on the topic, it was a quote that said: "Never send someone to charge over a hill you wouldn't yourself charge over." I think the kind of people who are worth working with are also the kind of people who don't seek to be led. They just follow their minds and their hearts to work on something that they deem of value. In that way, you are all working collaboratively on the same effort, and they "follow" you simply because you started marching toward the objective first, and they trust you not to send them on a fool's errand.

"I care deeply about the people I manage, and I want to see them happy, supported, and developing well, but this does take significant time."

Twitter: @davidrook • **Website:** securityleadership.ninja

David Rook

David Rook is the European security lead at Riot Games. He has worked in technology for 18 years and in the information security space full-time since 2006. Before moving into the computer games industry, David held various application security roles in the financial services industry. He has presented at leading information security conferences, including DEF CON and RSA.

43

Do you believe there is a massive shortage of career cybersecurity professionals?

I think the answer to this question is that it depends on what you're looking for. I do think we have a shortage of experienced (10+ years' experience) individual contributors and leaders but not of cybersecurity professionals. Cybersecurity Is still quite a young profession, so that's to be expected and something current leaders in this space should be focused on addressing.

I feel we're currently seeing more young people than ever interested in and studying toward becoming a cybersecurity professional. What we need to see is more leaders willing to give these people a chance without ridiculous requirements and expectations in job descriptions.

I also believe most hiring managers and leaders fail to look outside of the obvious pools of talent when hiring. If you understand the traits that are important in cybersecurity professionals, you can find them in people in every area of tech if you put the time into looking. My current team is a 50/50 split between those who had jobs in this industry before we hired them and those who didn't. We've hired excellent cybersecurity professionals from networking, IT, and software engineering backgrounds.

How do you make hard decisions? Do you find yourself more often making people, process, or technology decisions?

In an ideal world, I prefer to take time to think a lot about hard decisions I have to make. I prefer to collect all of the relevant information and speak to key people who can add additional context for me. Once I've got all of that, then I mainly just think multiple options over in my own head until I feel I've narrowed it down to the best one or two options. I'll often then share my thoughts with a few colleagues whose opinions I really respect before communicating my decision. I never like to rush hard decisions, so where possible I'll take as much time as I think is needed to consider options. We obviously don't live in an ideal world, though! At a recent large live event for my employers, I had to make some hard decisions about a core part of the event with very little time (I was in bed when I was called to help with this problem!). I still largely followed the same approach but with a more condensed timeline. I gathered all the people who could help troubleshoot and provide more context, and I found a quiet corner in the venue to think over the options before sharing my thoughts with a couple of senior leaders to get their thoughts.

My decisions nowadays tend to be process and people focused. I do provide input on technology decisions on a daily basis, but I defer to those closer to the problem than myself where I can.

What's something that you struggle with as a leader, and how do you overcome that?

This question is an easy one to answer but one I still struggle with. I moved into a people manager and leadership role at the same time, and I've often struggled with where to spend my time. I care deeply about the people I manage, and I want to see them happy, supported, and developing well, but this does take significant time. I find that some people will take more and more time without ever considering the impact on my day or plans. As a leader, I'm the one who needs to learn to say no more and offer an alternative time to chat or meet if it's not convenient.

I've found that explaining to my team what I'm actually working on and the deadlines I have helps with this. I also take advantage of flexible working hours and working from home to make sure I get the time I need to do work.

How do you lead your team to execute and get results?
I make sure my team sees the real me and not some manager/ leader act I've seen others put on. I focus on building positive relationships with the people I lead and ensure that they understand I care about them and actively support their development. If people feel psychologically safe and supported, they are able to perform at their best. Relationship building outside of my immediate team is also vital to ensure that we know what the business is doing and what they need from us, and it's an opportunity to champion our efforts.

Have you created a cohesive strategy for your information security program or business unit?
I've created and championed several important security strategies in the six years at Riot Games. My first strategy was for the application security program, and I spent a lot of time understanding the needs of the company before writing it. In this case, I spent time speaking to security and technology leadership to understand the goals of the product and discipline I was part of. This progressed to me meeting software engineers and product leads of key products to understand their goals and needs from security. This allowed me to develop and publish a strategy that launched an application security program that was aligned with the security and technology goals of the company. The strategy and vision for this team has been revisited over the years to ensure that this continues to be the case.

When I was writing our European security strategy, I iterated on this approach and spoke with many more people. I spoke with country managers, product leads, and individual contributors across Europe from every business unit we have. I could only create an impactful strategy by understanding their goals and needs.

What are your communication tips for interacting with executive leadership?

Understand what they care about in their role and in turn what they need to know about cybersecurity and how it impacts that. I think it's also important to tailor your messaging based on their view of the world and what they care about. You will often need to drop the technical jargon and description of issues, be factual, and drop a lot of the hype around problems. I've found that giving a high-level description of your concerns, the impact on a product/business, and an explanation of what you need from them works well.

How do you cultivate productive relationships with your boss, peers, direct reports, and other team members?

Be genuine, factual, and vulnerable. This has allowed me to create good relationships with people at every level in an organization. When it comes to the people I manage, I try to ensure that they understand where I see them fitting into the bigger picture, the value they deliver right now, and where they can grow going forward. If people feel you're supporting them and helping them progress, they'll go to great lengths to meet your expectations and deliver value for cybersecurity and the company.

Do you have any favorite books to recommend for people who want to lead cybersecurity teams?

- *The Leadership Pipeline* by Ram Charan, Stephen Drotter, and Jim Noel is a book that a friend gave me before I even became a leader. It's a book I feel all leaders should read, as it helps you understand how to identify and grow future leaders.
- *The Culture Map* by Erin Meyer is a fantastic book that will arm you with the knowledge you need to factor in cultural differences in your leadership role. It is easy to make mistakes when your worldview is limited to your own culture and experiences.
- *Leading Snowflakes* by Oren Ellenbogen is my final recommendation. It helped me make the transition from being a security engineer to being a security leader with people management responsibilities. It helped me figure out what my days should look like and how to redefine value/good work in my mind. It's a must-read for anyone making the transition from a purely technical role to one where you manage and develop others.

> "For me, on-the-job training is the best learning experience you can ever get, and I am lucky to work with leaders and in an environment that allows me to do so."

Twitter: @marfa_27 • **Websites:** www.linkedin.com/in/segalmarina and www.security-diva.com

Marina Segal

Marina Segal is the head of product management for cloud secops and compliance at Check Point Software Technologies.

Marina is focused on delivering cloud security and compliance products and has more than 13 years of global experience in security, compliance, and governance with Deloitte and other high-tech companies. She is the founder of WoSec and Bay Area Branch (formerly the Security Diva group), which promotes women in security and technology.

Marina has a bachelor of science degree in information systems and management and a master of business administration degree in technology, innovation, and entrepreneurship from Tel Aviv University.

44

Do you believe there is a massive shortage of career cybersecurity professionals?

Since we are part of a major digital transformation, there is an absolute need to ensure that all the newest technologies are protected. Since technological changes are happening as we speak, naturally we are in constant need of professionals who can secure all the innovation in healthcare, IoT, consumer business, and any other sector that affects our lives.

What's the most important decision you've made or action you've taken related to a business risk?

As part of my role as a product manager, I was involved in the M&A process. Being able to affect company decisions to invest or not to invest in another business involves a lot of steps, and I was only part of one aspect in this deal. My recommendation was to buy, and I chose it based on thorough data analysis, several discussions with relevant stakeholders, and of course a gut feeling that this was the right thing to do.

How do you make hard decisions? Do you find yourself more often making people, process, or technology decisions?

As part of my role, I often find myself making process and technology decisions. I usually try not to decide on a clear timeline for the decision-making process; I gather as much data as possible, consult with a few people that I believe have similar previous experience, think about the possible outcomes, and trust my intuition to make the right decision. I also strongly believe that in many cases, making any decision is much better than not making one and having to continue with ambiguity.

> I also strongly believe that in many cases, making any decision is much better than not making one and having to continue with ambiguity.

What's something that you struggle with as a leader and how do you overcome that?

Product management is one of the most challenging roles in the tech industry, and being 2.5 years into this role (after 12+ years spent mostly in various risk management and security capacities) makes me feel that I still have a long, long learning path ahead of me. For me, on-the-job training is the best learning experience you can ever get, and I am lucky to work with leaders and in an environment that allows me to do so.

How do you lead your team to execute and get results?

I let my team decide where they want to spend most of their time, since I strongly believe that if you enjoy what you are doing, that is where the motivation comes from. I also tend to give challenging tasks and let my team "figure it out" before I get involved so they can get out of their comfort zone and shine.

Do you have a workforce philosophy or unique approach to talent acquisition?

During the interviewing process, I do some technical and personality tests, but the most significant factor definitely includes soft skills that align with team/company culture.

What are your communication tips for interacting with executive leadership?

Transparency and no sugar-coating.

How do you cultivate productive relationships with your boss, peers, direct reports, and other team members?

Say whatever you mean and make sure to ask silly questions.

Have you encountered challenges collaborating with revenue-generating teams like sales and product development?

My approach is to understand the goals, the challenges, and the main drivers for these teams. Try to find out how you can make them successful and be sure you communicate any roadblocks up front.

Have you encountered challenges collaborating with technology teams like information technology and software development?

Yes, collaboration with R&D and IT can be challenging. My approach is to talk to a person first, get to know each other, and understand what drives each team member. Once you know all these, finding compromises will be much, much simpler.

Do you have any favorite books to recommend for people who want to lead cybersecurity teams?

How to Measure Anything in Cybersecurity Risk by Douglas W. Hubbard and Richard Seiersen.

"Managing hackers is hard work! But the results are worth it."

Twitter: @sehnaoui • **Websites:** www.khalilsehnaoui.com and en.wikipedia.org/wiki/Khalil_Sehnaoui

Khalil Sehnaoui

45 Khalil is a Belgian-Lebanese information security consultant and hacker who specializes in the Middle East, and he is the founder of Krypton Security, an InfoSec firm that helps test companies' security strengths, weaknesses, and loopholes.

He is also a member of the Chaos Computer Club (CCC), Europe's largest association of hackers, and was featured in *The Guardian*'s video series "The Power of Privacy" as well as on National Geographic's *Breakthrough*, in an episode called "Cyber-Terror."

Do you believe there is a massive shortage of career cybersecurity professionals?

There are certainly not enough information security experts in the labor market today. This is mainly because it is still a fairly new domain and many young people don't really know what it is about or are more attracted by app development. More importantly, there are not enough structured curriculums at universities. Information security expertise is as much about having some academic knowledge as it is about experience. It should also be noted that to be really good at InfoSec, you need to have a passion for it and

> Information security expertise is as much about having some academic knowledge as it is about experience.

also what I would call the "hacker mindset"—patience and an avidity to learn. We should encourage people by making some of the InfoSec conferences accessible, not only to a limited few but also to those who are curious about it and have never really thought they could make a career out of it.

What's the most important decision you've made or action you've taken related to a business risk?

Well, that would be starting my own business (Krypton Security, based in Lebanon) with my partner, Cyrus Salesse (who also took the same risk as myself), especially in an area of the world where information security awareness is still in its infancy. Most companies in the MENA region are still struggling with the idea that InfoSec should be considered a main part of their security posture and spending. Most of these countries do not yet have defined rules and regulations about information security. I chose that path because I saw a void in that area, and even though I knew we would be struggling in the beginning, and still are to this day, I wanted to build tenure and be ready for when consciousness around information security started to develop. I also felt, and still feel, that sharing my skills and knowledge (mainly gained outside of home) with my country was the right thing to do. In more general terms and relating to everyday business life, classic risk management tells us to minimize and mitigate business risk. However, in my view, being prepared for any eventuality is the most important factor in risk management.

How do you make hard decisions? Do you find yourself more often making people, process, or technology decisions?

The how depends a lot on the topic—sometimes alone but often with some teamwork and collaboration with the people involved in the decision's subject and repercussions.

Making decisions is the hardest when it comes to people in my experience. There is usually no easy answer. But nowadays, most decisions involve all of the above—that is, technology, people, and process—and it is becoming increasingly more difficult to separate them.

What's something that you struggle with as a leader and how do you overcome that?

I think one of the most difficult parts of the job is being able to pay enough attention and work on strategic issues as well as daily operational issues—not always easy. Also knowing when to delegate and to whom is tough, and I have learned that by trial and error mostly. The hardest thing is to always remember that to be a good leader, you have to lead by example, and that requires a lot of discipline that, as a hacker, I have to admit I never really mastered. This is why I rely a lot on my partner and friend Cyrus's experience and skills.

As for the most challenging role, certainly it has been about being/becoming an entrepreneur versus an employee.

How do you lead your team to execute and get results?

There is a distinction between leadership and management. Both are required, but they are not the same. To get people to do something specific, you need good management skills. Getting people to take the ball and run in a particular direction without you having to manage them in my view is leadership. The latter requires excellent communication skills to convey a vision and to motivate people. Management requires more managerial tools, such as planning, tracking, and control.

I try to contribute on an individual level to execution as much as time allows, if only to get a feel of the team and what they are going through on a daily basis on the ground—that will help me make more informed managerial and leadership decisions.

Do you have a workforce philosophy or unique approach to talent acquisition?

There are a number of key elements in selecting a person to work with or for you. In fact, one of the questions I ask myself when interviewing a candidate is, "Would you work with/for this person, or would you want this person working for you?" This is independent of any technical skills that the person may possess. The answer is often quite revealing. I also look for the passion I talked about and for the willingness to learn. You don't need to hire someone who is already at the peak of their technical talent, but if someone has the right mindset and the curiosity to learn, as well as a solid base, then they can be on the way to becoming a great asset to any team.

I think the key elements are more often cultural than technical. There has to be a compatible chemistry between the person and the work environment. It is even more difficult if the environment is multicultural/multilingual and even more so in an information security environment, where people often have different skills and mindsets. Managing hackers is hard work! But the results are worth it.

Have you created a cohesive strategy for your information security program or business unit?
We are in the business of information security, so we try not to be like the "shoemaker's children." (There is an old proverb about a shoemaker who was busy making shoes for his customers. However, he was so busy keeping them happy that his wife and children went shoeless.) The moral of the story is that we should not neglect ourselves or those around us—families or staff—while we care for others. So we try to structure our programs and business units in a way that takes into account everyone that is part of our company (or family).

Furthermore, given certain required certifications in the industry, we are obliged to meet certain standards. But it is not always perfect, as you might imagine.

What are your communication tips for interacting with executive leadership?
There is always an element of time constraint with executives. One has to know or learn how to get the message across, provide the required information, and help the executive understand what they need to know to make a decision—and all of this in the shortest amount of time possible.

My method is generally to put myself in the shoes of the executive and see how I would react to what I have to say to them. This is often my starting point.

How do you cultivate productive relationships with your boss, peers, direct reports, and other team members?
In one word, good communication. But there is something to be said about the information security field where all team members usually already share similar values and

passions. That makes it easy to cultivate relationships. In any given InfoSec conference, you will not be able to tell the difference between different members of a team, which is because they all melt together in one huge pot of hackers who are all indistinguishable from each other. So yes, good communication is paramount, but we are lucky to be in a field where it is more often than not amicable, and hence productive relationships already exist before someone even joins a team.

Have you encountered challenges collaborating with revenue-generating teams like sales and product development?

I think my approach is the same as my earlier response. Put yourself in their shoes to be able to collaborate via understanding.

Have you encountered challenges collaborating with technology teams like information technology and software development?

Not really, at least as teams...perhaps with individuals, such as those who are so caught up in the technical aspects that they cannot or do not wish to see the consequences for the business or other aspects of the mission. When this is the case, it becomes more difficult and requires more time and effort.

Do you have any favorite books to recommend for people who want to lead cybersecurity teams?

I cannot say that a particular book comes to mind. Obviously, one could cite all the self-teaching books about leadership, but in our world I think a good leader must lead by example and respect as well as be respected by his peers. That is enough to lead and, more importantly, be followed. That cannot be taught by a book.

I guess everyone defines "worthwhile reading" material differently. In my case, I enjoy reading books or material about the subjects that interest me and always need to learn something from the book I'm reading. I do not really enjoy just a good story; I need to take something useful away from my readings. So, it could be any subject on the spectrum of things I love or would like to learn more about, from lock picking to quantum theories and a lot of things in between!

"I adapt my style of leadership to the situation at hand. I attempt to distinguish whether instructing, coaching, supporting, or delegating is the best response at any given moment."

Twitter: @find_evil • **Websites:** www.spyglassltd.com and www.linkedin.com/in/FindEvil

Jackie Singh

Jackie Singh is the founder of Spyglass Security, a consultancy specializing in helping businesses develop and implement effective cybersecurity strategy.

46

Jackie became a Linux enthusiast at age 12 and became deeply involved in the world of hacking, eventually leading her to become an information security professional. Her most recent roles have led her to serve as principal consultant at Mandiant/FireEye, as global director of incident response at Intel Security/McAfee, and as a senior manager at Accenture.

Prior to her work in the commercial sector, Jackie served in the U.S. Army and spent several years in the Middle East and Africa working on technical projects.

Do you believe there is a massive shortage of career cybersecurity professionals?
The supposed gap between the raw availability of qualified information security professionals and increasing numbers of

cybersecurity jobs is overblown. Instead of a skills gap, I believe what we're actually experiencing is a misalignment between the true requirements of organizations, how those needs are represented outwardly to the marketplace, and the types of training available for job seekers.

Companies rarely dig deep to validate role requirements. This often creates a mismatch between actual roles and their descriptions. Job descriptions with incorrect or vague requirements can drive job seekers to consider training that may not be the most appropriate to support their actual chances of getting hired. Companies also often do not budget appropriately for the professional development of employees. Internal training teams are rare, concerted efforts to build internal training programs are few and far between, and external training programs are often criticized for their high costs in terms of both pricing and time away from the job. If you can't train an employee, you'll be incentivized to try to identify candidates who already have all the skills you need, which puts you at a severe disadvantage as the hiring manager and disincentivizes potentially qualified candidates from applying.

It's best not to open a new position to solve a problem if other members of the security operations team can develop a new skill or if a motivated employee from the IT department can gain a new responsibility and serve as a useful bridge to SecOps. Often, the need to hire a new employee can be shelved in favor of building or improving processes. Organizations sometimes prioritize technology as a "magic bullet" and fail to plan for staffing altogether, draining budget that could have been used for training or hiring.

The best answers for closing these gaps are more deeply embedded within the true needs of the organization, so my advice is to make sure you know what those are and align them well to your roles and job descriptions before making staffing decisions.

> Organizations sometimes prioritize technology as a "magic bullet" and fail to plan for staffing altogether, draining budget that could have been used for training or hiring.

How do you make hard decisions? Do you find yourself more often making people, process, or technology decisions?

Developing a personal library of decision-making models (for example, the Pareto principle) has been valuable for me over the past few years to support the data needed to answer difficult decisions well. Models help simplify and organize and are pragmatic. While they don't provide answers on their own, models help us structure chaos and reduce complexity by concentrating on what is most important.

I find technology decisions are often more straightforward than those involving people or process, which are more critical to get right and take more time to understand.

How do you lead your team to execute and get results?

I adapt my style of leadership to the situation at hand. I attempt to distinguish whether instructing, coaching, supporting, or delegating is the best response at any given moment. This follows the Hersey-Blanchard model for situational leadership, which suggests employees should be led in such a way that managers become superfluous. This means leading generously, sharing knowledge openly, and trusting the team to perform.

This is also similar to the way I contribute as an individual by maintaining flexibility and continually seeking the best collaborative approach.

Do you have a workforce philosophy or unique approach to talent acquisition?

Treat information security talent like any other talent. Have respect for the unique approaches that diverse individuals and their experiences can bring to your organization. Compensate them fairly and equally.

Have you created a cohesive strategy for your information security program or business unit?

Developing a diplomatic approach is critical for any leader. While your team is critical to the functioning of your program, you won't get it off the ground and continue to grow its scope and budget unless you are skilled at the art of obtaining buy-in from executive staff, other critical pillars/junctures within your organization, and your peers.

Finding out more about the day-to-day business and responsibilities of other teams outside of security will improve your ability to find areas of mutual interest, which are critical to advancing your team's agenda.

What are your communication tips for interacting with executive leadership?
My most helpful communication tip is to cut down any information that isn't necessary to understand the big picture of what you are attempting to convey. Tailoring your message for an executive audience means limiting technical detail and elevating the most important statistics.

It is also important to distinguish problems from opportunities and to show you know the difference.

How do you cultivate productive relationships with your boss, peers, direct reports, and other team members?
The human side of this work is often overlooked. Seemingly small actions, such as ensuring that credit is given when due, recognizing hard work, being giving of your time to share knowledge, or getting in touch if you suspect someone is going through a hard time can go a long way toward creating lasting relationships.

This is a small industry, and you are likely to run into the same people again and again over the course of your career.

Have you encountered challenges collaborating with revenue-generating teams like sales and product development?
I encourage you to try to identify areas of mutual interest. Understanding other teams' definition of success is valuable information you can use to help drive outcomes.

Have you encountered challenges collaborating with technology teams like information technology and software development?
IT and development teams don't have a great grasp on security. Leaders who can reduce complexity, keep their ego in check, and provide supportive reassurance will be most successful in working with teams with competing priorities. We're all in this together.

"The cold, hard reality is that one or two talented folks and some automation tooling could easily replace a SOC or security department of a dozen people who have no clue what they're doing."

Twitter: @viss • **Website:** phobos.io

Dan Tentler

Dan Tentler is the executive founder of Phobos Group. He has a long history of both attack and defense roles, as well as public speaking engagements and press interviews. Dan has made a name for himself and Phobos Group by approaching security from an entirely new direction, resulting in routine discoveries that have had a major impact on customers as well as the greater security landscape.

47

Do you believe there is a massive shortage of career cybersecurity professionals?

I think that there are several moving parts here and that it is not as simple as "there aren't enough people." I think that the influx of candidates who are comfortable being dishonest when representing themselves and their abilities is polluting the job market. I also think that recruiters are amplifying this problem by forcing unqualified people into positions that require experience, and I also believe that businesses are happy to hire people who have little to no experience and call them "seniors," because the vast majority of businesses in the United States are, for some reason, comfortable putting their safety and well-being into the hands of dilettantes.

It is unfortunate when businesses elect to take the "Whatever, we're insured" or "We'll just do the absolute bare minimum that the compliance statutes require of us and not a hair more" path. All of this results in a situation where businesses "can't seem to find enough talented people" and will complain about that. The cold, hard reality is that one or two talented folks and some automation tooling could easily replace a SOC or security department of a dozen people who have no clue what they're doing because they paid some guy in India to take their OSCP exam for them or bought a CISSP boot camp so that they could get past the HR firewall and land a job they aren't qualified for to work for an organization that only cares about doing whatever the bare minimum is to make the auditors go away for another year. Changing this means a massive, fundamental change in how security is conducted, and it starts with throwing away the status quo, which won't be comfortable for everyone playing security theater.

What's the most important decision you've made or action you've taken related to a business risk?

Almost every other startup founder has told me horror stories about taking VC money. I think we dodged a bullet by not seeking funding out of the gate, and this keeps getting reinforced every time I hear about another startup who took funding and fizzled out or got "acqui-hired" or otherwise didn't get where they wanted to go.

How do you make hard decisions? Do you find yourself more often making people, process, or technology decisions?

It took me literally years to rewire my brain. The only way to get things done is to presume that the folks you're working with are adults and will behave appropriately. Sometimes hard decisions have to be made, and the wrong choice will devastatingly hurt your business. You just have to be okay with telling people things that suck sometimes.

What's something that you struggle with as a leader and how do you overcome that?

They say never hire your friends. I didn't believe that saying. I was wrong.

How do you lead your team to execute and get results?

Setting goals and objectives with deadlines in plain English. Make it simple for everybody, and make it clear and easy to understand. Being part of a small company means wearing lots of hats, so just being clear and communicating well applies no matter what the job is.

Do you have a workforce philosophy or unique approach to talent acquisition?

Referring to the first question, we've found it challenging finding honest candidates. The signal to noise ratio is terrible. The "right people," when presented with the work we do, will find it fulfilling and interesting, so that part is handled.

Have you created a cohesive strategy for your information security program or business unit?

Yes. Taking into account the sentiments from folks like Haroon Meer and Alex Stamos, the enemy of productivity is complexity, so we're redefining security by throwing away all the fluff and complexity added by companies that exist only so that those companies can sell the "decoder ring" to solve that complexity. Fortunately, as a security consulting firm, our corporate strategy is pretty straightforward: do what makes the customers happy and improves their security posture!

What are your communication tips for interacting with executive leadership?

Get to the point, and decide what is important. Surface problems and concerns early; be prepared to make hard decisions. I'm the executive founder, so from where I sit, my communication strategy is essentially the same for everybody.

How do you cultivate productive relationships with your boss, peers, direct reports, and other team members?

Find out what folks are interested in. Encourage people to adopt hobbies. Talk to folks about their hobbies. Avoid playing devil's advocate all the time, and avoid being snarky all the time. Constant, persistent contrarianism makes people think you have a terrible attitude, and attitude counts for everything.

Do you have any favorite books to recommend for people who want to lead cybersecurity teams?

Yeah, but they're all sysadmin books. I feel strongly that if you have no idea how a system works at all, you are going to be a terrible defender or attacker. Understanding the systems you want to either attack or defend is a critical prerequisite.

"The company I work for has a 'people-first' culture with the belief that if you take care of your people, they will take care of you, you will see results, and you will have a successful team. I believe in this philosophy too."

Twitter: @eugeneteo • **Websites:** www.linkedin.com/in/eugeneteo and www.temasek.org

Eugene Teo

48

Eugene Teo is a seasoned information security leader with extensive experience in building information security programs and leading global security teams. Possessing both entrepreneurship spirit and drive, Eugene works with technology companies to develop their security capabilities in the Asia-Pacific region. He is a senior director at a U.S.-based software-as-a-service company. They brought him in to build and mature their global threat detection and incident response capabilities. Eugene is best known for his past contributions to the security of the Linux kernel. Eugene has been interviewed in the media, has spoken at security conferences, has mentored security professionals, and has advised technology startups.

Do you believe there is a massive shortage of career cybersecurity professionals?

Cybersecurity professionals with a strong technical background and high-value skills are in short supply. Depending on where you are, the skill set of the talent pool may skew toward where most of the security jobs are.

Singapore is home to a large number of regional headquarters for some of the largest global companies in the world. Most of the security job opportunities are in the area of compliance, audit, and consulting. If you are building a team that focuses on niche areas such as vulnerability research and malware reverse engineering, you will draw from a limited applicant pool. You may even have to hire from abroad!

When I was building a security R&D center at my previous company, we had to hire very technical security engineers to work on our security detection technologies. It was incredibly challenging to find the right people with the right skills and experience. One way to overcome this issue is to look for nonsecurity professionals whose skills are transferable and who have a strong passion for cybersecurity. One of my successful hires was a software engineer who developed microscopy software modules for cameras. With great work and commitment, he developed new skills to analyze spams and phishing emails for improving our email security detection technologies.

A diverse workforce helps to bring in new ideas and different perspectives. It can also help to overcome the talent shortage that our industry is experiencing.

> A diverse workforce helps to bring in new ideas and different perspectives.

How do you make hard decisions? Do you find yourself more often making people, process, or technology decisions?

One thing I have learned about leading teams is that you need to develop metrics right from the outset. You need to understand your team's work and its performance in a way that is measurable so that you can demonstrate ongoing proof of value to the business. It would help if you also had indicators to highlight potential risks that may impact the business goals and initiatives. Use business-relevant metrics that are tied to your strategic objectives so that you can use them to guide informed decisions or drive continuous improvements. Let the numbers do the talking.

What's something that you struggle with as a leader and how do you overcome that?

Through an executive presence program at work, I learned that sometimes we might be perceived differently from our intentions even if they are right. Executive presence is all about my ability to inspire confidence and to exude authority at work. I became conscious of how I demonstrate my personality in the way I carry myself. Fortunately, executive presence is a skill that I can strengthen through practice. I have to also work on my people-oriented leadership skills so that I can build lasting relationships with my team.

Do you have a workforce philosophy or unique approach to talent acquisition?

In an employees' market, I prefer to take a proactive approach when it comes to acquiring talent. I can get a better feel of the market. I can also reduce the time to hire. I have a bias for this approach partly because I have successfully built my dream team twice this way.

When it comes to hiring, I look for honesty, passion, and aptitude. I also look for integrity and a reasonably good technical background. These qualities apply to people managers too. I believe that to have motivated and engaged employees at work, managers and leaders need to have a sound technical background. You will make better decisions and be a role model for your team. You will also have better employee retention.

The company I work for has a "people-first" culture with the belief that if you take care of your people, they will take care of you, you will see results, and you will have a successful team. I believe in this philosophy too.

Have you created a cohesive strategy for your information security program or business unit?

We used a variation of objectives and key results (OKRs) to develop goals and milestones that align with our organizational objectives and initiatives. We share the progress of our OKRs at our quarterly business reviews. I find this an excellent way to communicate our strategy and have everyone on the same page. It is also easy for everyone to know what is important and how our work contributes to our success.

What are your communication tips for interacting with executive leadership?

Know your leaders and frame your conversations accordingly. Be specific and consistent but not overly detailed. Nobody enjoys one-way communication. Always provide a context so that they know what you are trying to convey. Speak in their language. Use layman's terms and avoid technical speak unless they come from a technical background too. More importantly, just be yourself.

How do you cultivate productive relationships with your boss, peers, direct reports, and other team members?

Be authentic and respectful. Make an effort to build cordial work relationships. If you have an opportunity to travel for work and meet your team, do that. People tend to be more approachable when they can put a name to a face. In a global team setting, be conscious and sensitive about different cultures. Find out if they have preferred communication styles. Sometimes misunderstandings can be avoided if you understand their needs. Place the needs of others at the same level as your needs. If you say you are going to commit to doing something, then make it happen.

Sometimes things do not work out for you, and that is all right. Such is life. We do not often get to work with people that we like, nor do we have control over what others think of us. It is up to us to do the best we can so that our work is enjoyable.

Have you encountered challenges collaborating with revenue-generating teams like sales and product development?

In a paper written by Giampaolo Bella, he used the idea of cities as an analogy to describe two different approaches to cybersecurity. The first approach is to make cybersecurity "beautiful." In this city, cybersecurity is something visible. It is supposed to be a positive and desirable thing to have. People have to embrace cybersecurity because it is right for them. The second approach is to make cybersecurity invisible. Cybersecurity is transparent to the user. Users may not know that, but it is there.

For us to be great partners with the revenue-generating teams, we should look at cybersecurity not as a technical issue but as a business problem. By making cybersecurity invisible, we can focus on becoming a business enabler that drives business value to the organization.

Have you encountered challenges collaborating with technology teams like information technology and software development?

It is not uncommon to hear stories of technology teams that bypass their cybersecurity team to get things done. It is also not a surprise to know that cybersecurity is often involved in the final phases of a project so that they do not impede the technology teams.

Technology teams that do that perceive cybersecurity as being slow and not keeping up with the times, especially with methodologies like agile.

Cybersecurity needs to evolve and adapt so that we can become partners and advisers to the technology teams. Cybersecurity is everyone's business. Instead of saying no to whatever it is that they are trying to implement, we should look at managing risks. Is there anything that we can do to reduce the risk to an acceptable level? Is this a risk that the business is willing to accept? These are the types of questions we should be asking.

Do you have any favorite books to recommend for people who want to lead cybersecurity teams?

If you are serious about security and leadership, you cannot afford not to read regularly. I remind myself all the time. I am also trying to improve the way I read books by engaging with the text so that I can retain the information I learn better. When I read a book that I no longer find interesting, I move on to the next book.

I have three books to recommend.

- *Getting Things Done* by David Allen
- *Measure What Matters* by John Doerr
- *CISO Compass* by Todd Fitzgerald

I used Getting Things Done (GTD) with Kanban to organize my work. When I was at Red Hat, we used a variation of GTD to track our work, and it worked very well for a global remote team. John Doerr's book introduces how Google sets goals and measures its success by using OKRs. I mentioned earlier that we had implemented a variation of OKRs at work to achieve organizational alignment and success. As for the last book, the author provides guidance, insights, and lessons that a CISO could learn from other leaders' experiences. It gives me a holistic view of the areas I have to work on as I work toward my career aspiration to be a CISO.

"I follow the golden rule of treating others the way you want to be treated."

Twitter: @domyboo • **Websites:** www.linkedin.com/in/dominiquewest and www.securityincolor.com

Dominique West

Dominique West is the creator of SecurityinColor.com, a cybersecurity platform that provides weekly industry news and professional guidance to those aiming to navigate a career in cyber. Currently a senior cloud security consultant based in Atlanta, Georgia, Dominique has eight years of experience in information technology, five of which are in cybersecurity with experience spanning risk assessments, vulnerability assessments, incident and response, and cloud transformation and security across the commercial industries.

49

   A Certified Information Systems Security Professional (CISSP), Dominique holds a variety of technical certifications as well as a master's degree in cybersecurity from the University of Dallas. Dominique also is the chapter lead for various nonprofit and volunteer organizations, notably the Women's Society of Cyberjutsu and Women in Security. Outside of all things cybersecurity, Dominique enjoys traveling, reading, video games, and sky diving.

Do you believe there is a massive shortage of career cybersecurity professionals?

Professionals, yes, if we are strictly taking that word in its literal definition of any person who earns their living from a specified professional activity. Organizations are unable to hire enough experienced professionals for the roles that they are looking for. But that is not to say there is a shortage of willing and earnest cybersecurity enthusiasts who just need tangible resources and opportunities to help bridge this gap.

How do you make hard decisions? Do you find yourself more often making people, process, or technology decisions?

Typically, I am a literal pros versus cons person. If faced with a hard decision, I write down the positives and negatives, along with any risks and possible consequences, before proceeding. It helps me draw the big picture and thoroughly understand the decision I am trying to make. More often I find myself making people-related decisions, giving my time and resources to help someone out.

> If faced with a hard decision, I write down the positives and negatives, along with any risks and possible consequences, before proceeding.

What's something that you struggle with as a leader and how do you overcome that?

For quite some time I found myself succumbing to imposter syndrome—questioning if I belonged in a certain room or should be accepting accolades I know I rightfully earned. For me, it was an issue not only of confidence but of not wanting to sound like I am bragging. Overcoming this feat wasn't easy but became important to me, as imposter syndrome can affect the way you show up—at first you realize you are just speaking negatively in your mind, until you realize you are downplaying yourself out loud as well, and that, to me, is unacceptable. Showing up for myself and believing in myself became my first priority—so I write down and acknowledge all of my accomplishments and share them with friends and family I know will support me.

Imposter syndrome attempted to rear its ugly head recently when I was offered, and accepted, a senior position within a well-established firm. This time, though, instead of telling myself, "You might not belong here," I told myself, "You belong in every room you decide to step into."

What are your communication tips for interacting with executive leadership?

I have been in unique positions where I was not far removed from the executive leadership in the organizations I worked for, meaning many times I had direct access to speak to executive members one-on-one or in group settings. What I've learned is that everyone does not understand and communicate at the same level. The concerns of leadership may not be the concerns of your department, but you both are on the team. If given the opportunity to interact with leadership, take the time to be reciprocative in communication—make your concerns heard but also listen to what is keeping them up at night. Everyone is human, and a simple conversation can bridge the gap often seen between leaders and the rest of the organization.

How do you cultivate productive relationships with your boss, peers, direct reports, and other team members?

I follow the golden rule of treating others the way you want to be treated. We spend the majority of our daily lives at work, and if I have to report somewhere for eight hours, I'd like to think I would enjoy it. Sure, every day won't be easy, but what makes it worthwhile are the relationships I have been able to forge with my colleagues. Making sure to carve out time, once a week or bi-weekly, for non–work-related conversations is important. Get away from the desk and meet up with someone for coffee for 15 minutes. I found this to be effective in developing better relationships and understanding with my peers.

> Making sure to carve out time, once a week or bi-weekly, for non–work-related conversations is important.

Have you encountered challenges collaborating with technology teams like information technology and software development?
There is this negative narrative that the security teams in organizations are the bad gatekeepers, and therefore that automatically makes other departments stay away and not want to work with us. I believe, and have experienced firsthand, that this is a narrative built upon a lack of communication and understanding. When I realized that, I immediately took the time to call all parties involved to a

> When I took the time to stop, listen, and understand where the divide was coming from, the project began to come to fruition much more smoothly.

meeting to really understand where the rift was coming from. We all want the same objective in the end; how do we do this peacefully? When I took the time to stop, listen, and understand where the divide was coming from, the project began to come to fruition much more smoothly. It is easy to get caught up in the us versus them mentality in cybersecurity, but I believe it is an opportunity to engage in thoughtful and communicative collaboration.

Do you have any favorite books to recommend for people who want to lead cybersecurity teams?
Some great books I recommend are:
- *The 7 Habits of Highly Effective People* by Stephen Covey
- *Becoming* by Michelle Obama
- *I Am Malala* by Malala Yousafzai
- *Emotional Intelligence* by Jean Greaves and Travis Bradberry

These are four very different books, but all of them were impactful in telling a story about overcoming and becoming someone great. I believe effective leading starts with the relationship of self, and these are great books that help you process and analyze that relationship.

Jake Williams

"My biggest challenge is letting the little things go."

50

InfoSec professional. Breaker of poorly written software. Incident responder. Digital defender. Business bilingual. Jake Williams treats InfoSec like the Hippocratic oath: first do no harm. By addressing realistic risks, Jake helps businesses create secure environments that actually function. He penetration tests organizations so they can find the weak spots before an attacker does. When an attacker does find a weak spot first, Jake works with the organization to remove the attacker, assess the damage, and remediate the vulnerabilities that allowed the attacker access in the first place. Jake is also a prolific conference speaker, an instructor, and an InfoSec mentor.

Do you believe there is a massive shortage of career cybersecurity professionals?
This is such a hard thing to answer, because if you left "career" out of it, I would have said no. But by adding "career,"

I think the answer is yes. I think there are plenty of people who want to get an InfoSec job because they want the money the field promises. But I think InfoSec salaries are more a result of supply and demand than skills. For example, many InfoSec jobs don't require more expertise than systems engineering, yet in many cases we're compensated differently. Bridging the gap will be difficult but will largely involve mentoring those who truly have passion for the *job* and not the money.

What's the most important decision you've made or action you've taken related to a business risk?
Recognizing that we can't do everything well. We're usually resource constrained and have to make compromises. If you prioritize everything, you prioritize nothing. We like to joke about "accepting the risk" in InfoSec, but there's nothing wrong with accepting risk. The issue is when you "accept" the risk because you ignored it. But choosing to accept a risk because you lack the resources to do everything well can be a good decision. Given the resourcing choice between doing everything in a mediocre way and simply not doing some things at all, I'll choose the latter. Then we need to brief decision-makers as to why we chose our priorities and what we chose *not* to do. Unsurprisingly, "We aren't doing this at all because we lack resources" gets more attention than "We are doing a lot of things suboptimally because we need more resources."

> If you prioritize everything, you prioritize nothing.

How do you make hard decisions? Do you find yourself more often making people, process, or technology decisions?
If it's a hard decision, I probably shouldn't be making it alone. I should be involving others in the org. At Rendition Infosec, we have Voltron—the group of people who come together to make those "hard decisions." The Voltron name is a nod to the fact that while we're each capable and accomplished on our own, we can come together to form something so much more powerful than any one of us alone.

Process is where I spend most of my time. In a pure leadership role, you probably shouldn't be making technology decisions. Those should almost always be delegated (with appropriate oversight). Get your team to research and justify the correct technology decisions. People decisions should also largely be made by the team. Especially if they aren't direct reports, they'll be working more with the team than with you. Get the team involved in the people selections.

> In a pure leadership role, you probably shouldn't be making technology decisions. Those should almost always be delegated (with appropriate oversight).

What's something that you struggle with as a leader and how do you overcome that?

My biggest challenge is letting the little things go. My company, Rendition, was founded by intelligence veterans, and extreme attention to detail is often the difference between success and abject failure in operations. That's not to say that I'm a crisis person (someone who sees everything as a crisis). It's a balancing act understanding what you can and can't let go without risking an operation (yes, we often internally refer to engagements as operations).

How do you lead your team to execute and get results?

Delegate, delegate, delegate. Delegation is a real force multiplier. Get out of the way and let mid-level management do their thing. But also ensure that they know you're there for them. One of the rules I have is "I'd rather you bring an issue to me early if you don't know you can handle it." Most operational risks were identified early by *someone* but not addressed correctly or in a timely manner. Good leaders are like good parents—provide direction, but get out of the way so you can grow mini-mes (who despite your best efforts will sometimes make mistakes).

Do you have a workforce philosophy or unique approach to talent acquisition?

Relationship counselors often advise their clients to learn their partners' love languages (side note: you totally should; that totally would have saved one of my marriages). Learning your co-workers' and reports' affirmation languages is equally valuable. Beyond a certain dollar point, the money doesn't matter. But people want to feel valued, and different things make different people feel valued. Learn what those things are, and apply them on a regular basis.

What are your communication tips for interacting with executive leadership?

Don't sell executives fear, uncertainty, and doubt (FUD), and don't try to impress them with technical wizardry. Executives by and large understand that security is an issue. They're not looking for FUD; they're looking for ways to address their issues that make sense from a business standpoint. InfoSec is a cost center, and we're only here to protect the profit centers. Stop pretending solutions don't have costs—the least of which is usually licensing. If a product/process/policy impacts the business negatively, you need to address that up front. Anything less will be seen for what it is—disingenuous.

How do you cultivate productive relationships with your boss, peers, direct reports, and other team members?

Listen. No really, listen. My employees will tell you that I'm regularly in the office (even off-hours for the SOC night shift) discussing operations with them. I'm not the CEO of the company, though, so I have to continue the relationship with my CEO. Most of that is listening as well. Empathy plays a big role here too. Sometimes I'm not happy with a decision or outcome, but if I can empathize, that makes a big difference in not sounding judgmental.

Have you encountered challenges collaborating with revenue-generating teams like sales and product development?

I don't personally, but it's only because I always remember that revenue-generating units are the only reason the organization exists. Instead of saying "No, you can't," I'm all about "How can I help you meet your business requirements most safely?" If you adopt that attitude, it's amazing how much less friction you'll encounter.

Have you encountered challenges collaborating with technology teams like information technology and software development?

You might have already figured this out from my earlier answers, but I'm big on understanding motivators. Nobody says, "Let's go do this horribly insecurely!" Either they don't know better or they have competing objectives (most often it's the latter).

Development teams are concerned with release schedules. Penetration testers can derail those schedules or put them in a position where they have to ship software with known vulnerabilities. Embedding a penetration tester on the development team (even just one day a week) can help find issues early when they're easier to fix (and before a code freeze).

Likewise, IT is primarily concerned with availability of assets. If security tries to mandate things that jeopardize availability, they're likely to be met with resistance. There are three ways I overcome resistance from IT. First, I work with business leadership to get vulnerability management and security architecture written into IT job descriptions. Now it's not "my priorities versus your priorities." Second, we prioritize realistic risk. If we need to fix a real issue, I'm not reporting "insecure cipher suite" vulnerability scan results like they're the end of the world. Focusing on realistic risk keeps me and IT marching in step together. Finally (and this is most important), don't talk down to IT like "You just don't get it." Take the time to explain why a vulnerability is serious and how it can be exploited. When I hear "Nobody would ever think to do that," I have a slight advantage in that I've been a nation-state hacker and can just say "Um, I thought to do that...."

Do you have any favorite books to recommend for people who want to lead cybersecurity teams?
Obviously the original *Tribe of Hackers*. There's a ton of wisdom there. Outside of that, I'd recommend *A More Beautiful Question* by Warren Berger—this book helps you assess whether you're even asking the right question in the first place. Another book I recommend to everyone is *Good to Great* by Jim Collins— it's packed full of business wisdom and *every* executive you meet is likely to have read it. If you know the contents well, you immediately have common ground you can build your communications on. Finally, I recommend *Principles* by Ray Dalio. It' a fantastic book on building an organization from the ground up. Though it's a newer book, many in management have also read it (providing you more common ground).

Twitter: @DHAhole

Wirefall

51

Some are born leaders, some achieve leadership, and some have leadership thrust upon them. I fall firmly into that last category.

Do you believe there is a massive shortage of career cybersecurity professionals?

There is only a massive shortage of qualified cybersecurity professionals because the definition of "qualified" is flawed.

I'm very involved in my local InfoSec and hacker scenes. Those organizations that have embedded themselves within our community, and that understand potential can be as valuable as referenceable experience or certifications, have been able to attract and retain some amazing talent even in this "negative unemployment" market.

Another step organizations should be taking to fill their open positions is to ensure that everyone is welcome at the table. Diversity and inclusion can't just be an HR mission statement. These aspirations must go hand in hand with equality in pay and opportunity for promotion.

> "I strive to put the organization's interests above my own, but I'm not an automaton."

How do you make hard decisions? Do you find yourself more often making people, process, or technology decisions?

If it isn't difficult, then it's not a decision; it's merely selecting the best answer from a list of options. Decisions imply consequences, and determining the gravity of those consequences is often what determines how hard the choice will be to make.

Some of the most challenging decisions are those where unpredictable externalities are involved or the information required to make an informed decision just isn't available. In those cases, your "gut feeling" may be the best you can hope for.

The hardest decisions of all for me are personal. I strive to put the organization's interests above my own, but I'm not an automaton. While I respect the privacy of those on my teams, I hope to be close enough to know their family situations and the names of their significant others and children or pets, if any. I want to know their passions, dreams, and hobbies.

I've had to let folks go who felt more like family than colleagues. While making that decision is extremely difficult, putting my entire social network behind finding them a soft landing isn't. That's just a given.

What's something that you struggle with as a leader, and how do you overcome that?

I find everything related to leadership a struggle. I don't believe that I will ever overcome that, but I can continue to work on it. Open communications, building trust, and being accepting of honest feedback are how I determine what areas to focus my efforts on.

The most difficult leadership position I've ever been thrust into was at my last duty station. Our sergeant rotated out a full six months before his replacement was scheduled to arrive. We were a small shop of four airmen. We were all equals and had formed a cohesive team. One of our team was the natural selection for the position, as his goal was to make the Air Force a career and rise through the ranks as quickly as possible. Unfortunately, I outranked him by a day, and that's all that mattered in assigning me the temporary acting-sergeant role. This changed the dynamics of the shop instantaneously, and I lost a valued friendship because of it. I was able to finally convince the base commander to have the sergeant of another shop serve part-time over our team so that I handled the day-to-day assignments and he managed the personnel issues, but the damage had already been done. Twenty-five years later I still second guess my decision to put duty first, and I'll likely take that doubt to my grave.

How do you lead your team to execute and get results?

The most important factor for any successful team is trust. In this aspect, the only difference between how I lead a team and how I contribute as an individual is that as the leader it isn't just the most important factor; it's all that matters. Every promise and commitment must be met. If they are not, then it's imperative to immediately engage the team on why they weren't. If it was due to unforeseen circumstances, then share those. If it was because I dropped the ball, because none of us are perfect, then I will own up to it and explain how I intend to make sure that it doesn't happen again. The corollary of this is also true. If one of your team members doesn't meet their commitments, then give them the opportunity to explain why and work with them on how they can prevent future occurrences.

Finally, when briefing management, always credit the team for its successes while taking the blame for its failures.

Do you have a workforce philosophy or unique approach to talent acquisition?

Of all of my responsibilities as a team leader, this is one of the most critical. Often you'll just be handed a team, which can be quite challenging. There are existing dynamics that must be considered, and many times there will be members that you would have never chosen if given the option. Work with what you have. Find ways to motivate underperformers, but don't be afraid to let toxic team members go.

The most ideal situation is a greenfield opportunity. I've had this occur only once in my career. You should already know who you want on your team before this opportunity ever presents itself. Successfully building a dream team often depends on how plugged in you are to the community, whether that's your local meetups or social media outlets. I'm not advocating for nepotism. It's not about hiring your friends; rather, it's about who you know and trust that can meet the demands placed before the team.

Once the team is in place, the best way to retain your top talent is to challenge them, provide them with an attainable career path within the organization, and provide meaningful training opportunities. The latter is something I focus on as a team leader. I know many managers who discount conferences like Defcon or BSides as nothing but opportunities to party, but I feel that it's during these social events that true relationships are formed, which then become the potential for future hires.

This brings me to my final recommendation on this subject. You shouldn't just rely on your network; you should leverage the network of the entire team. If, as a leader, you've properly set the expectations of accountability, then nobody is going to recommend somebody just because they're a friend. You're going to get referrals for people who are going be outstanding contributors.

What are your communication tips for interacting with executive leadership?
All communications with executive leadership should be the culmination of your interactions with your boss, peers, direct reports, and the rest of your team members. It should be a bottom-up approach. Your team members and direct reports will provide the information you need to formulate the best options available. Leverage your peers to vet any and all recommendations, and work with your boss to help massage the message into a format that will be most readily digestible by executive leadership.

The goal should be to make this less of a decision for the executives and more of a selection of the best option from those provided.

How do you cultivate productive relationships with your boss, peers, direct reports, and other team members?
Again, it's all about trust. All of your promises, commitments, and actions should be focused on increasing your trustworthiness. It's good to be liked, but it's better to be trusted.

Have you encountered challenges collaborating with revenue-generating teams like sales and product development?
This can be one of the most challenging relationships. As a delivery consultant for penetration tests or as a leader of a

pentest team, I am also revenue-generating. We don't get the gig in the first place, though, without sales.

The sales team always seems to be chasing the pretty penny. Red team? Yes, we do that! And then they scope it as a traditional vulnerability scan or penetration test. Most of the time, though, the client doesn't understand what they want either. In the end, it boils down to education of the sales team and expectation management of the client.

Have you encountered challenges collaborating with technology teams like information technology and software development?

In my roles I've had limited experience with this. When our company was first acquired, the acquiring company had a strict data security policy. Only authorized applications were allowed on corporate assets, and client data could not be stored on noncorporate assets. Unfortunately, at the time, the only tangentially related security applications allowed on corporate assets were PasswordSafe and Ethereal. We couldn't have a BackTrack instance or install Nessus because those weren't authorized on corporate devices, and if we installed them on noncorporate devices, then we were violating the policy regarding client data collection. Imagine performing a penetration test with just a password vault and a packet capture application! We successfully worked with the CISO to create a policy exception. Our testing laptops would adhere to the intention of the corporate security policy but would not be restricted to authorized software. The only caveat was that these devices could never connect to the corporate network.

Do you have any favorite books to recommend for people who want to lead cybersecurity teams?

While we should always be learning, one's preferred format for ingesting information is irrelevant. It doesn't matter if it's from a book by an expert in the field or from formal education, online videos, podcasts, on-the-job training, interaction with our self-selected mentors, or even just our day-to-day experiences. How we learn is less important than what we learn.

That said, *The Phoenix Project* by Gene Kim has done more to inspire and help me become an effective security leader than anything else.

Appendix: Recommended Reading

We've compiled all the great reading materials that our experts have mentioned throughout the book, in the hopes that you'll use it to further your study of cybersecurity leadership.

Adams, Douglas. *The Hitchhiker's Guide to the Galaxy*. Gollancz, 2012.

Adams, Scott. *The Dilbert Principle*. Harper-Collins, 1996.

Allen, David. *Getting Things Done: The Art of Stress-Free Productivity*. Penguin Books, 2001.

Allen, David. *Making It All Work: Winning at the Game of Work and the Business of Life*. Penguin Books, 2008.

The Arbinger Institute. *Leadership and Self-Deception: Getting Out of the Box*. Berrett-Koehler Publishers, 2018.

The Arbinger Institute. *The Anatomy of Peace: Resolving the Heart of Conflict*. Berrett-Koehler Publishers, 2006.

Anastasi, Shane. *The Seven Principles of Professional Services*. PS Principles, 2014.

Bace, Rebecca Gurley. *Intrusion Detection*. Sams, 1999.

Bennis, Warren. *On Becoming a Leader*. Basic Books, 2009.

Bennis, Warren G., and Biederman, Patricia Ward. *Organizing Genius: The Secrets of Creative Collaboration*. Basic Books, 1997.

Berger, Warren. *A More Beautiful Question: The Power of Inquiry to Spark Breakthrough Ideas*. Bloomsbury USA, 2016.

Bergeron, Ben. *Chasing Excellence: A Story About Building the World's Fittest Athletes*. Lioncrest Publishing, 2017.

Blanchard, Ken, and Johnson, Spencer. *The One Minute Manager*. William Morrow, 2015.

Blank, Warren. *Leadership for Smart People: Book 1: The Five Truths*. The Leadership Group Press, 2006.

Bock, Laszlo. *Work Rules*. Twelve, 2015.

Bolles, Richard N. *What Color Is Your Parachute?* Ten Speed Press, 2019.

Bonney, Bill, et al. *CISO Desk Reference Guide Volume 1: A Practical Guide for CISOs. Volume 1*. CISO DRG, 2019.

Bonney, Bill, et al. *CISO Desk Reference Guide Volume 2*: A Practical Guide for CISOs. CISO DRG, 2018.

Brafman, Ori, and Beckstrom, Rod. *The Starfish and the Spider: The Unstoppable Power of Leaderless Organization*. Portfolio, 2006.

Brown, Brené. *Dare to Lead*. Random House, 2018.

Brown, Brené. *Daring Greatly: How the Courage to Be Vulnerable Transforms the Way We Live, Love, Parent, and Lead*. Avery, 2012.

Buckingham, Marcus. *First, Break All The Rules: What the World's Greatest Managers Do Differently*. Gallup Press, 2016.

Bundy, Liza. *Code Girls: The Untold Story of the American Women Code Breakers of World War II*. Hachette Books, 2017.

Cain, Susan. *Quiet: The Power of Introverts in a World That Can't Stop Talking*. Crown, 2012.

Cairo, Alberto. *How Charts Lie: Getting Smarter about Visual Information*. W. W. Norton & Company, 2019.

Carey, Marcus J., and Jin, Jennifer. *Tribe of Hackers: Cybersecurity Advice from the Best Hackers in the World*. Wiley, 2019.

Carnegie, Dale. *How to Win Friends and Influence People*. Simon & Schuster, 2019.

Charan, Ram, et al. *The Leadership Pipeline: How to Build the Leadership Powered Company*. Jossey-Bass, 2011.

Clark, Ben. *RTFM: Red Team Field Manual*. CreateSpace, 2014.

Collins, Jim C. *Good to Great: Why Some Companies Make the Leap and Others Don't*. HarperBusiness, 2001.

Covey, Stephen. *The 7 Habits of Highly Effective People*. Free Press, 1989.

Covey, Stephen. *The Speed of Trust: The One Thing That Changes Everything*. FranklinCovey, 2006.

Cuddy, Amy. *Presence: Bringing Your Boldest Self to Your Biggest Challenges*. Little, Brown Spark, 2015.

Dalio, Ray. *Principles*. Simon & Schuster, 2017.

Doerr, John. *Measure What Matters*. Portfolio, 2018.

Dreeke, Robin. *It's Not All About Me: The Top Ten Techniques for Building Quick Rapport with Anyone*. Dreeke, 2011.

Dweck, Carol. *Mindset: The New Psychology of Success*. Random House, 2006.

Ellenbogen, Oren. *Leading Snowflakes: The New Engineering Manager's Handbook*. Ellenbogen, 2013.

Ekman, Paul. *Emotions Revealed: Recognizing Faces and Feelings to Improve Communication and Emotional Life*. Holt Paperbacks, 2004.

Fagone, Jason. *The Woman Who Smashed Codes: A True Story of Love, Spies, and the Unlikely Heroine Who Outwitted America's Enemies*. Dey Street Books, 2017.

Field Manual 22-100, "Military Leadership." Washington, DC.: U.S. Army, 1990.

Fitzgerald, Todd. *CISO Compass: Navigating Cybersecurity Leadership Challenges with Insights from Pioneers*. Auerbach Publications, 2018.

Forsgren, Nicole, et al. *Accelerate: The Science of Lean Software and DevOps: Building and Scaling High Performing Technology Organizations*. IT Revolution Press, 2018.

Fournier, Camille. *The Manager's Path: A Guide for Tech Leaders Navigating Growth and Change*. O'Reilly Media, 2017.

Fried, Jason. *Rework*. Currency, 2010.

Gawande, Atul. *Checklist Manifesto*. Metropolitan Books, 2009.

Gentile, Michael, et al. *The Ciso Handbook: A Practical Guide to Securing Your Company*. Auerbach Publications, 2005.

Gladwell, Malcolm. *Talking to Strangers: What We Should Know About the People We Don't Know*. Little, Brown and Company, 2019.

God, *The Scriptures* (66 books of the Textus Receptus)

Goden, Seth. *Linchpin: Are You Indispensable?* Portfolio, 2011.

Goldsmith, Marshall. *What Got You Here Won't Get You There.* Hachette Books, 2007.

Franks, Gen. Tommy. *American Soldier.* Regan Books/Harper Collins, 2004.

Greaves, Jean, and Bradberry, Travis. *Emotional Intelligence 2.0.* TalentSmart, 2009.

Glen, Paul. *Leading Geeks.* Jossey-Bass, 2002.

Green, Tim. *First Team.* HarperCollins, 2014.

Greenburg, Andy. *Sandworm: A New Era of Cyberware and the Hunt for the Kremlin's Most Dangerous Hackers.* Doubleday, 2019.

Grove, Andrew S. *High Output Management.* Random House, 1983.

Hadnagy, Christopher. *Unmasking the Social Engineer: The Human Element of Security.* Wiley, 2014.

Hallowell, Edward. *Crazybusy: Overstretched, Overbooked, and About to Snap! Strategies for Handling Your Fast-Paced Life.* Ballantine Books, 2006.

Harari, Yuval Noah. *Sapiens: A Brief History of Humankind.* Harper, 2015.

Heath, Chip, and Heath, Dan. *Switch: How to Change Things When Change Is Hard.* Crown Business, 2010.

Hoefling, Trina. *Working Virtually.* Stylus, 2017.

Holiday, Ryan. *Ego Is the Enemy.* Portfolio, 2016.

Horowitz, Ben. *The Hard Thing About Hard Things.* Harper Business, 2014.

Horstman, Mark. *The Effective Manager.* Wiley, 2016.

Hubbard, Douglas W., and Seiersen, Richard. *How to Measure Anything in Cybersecurity Risk.* Wiley, 2016.

Jaquith, Andrew. *Security Metrics: Replacing Fear, Uncertainty, and Doubt.* AddisonWesley Professional, 2007.

Johnson, Spencer. *Who Moved My Cheese: An A-Mazing Way to Deal with Change in Your Work and in Your Life.* G. P. Putnam's Sons, 1998.

Kaplan, Fred. *Dark Territory: The Secret History of Cyberwar*. Simon & Schuster, 2016.

Kennedy, David. *Metasploit: The Penetration Tester's Guide*. No Starch Press, 2011.

Khalsa, Mahan. *Let's Get Real or Let's Not Play*. Portfolio, 2008.

Kim, Gene. *The DevOps Handbook: How to Create World-Class Agility, Reliability, and Security in Technology Organizations*. IT Revolution Press, 2016.

Kim, Gene. *The Unicorn Project: A Novel about Developers, Digital Disruption, and Thriving in the Age of Data*. IT Revolution Press, 2019.

Kim, Gene, et al. *The Phoenix Project: A Novel about IT, DevOps, and Helping Your Business Win*. IT Revolution Press, 2013.

Kim, Peter. *The Hacker Playbook: Practical Guide To Penetration Testing*. CreateSpace, 2014.

Knuth, Donald E. *Things a Computer Scientist Rarely Talks About*. Center for the Study of Language and Information, 2003.

Krawcheck, Sallie. *Own It: The Power of Women at Work*. Currency, 2017.

Kua, Patrick. *Talking with Tech Leads: From Novices to Practitioners*. CreateSpace, 2015.

Larsson, Stieg. *The Girl with the Dragon Tattoo*. Knopf, 2008.

Lencioni, Patrick. *Death by Meeting: A Leadership Fable about Solving the Most Painful Problem in Business*. Jossey-Bass, 2004.

Lencioni, Patrick. *The Five Dysfunctions of a Team: A Leadership Fable*. Jossey-Bass, 2002.

Lewis, Michael. *The Fifth Risk: Undoing Democracy*. W. W. Norton & Company, 2018.

Logan, David. *Tribal Leadership: Leveraging Natural Groups to Build a Thriving Organization*. Harper Business, 2008.

Luecke, Richard. *Harvard Business Essentials: Negotiation*. Harvard Business School Press, 2003.

Marquet, L. David. *Turn the Ship Around!* Portfolio, 2013.

Maxwell, John. *The 21 Irrefutable Laws of Leadership: Follow Them and People Will Follow You*. HarperCollins, 2007.

McChesney, Chris, et al. *The Four Disciplines of Execution*. Free Press, 2012.

McChrystal, Stanley. *Team of Teams: New Rules of Engagement for a Complex World*. Portfolio, 2015.

McKeown, Greg. *Essentialism*. The Disciplined Pursuit of Less, 2014.

Menn, Joseph. *Cult of the Dead Cow: How the Original Hacking Supergroup Might Just Save the World*. PublicAffairs, 2019.

Meyer, Erin. *The Culture Map*: *Breaking Through the Invisible Boundaries of Global Business*. PublicAffairs, 2014.

Mitnick, Kevin D., and Simon, William L. *The Art of Deception and the Art of Intrusion*. Wiley, 2002.

Moreland, J. P., et al. *Theistic Evolution: A Scientific, Philosophical, and Theological Critique*. Crossway, 2017.

Morrison, Terri, and Conaway, Wayne A. *Kiss, Bow, or Shake Hands: How to Do Business in Sixty Countries*. Bob Adams, Inc., 1994.

Navarro, Joe. *Louder Than Words: Take Your Career from Average to Exceptional with the Hidden Power of Nonverbal Intelligence*. William Morrow, 2010.

Navarro, Joe. *What Everybody Is Saying: An Ex-FBI Agent's Guide to Speed-Reading People*. William Morrow, 2008.

Obama, Michelle. *Becoming*. Crown Publishing Group, 2018.

Pacetta, Frank. *Don't Fire Them, Fire Them Up*. Simon and Schuster, 1994.

Patterson, Kerry. *Crucial Conversations*. McGraw-Hill, 2002.

Pink, Daniel H. *Drive: The Surprising Truth About What Motivates Us*. Riverhead Books, 2009.

Ripley, Amanda. *Unthinkable: Who Survives When Disaster Strikes—and Why*. Harmony, 2009.

Ruiz, Don Miguel. *The Four Agreements: A Practical Guide to Personal Freedom*. Amber-Allen Publishing, 2001.

Scalzi, John. The Interdependency Series. Various dates.

Schneier, Bruce. *Applied Cryptography: Protocols, Algorithms and Source Code in C*. Wiley, 2015.

Schulze, Horst. *Excellence Wins*. Zondervan, 2019.

Schwartau, Winn. *Analogue Network Security*. SchwartauHaus, 2018.

Schwartz, Mark. *War and Peace and IT: Business Leadership, Technology, and Success in the Digital Age.* IT Revolution Press, 2019.

Scott, Kim. *Radical Candor: Be a Kick-Ass Boss Without Losing Your Humanity.* St. Martin's Press, 2017.

Shostack, Adam. *The New School of Information Security.* Addison-Wesley Professional, 2008.

Sinek, Simon. *The Infinite Game.* Portfolio, 2019.

Sinek, Simon. *Leaders Eat Last: Why Some Teams Pull Together and Others Don't.* Portfolio, 2014.

Smith, Jeremy. *Breaking and Entering: The Extraordinary Story of a Hacker Called "Alien."* Eamon Dolan/Houghton Mifflin Harcourt, 2019.

Stoll, Cliff. *The Cuckoo's Egg: Tracking a Spy Through the Maze of Computer Espionage.* Doubleday, 1989.

Stone, Douglas, and Heen, Sharon. *Thanks for the Feedback: The Science and Art of Receiving Feedback Well.* Viking, 2014.

Stuttard, Dafydd. *The Web Application Hacker's Handbook.* Wiley, 2011.

Syed, Matthew. *Black Box Thinking: The Surprising Truth About Success.* Portfolio, 2015.

Voss, Chris. *Never Split the Difference: Negotiating As If Your Life Depended On It.* Harper Business, 2016.

Walker, Matt. *CEH Certified Ethical Hacker Bundle 4th Edition.* McGraw-Hill Education, 2019.

Wallace, David Foster. *This Is Water: Some Thoughts, Delivered on a Significant Occasion, about Living a Compassionate Life.* Little, Brown and Company, 2009.

Walsh, Bill. *The Score Takes Care of Itself: My Philosophy of Leadership.* Portfolio, 2009.

Warsinske, John, et al. *The Official (ISC)² CISSP CBK Reference.* Wiley, 2019.

Watkins, Michael. *The First 90 Days: Proven Strategies for Getting Up to Speed Faster and Smarter, Updated and Expanded.* Harvard Business Review Press, 2013.

Weidman, Georgia. *Penetration Testing: A Hands-on Introduction to Hacking.* No Starch Press, 2014.

Wheatley, Margaret. *Leadership and the New Science: Learning about Organization from an Orderly Universe*. BK Berrett-Koehler, 1993.

White, Alan J. and Clark, Ben. *BTFM: Blue Team Field Manual*. CreateSpace, 2017.

Willink, Jocko, and Babin, Leif. *Extreme Ownership: How U.S. Navy SEALs Lead and Win*. St. Martin's Press, 2017.

Yousafzai, Malala. *I Am Malala*. Little, Brown Books for Young Readers, 2014.

Get the Whole *Tribe of Hackers* Series!

The book that started it all, *Tribe of Hackers: Cybersecurity Advice from the Best Hackers in the World* is your guide to joining the ranks of hundreds of thousands of cybersecurity professionals around the world. Wherever you are in your cybersecurity career, *Tribe of Hackers* offers the practical know-how, industry perspectives, and technical insight you need to succeed in the rapidly growing information security market. It includes inspiring interviews from 70 security experts, including Lesley Carhart, Ming Chow, Bruce Potter, Robert M. Lee, and Jayson E. Street. ISBN: 9781119643371

The Tribe of Hackers team is back with a new guide with insights from dozens of the world's leading Red Team security specialists. With their deep knowledge of system vulnerabilities and innovative solutions for correcting security flaws, Red Team hackers are in high demand. *Tribe of Hackers Red Team: Tribal Knowledge from the Best in Offensive Cybersecurity* dives deep into penetration testing and ethical hacking with interviews from specialists including David Kennedy, Rob Fuller, and Georgia Weidman. ISBN: 9781119643326

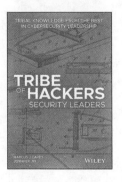

The Tribe of Hackers series continues, sharing what CISSPs, CISOs, and other security leaders need to know to build solid cybersecurity teams and keep organizations secure. Dozens of experts and influential security specialists reveal their best strategies for building, leading, and managing information security within organizations. *Tribe of Hackers Security Leaders: Tribal Knowledge from the best in Cybersecurity Leadership* looks at organizational security impact with Mike Chapple, Kimber Dowsett, Andrew Hay, Tanya Janca, Rafał Łoś, Tracy Z. Maleeff (@InfoSecSherpa), Ray [REDACTED], Khalil Sehnaoui, and many others. ISBN: 9781119643777

Coming July 2020! The Tribe of Hackers team is back. This new guide is packed with insights on blue team issues from the biggest names in cybersecurity. Inside, dozens of the world's leading Blue Team security specialists show you how to harden systems against real and simulated breaches and attacks. You'll discover the latest strategies for blocking even the most advanced red-team attacks and preventing costly losses. The experts share their hard-earned wisdom, revealing what works and what doesn't in the real world of cybersecurity. ISBN: 9781119643418